Graham Greene

WINC.

Also Available from Continuum:

Such Deliberate Disguises: The Art of Philip Larkin
Richard Palmer

Faith and Doubt of John Betjeman
Kevin Gardner

Graham Greene
Fictions, Faith and Authorship

Michael G. Brennan

continuum

Continuum International Publishing Group

The Tower Building   80 Maiden Lane
11 York Road   Suite 704
London SE1 7NX   New York, NY 10038

www.continuumbooks.com

British Library Cataloguing-in-Publication Data
A catalogue record for this book is available from the British Library.

Library of Congress Cataloging-in-Publication Data
A catalog record for this book is available from the Library of Congress.

ISBN: 978-1-8470-6338-0 (hardback)
      978-1-8470-6339-7 (paperback)

Typeset by Newgen Imaging Systems Pvt Ltd, Chennai, India
Printed and bound in Great Britain by CPI Antony Rowe Ltd, Chippenham, Wiltshire

For Christina and Alice

Contents

Preface

What have we gained then by our unbelief
But a life of doubt diversified by faith,
For one of faith diversified by doubt?
We called the chessboard white, – we call it black.

[I]f Literature is to be made a study of human nature, you cannot have a Christian Literature. It is a contradiction in terms to attempt a sinless literature of sinful man.[1]

This study of Greene's literary explorations of faith, doubt and authorial versatility does not seek to offer a spiritual biography of the writer. Rather, it traces how elements of Catholic belief, theology and liturgy consistently provided him with an inspiring source of narrative creativity and intellectual scepticism. For over sixty years, Greene depended upon religious issues to formulate dominant narrative and thematic concerns in his fictions and also insistently wove elements of Catholic theology and tradition into the fabric of his novels, entertainments, short stories, plays, prefaces, journalism and private correspondence. While the religious mode of thought often endows his writings with a tone of questioning and uncertainty, the interplay in his narratives of three key dualities – faith and doubt, hope and despair, and love and betrayal – draws the reader into his sustained interrogation of the intellectual and spiritual demands of twentieth-century English Catholicism. The most important question is not whether Greene may be classified as a 'Catholic novelist' but rather how Catholicism provided him with such a diverse and sustained source of inspiration for his writings. In this respect, Greene's conversion to Catholicism in February 1926 becomes of less significance – since one may become a devout, doubting or even indifferent convert – than the fact that the theology, iconography and psychological potency of Catholicism continually pervaded his creative imagination.

Greene's constantly evolving views on the role of the writer and his testing attitudes towards the author-reader relationship are also explored in this study. He persistently challenges readers by making implicit and often elusive reflections on his own relationships, religious beliefs and psychological preoccupations.

As one of the most generically ambitious prose writers of the twentieth century, he experimented not only with ways of reinterpreting the established modes of prose fiction, especially through his blending of traditional novel forms with thriller-inspired entertainments, but also immersed himself in an impressive diversity of other categories of literary endeavour. As well as publishing over twenty major novels, novellas and entertainments, Greene wrote poetry, travel memoirs, film scripts, plays, short stories, biographical and critical essays, children's stories, autobiographical works, polemical letters to the press, reviews of films and books and a sustained range of journalism. Early in his career, he gained valuable experience as an editor of newspapers and periodicals, contributed introductions to the works of other writers and edited their works for publication. Of no less importance for modern criticism is his impressively diverse (and now more accessible) range of private correspondence and his sustained friendships with other notable literary figures.

As an energetic and systematically disciplined writer, Greene's generic diversity as an author was a direct product of his determination to sustain a decent financial living as a man of letters. As demonstrated by the Greene papers in the archives of his literary agent, Laurence Pollinger, he was always keenly involved in the business side of his career, monitoring royalties, maintaining a close eye on translation and film rights, and even selling at commercially opportune moments successive manuscript and proof drafts of his publications.[2] On a more introspective level, fictional writing seems to have answered a persistent psychological need in Greene for self-analysis, providing him with the means to explore and define his responses to testing private and public issues, especially religious ones. Greene's subjective presence is often traceable in his fictional worlds – whether echoing the Catholic devotions of his young wife, Vivien, in his earliest novels from *The Man Within* (1929) to *Brighton Rock* (1938), his horror at the murderous persecution of the Catholic Church in Mexico in *The Lawless Roads* (1939) and *The Power and the Glory* (1940), his adulterous affair with the Catholic convert Catherine Walston in *The End of the Affair* (1951) or his later fascination with Latin American politics and 'liberation theology'. Within this personalized framework of literary creativity, he consistently drew for creative inspiration – sometimes seriously and at other times in comic, ironic or despondent modes – upon issues of Catholic theology, liturgy and spirituality.

It is sometimes all too easy, of course, to tease out religious references and echoes once such a dominant strand of creative influence has been identified in a writer's works. Greene developed a strong antipathy towards being regarded as a 'Catholic novelist' and, after the international success of *The Power and the Glory*, he remained wary of readers and critics who assumed that his fictions invariably explored issues of religious doctrine and faith. Indeed, such assumptions could prove comically wide of the mark. For example, in his memoir *A Sort of Life* (1971) Greene recalled how, soon after graduating in 1925 from Oxford University, he had taken a temporary post in Derbyshire as tutor to an eight-year-old boy. He befriended a girl in the private hotel where he was accommodated and she gave him a mongrel terrier called Paddy as a souvenir of their acquaintance. Over thirty years later, he revived fond memories of this gift by giving the dog a brief off-stage 'barking' role in his west-end drama, *The Potting Shed* (1958). He was amused when *The Observer*'s theatre critic, Kenneth Tynan, declared in his review that this visibly non-present canine must represent God, even though Greene insisted that had simply been amusing himself by making reference to a long-dead pet.[3]

Despite Tynan's misguided deification of Paddy the dog, there remains a pressing need for a comprehensive reassessment of what Greene's Catholicism meant to him – not so much as a private or devotional individual but rather as a prolifically published writer who habitually used Catholic issues and beliefs as a source of creative inspiration and self-interrogation. Following the recent publication of major biographical studies of Greene by Norman Sherry, Michael Shelden, W. J. West, Anthony Mockler and others, along with more open access to the key collections of primary Greene materials in academic libraries (especially at Texas at Austin, Georgetown, Boston and Leeds universities), it is feasible to begin a fresh reconsideration of Greene's entire literary career. At the same time, it has become all the more important to differentiate between these biographers' revelations of intimate details from Greene's private life, especially in terms of his personal relationships and ever-fluctuating religious faith and doubts, and the fictive creations and ideas encapsulated in his writings. While Greene's own life and his fictional characters often interacted productively and self-consciously, he repeatedly emphasized that he should not be regarded as a 'Catholic writer'. Such a terminology implies a conformist promulgator of established devotional truths. Instead, he viewed himself as a writer who happened to be a convert to Catholicism and who was intellectually fascinated by the demands, paradoxes and spiritual solaces of Catholic communities, theology and liturgy.

Henry Graham Greene was born into an upper-middle class Hertfordshire family on 2 October 1904 at St. John's House, Berkhamsted School (28 miles north-west of London), where his father was a housemaster. He was the fourth surviving child of Charles H. Greene (1865–1942) and Marion Raymond Greene (1872–1959), who were first cousins once removed and members of a large and close-knit family circle. Although originally from a dissenting background, by the late-nineteenth century most of the Greenes regarded themselves as conforming members of the Church of England. Certainly, their extensive family records reveal no personal associations with Catholicism prior to Greene's adoption of the Roman Catholic faith in February 1926. Although he habitually chose to present his religious conversion as being primarily motivated by a desire to please his future wife, Vivien(ne) Dayrell-Browning, it seems likely that Catholicism also offered a convenient way of distancing himself from what he regarded as the claustrophobic world of traditional English Anglicanism.

Although Greene retrospectively viewed his early childhood as generally untroubled, his entry into the upper school at Berkhamsted was in sharp contrast. His growing unhappiness and depressions as a teenager led him into bouts of truancy and even some ineffectual attempts to commit suicide, including drinking a bottle of hay-fever drops and swimming in the school baths while dazed from an overdose of aspirin.[4] His concerned parents accepted the advice of their older son, Raymond (who had begun medical training), and sent Greene in summer 1921 to be treated by Kenneth Richmond, a Jungian psychiatrist with interests in both spiritualism and the literary world. Greene went to live with Richmond and his wife, Zoe, in their bohemian London home and his cousin, Ave Greene, was also treated there. At the heart of Richmond's methods was a belief in the efficacy of dream analysis. His insistence that written records of dreams should be kept by his patients led Greene into just such a daily habit. Greene also resumed this practice during the last 25 years of his life, leading in 1992 to the posthumous publication (as a deathbed request) of his dream anthology, *A World of My Own. A Dream Diary*.[5]

Richmond's brand of Jungian psychiatry was less concerned than Freudian methodologies with unearthing sexually based neuroses and repressions. Instead, it placed a more holistic emphasis upon the therapeutic value of spiritualism and dream analysis as a means of penetrating the personal unconscious, thereby achieving access to the illuminating mythologies of humanity's collective unconscious. Inevitably, such treatments fostered in Greene's impressionable teenage mind the idea that all answers to personal dilemmas lay buried deep within the self, in contrast to the more trusting reliance upon an external deity of Anglicanism and other Christian denominations. As Zoe Richmond explained, she and her husband (the alienated son of an Anglican canon of Winchester) believed only in the concept of humanity's inner God:

> You had to decide all by yourself. That was the whole treatment. To listen to the God in you, and you are told what to do. Kenneth would have told Graham to listen to his own voice – listen to the God in him. That's the whole point of Jung's analysis – to unite your conscious mind with an unconscious God in you.[6]

Greene himself confirmed that he emerged from his psychoanalysis bereft of any lingering religious beliefs in the 'Jesus of the school chapel'.[7]

The Richmonds also provided Greene with his first access to a wide and supportive literary circle of friends, including Walter de la Mare and Naomi Royde-Smith who published some of Greene's earliest attempts at poetic prose in the *Weekly Westminster Gazette*.[8] Hence, the Richmonds were responsible not only for offering encouragement to his adolescent writing ambitions but also for placing the first seeds in his mind of a lifelong preoccupation with using his dreams and fictions (with the former often included in the latter) as a means of reflecting upon his personal relationships and religious beliefs. For Greene, the writer's art became not only one of storytelling, social commentary and stylistic experiment but also an implicit and sometimes obscurely covert means of authorial and psychological self-analysis. In this sense, his conversion to Catholicism at the outset of his literary career enabled him to begin the (always elusively incomplete) process of psychologically detaching himself from the Greene family's considerable social distinctions, personal wealth and conventional religious devotions at Berkhamsted.[9] Hence, Greene's youthful embracing of Catholicism may be interpreted as one of his various 'ways of escape' from his suffocating English upper-middle-class background. While Greene certainly wished to please his future wife in becoming a Catholic, he also seems to have experienced a personal and subversive satisfaction in becoming, as far as he knew, the first Catholic member of the extended Greene family.

Acknowledgements

I am grateful to Bernadette Barnett and Geraldine Brennan for their expertise on matters of Catholic theology and literature; and to Bernard Bergonzi, Wm Thomas Hill, Mary Reichardt and Alistair Stead for their shared interests in Greene's literary career. Christopher Sheppard (Brotherton Library, University of Leeds) has been consistently supportive of this study. I owe much to the generosity of Fay and Geoffrey Elliott whose major bequests to the Brotherton Library include a wealth of important primary materials on Greene. The student members of my MA seminars on Graham Greene have also provided me with illuminating readings of his writings.

I have drawn extensively from Norman Sherry's three-volume biography and from the publications of Yvonne Cloetta, Leopoldo Duran, Shirley Hazzard, Anthony Mockler, Michael Shelden and W. J. West. *The Oxford Dictionary of National Biography* has proved an invaluable research resource. I acknowledge my frequent reliance upon *A Preface to Greene* by Cedric Watts; and I am indebted to instructive readings of Greene by Cates Baldridge, Bernard Bergonzi, Mark Bosco, S.J., A. A. DeVitis, Quentin Falk, Robert Hoskins, Samuel Hynes, Ian Ker, David Lodge, Paul O'Prey, Roger Sharrock, Neil Sinyard, Grahame Smith, Philip Stratford and Tom Woodman. I have received helpful advice during the compilation of this book from Anna Fleming (Publisher) and Colleen Coalter (Editorial Assistant) at The Continuum International Publishing Group. I am grateful to Bruce Hunter (David Higham Associates) for his assistance when requesting permission from the Greene Estate and Vintage Books to quote from Greene's writings.

All page references given in the text are to the editions of Greene's work listed in the Bibliography.

Chapter 1

The Writer in Search of a Career: 1923–1929

Personal Religious Background: 1904–1924

By autumn 1922, when Greene matriculated at Balliol College, he had developed a firm aversion to what he regarded as the tedium of Anglican worship. He adopted at Oxford the casual pose of an atheist socialist and, briefly, a communist. This sense of youthful rebellion against the stifling conventionality of his upbringing at Berkhamsted (sometimes attendance at early-morning school chapel, literally, made him faint) is apparent in two anti-religious short stories published during his first year as an undergraduate.[1] The first, 'The Trial of Pan', appeared in the student magazine *Oxford Outlook* (February 1923) – Greene became its assistant editor that autumn – and tells how this pagan nature-deity is brought to Heaven to appear before God's ludicrous law court. With Archangel Michael prosecuting and Archangel Gabriel defending, this divine court has already dealt with six prostitutes, fourteen murderers, two robbers and a swindler. They have all been speedily acquitted, with only a curate, a bank manager and Lady Hope-Smithies deemed fallen enough to be found guilty as charged. Surely Pan will also be rapidly condemned? But he pre-empts God's moment of triumph by singing an alluring song. Everyone in Heaven is seduced into following him, leaving the pathetic figure of a white-bearded God (50) sitting alone, idly playing noughts and crosses.[2]

This mischievous mockery of divine omnipotence reduced to impotence was followed by a more sombre short story, 'The Improbable Tale of the Archbishop of Canterbridge', published in another Oxford student magazine, *The Cherwell* (15 November 1924). In this tale Satan arrives in Britain to stir up insurrection so that poppies may be made a brighter colour of scarlet by being dipped in the fresh blood of fallen soldiers. The archbishop considers it his duty to shoot Satan, even though he fears retribution for this murderous act. But as Satan dies, in a 'bubble of bloodstained laughter' (191), he assures the archbishop that divine punishment will not be forthcoming since he is also God. This startling denouement provides the first published illustration of Greene's lifelong fascination with the concept of deistic dualism and how in his fictions the tangible forces of darkness often seem more insistently present than the intangible powers of goodness.

Throughout his literary career, Greene was fascinated by the creative potential of the third-century Christian heresy of Manichaeism, founded by the Persian prophet Mani or Manichaeus and vigorously opposed by one of its former disciples, St Augustine of Hippo. It envisaged a materialistic duality and primordial conflict between two eternal principles of good (or spirit and light) and evil (or matter and darkness). It supported the efficacy of pure reason as opposed to a Christian emphasis upon virtuous credulity and trusting faith. In the Manichaean view of the world, the forces of evil were ever-present, Adam and Eve were the offspring of devils, women were sent by demons to lure men into fornication and even marital procreation merely produced more material servants of the prince of darkness. Only the soul of man possessed inherent virtue and was seen as an elemental particle of light tragically entangled in darkness. Claiming to be the true Christianity, Manichaeism preached that Christ the Redeemer was sent to earth by the prince of light to enable some imprisoned particles to escape and return to their proper region.

In her series of face-to-face interviews with Greene, published in French as *L'Autre et son double* (1981) and in English as *The Other Man* (1983), Marie-Françoise Allain suggests that as a writer he seems balanced on the edge of 'darkness rather than of light'. She asks if he is essentially a 'Manichean' who had never 'succumbed to his vice'? A verbal slip in Greene's reply is revealing, as he explains that from a Manichaean perspective the world was entirely in the 'hands of God . . . I mean of the devil'. Allain pounces on this error and asks whether he did sometimes 'confuse God with the devil' (165). This question seems reasonable since, almost fifty years after his student story in *The Cherwell*, Greene included in *The Honorary Consul* (1973) a guerrilla priest who believes that God and the devil are one unified individual. Father León Rivas envisages God as having a day-time and night-time face and views him as responsible for both the saints and all the evil in the world. Only the virtuous acts of men, Rivas argues, can evolve this God towards the benign world of light since: 'We belong to Him and He belongs to us' (228).

Similarly, reviving memories of his unhappy childhood, Greene describes in *A Sort of Life* (1971) the Reverend Doctor Thomas Charles Fry, his father's 'sinister sadistic predecessor' as Headmaster of Berkhamsted School, as a 'Manichaean figure' wearing black gaiters and a 'long white St Peter's beard' (50). This comment carries a bitter personal nuance since Fry had baptized the infant Greene in the chapel of Berkhamsted School on 13 November 1904.[3] To cite a final example, in his 1950 essay on 'The Young Dickens', Greene concludes that *Oliver Twist* is set in a heavily 'Manichaean world', in which goodness always seems insubstantial while the evils of the material world are tangibly present: 'The world of Dickens is a world without God.' His early fictions are seen as irrevocably tainted by the 'Manichee', with Dickens despairingly teaching us that the 'world was made by Satan and not by God'.[4]

However, Greene's abiding interest in the imaginative potential of Manichaeism does not entirely explain his handling of deistic dualism in one crucial respect – his treatment of female characters. Deeply misogynistic, the Manichaeans believed that women were sent by the devil specifically to tempt mankind. Eve was viewed as responsible for the fall of Adam and for this act she had been condemned to eternal damnation, thereby denying the possibility of redemption for all other women. Although some of Greene's sexually seductive female characters seem to conform to this crude stereotype (Lucy in *The Man Within*, Anne-Marie in *The Name of Action*, Sylvie in *Brighton Rock* and Kay in *It's a Battlefield*), *Brighton Rock* offers evidence that Greene's perspectives cannot be regarded as consistently Manichaean. The fundamental decency of Rose and Ida confounds the idea that the female can only lure the male into a sinful fall. Instead, Rose's ingrained innocence offers Pinkie a route towards possible salvation, even though his views of women remain darkly Manichaean in perspective. Just as significantly, the stylized figure of Ida radiates the essential human qualities of kindness and honesty and, in contrast to Brighton's indifferent male police force, she becomes Pinkie's moral nemesis. As the novel's most potent force for good, she purges Brighton of Pinkie's malevolence, even though, as Greene acknowledged, the film-star Mae West inspired her comically sexualized physicality and we first meet her in a public bar slightly drunk, singing popular ballads to a riotous group of predatory men (5).

Similarly, some of Greene's other female characters in his early novels, notably the saintly Elizabeth (*The Man Within*) and the two decent showgirls, Coral Musker (*Stamboul Train*) and Anne Crowder (*A Gun for Sale*), are formulated neither as psychologically realized individuals nor as destructively seductive threats to the male characters. Instead, they are sketched as stylized moral centres for the unfolding dramatic action. They offer to their male counterparts the chance of stability and affection and even fleeting glimpses of the possibility of personal redemption through an escape with them from their dismally materialistic worlds.

How, then, is this persistent divergence in Greene's writings from Manichaean misogyny to be explained? The practical need to offer some attractive female characters is self-evident for an ambitious young novelist, keen to cultivate a popular readership. But Greene was also intrigued during the 1920s by the views of another heretical Christian sect. The Cathars (or Albigenses) appeared in Europe during the eleventh century and became firmly rooted in the Languedoc region of France before they were ruthlessly eradicated by the Catholic Church. The Cathars believed in a neo-Manichaean dualism of a good God and a bad god, comparable to the God and Satan of mainstream Christianity. The good God, strongly identified with the New Testament, was the God of all immaterial things, including souls and light. The bad god, essentially a figure from the Old Testament, was viewed as the god of all material things, including the created world and everything in it. Human bodies were seen as mere lodgings of clay, in which our divine and immaterial spirits were imprisoned. While the bad god could endlessly torment the body with temptations, disease and other tribulations, it had no power over the souls of men and women which remained a divine spark of the Good God. Heaven was the domain of the intangible good God while Hell was the creation of the bad god and, therefore, found only within the material world of the earth.

Significantly for Greene, in contrast to Manichaeism the Cathars denoted no essential differences between the souls of men and women. Their elect included men (*parfaits*) and women (*parfaites*) and both genders were deemed capable of aspiring towards the light or descending into spiritual darkness. They also they shared with Manichaeism the idea that marital sexuality brought forth more potential fallen humans. In just the kind of theological paradox that appealed to Greene in his fictions, they argued that non-procreative sexual activities (including homosexuality) were less culpable than procreative sex between a husband and wife.

An acclaimed life of the Cathars's most prominent opponent, St Dominic (*c.*1170–1221), by Father Bede Jarrett was published in 1924 (when Greene was still a history undergraduate). Jarrett, who was the first Dominican to study at Oxford University since the Reformation, became of great personal and spiritual significance to the young Greene and his wife. He had given daily Catholic instruction to Vivien before her conversion in 1922 and he remained close to the Greenes after their marriage in 1927, acting as godfather to their daughter, Lucy Caroline (b.1933). In his *Life of St Dominic* Jarrett offered, in terms that would have aroused Greene's curiosity as a novelist, a succinct definition of the Cathars's perspectives upon the material and spirit worlds:

> Matter was evil; hence every living thing was unclean; and physical life was in itself evil, and therefore to prolong the existence of matter was evil and to reproduce matter was an even greater evil. The only real act of goodness was the getting rid of life.[5]

Clearly, Greene never espoused in any sustained sense either Manichaean or Cathar heresies, but their polarized beliefs were readily fed into several of his more extreme characterizations and dramatic situations during his long career as a novelist.

For most of his time at Oxford, Greene outwardly cultivated the stance of a rational atheist. His friend at Balliol, the politician Robin Turton (later Lord Tranmire), recalled how Greene always seemed confidently committed to his rejection of the orthodoxy of his Anglican upbringing:

> Careful thinking led him to it and he would propound his own strong atheism. I think in my life I've never heard atheism put forward better than by Graham, although one was fighting it at that time. But he was, apparently, a convinced atheist – not arguing but merely explaining it.[6]

Such a view seems entirely innocent of Greene's private preoccupations with deistic dualities. One of his earliest religious poems, 'Après Vous' (*The Cherwell*,

22 November 1924), contemplates the dangers of such heretical thoughts by describing how a lover wishes to reach Heaven only if his beloved has preceded him. He hopes that she will intercede on his behalf in advance with the Archangel Michael and ensure that he does not pontificate to God about his dualistic views of Heaven and Hell: 'And do not, do not let him talk to God/Of the superiority of Hell's constitution!' The poet seems here almost embarrassed by the overwrought heretical perspectives of 'The Improbable Tale of the Archbishop of Canterbridge'. He pleads with his love: 'when I skate on thin ice talking of Satan,/Warn me with that little twisted frown of yours.'[7]

Early Poetry and Unpublished Novels: 1925–1929

Greene made systematic attempts for over sixty years to suppress some of his earliest published works, ensuring that a substantial amount of his youthful writings still remain inaccessible today. This is a significant problem for modern criticism since some of his key literary preoccupations – especially his fascination with religious and psychological issues – were firmly established during the 1920s. Apart from his periodical publications as a schoolboy and undergraduate, Greene's first volume in print was a collection of poems, *Babbling April*, published in 1925 by Basil Blackwell, the Oxford firm which had produced four years earlier Vivien Dayrell-Browning's poetic selection, *Little Wings*. His own selection proved so embarrassing that in later years Greene bought and destroyed copies whenever he found them.[8] Nevertheless, the collection conveys the already eclectic range of Greene's literary ambitions, including some predictable influences, such as Shakespeare and T. S. Eliot (whose admiration for the Metaphysical poets was enthusiastically adopted by Greene), and also others less immediately obvious today.[9] This latter category includes the imagist poetry, art criticism and psychoanalytic interests of Herbert Read; and Greene insisted that Eliot and Read were the 'two great figures of my young manhood'.[10] He was also stimulated by the creative eccentricities of Edith Sitwell. These encompassed dabblings with dadaism, cubism and futurism and a devotion to Verlaine, Rimbaud and Mallarmé, culminating in her idiosyncratic poetic collection *Bucolic Comedies* (1923).[11]

Of most relevance to Greene's own verses was the American lyric poet, Edna St. Vincent Millay, whose *Second April* (1921) and its line, 'It is not enough that yearly, down this hill, April/Comes like an idiot, babbling and strewing flowers', inspired the mawkish title of Greene's collection. Poetic lyricism was an essential stimulus for his imaginative creativity and prose style at this period, so much so that he admitted in *A Sort of Life* that he became addicted in his early novels to deploying exaggerated poetic effects. He grew to depend upon Vivien's copy-editing skills to eradicate posturing 'leopards' in his prose, so called because he once compared 'something or someone in the quiet

landscape of Sussex to a leopard crouching in a tree' (138). Yet, despite its
stylistic importance to Greene, for modern criticism his poetry (composed
sporadically throughout his life) still remains a largely hidden undercurrent in
his literary output.

Greene had originally sent to Basil Blackwell in May 1923 a selection of his
prose and verse. Although all the prose was eventually dropped from *Babbling
April*, Blackwell was impressed enough with these samples to suggest that he
should try his hand at novel writing.[12] His first attempt, completed in late-1924
while still a second-year undergraduate, was given both a secular ('Anthony
Sant') and devotional ('Prologue to Pilgrimage') working-title in early drafts.
This deeply self-reflective novel focuses upon an alienated black child who,
mysteriously, has white parents. He is unhappy because of bullying at a
Berkhamsted-like school, not least for the Greeneian 'crimes' of reading poetry
and keeping a psychologically revealing diary. Understandably, Blackwell was
not impressed and the novel was rejected but Greene then managed to find for
himself a newly established literary agent, A. D. Peters.

A novel focusing upon a schoolboy's loneliness was ideally pitched at Peters
(born August Detlef in Schleswig-Holstein). He had come to England as a child
to be educated as the only boy at a girls' school in Brighton, run by his paternal
aunt who had adopted him following his father's bankruptcy. By the late-1920s
Peters's list of authors included Hillaire Belloc, the Catholic son of a Catholic
convert mother and, like Greene, a graduate of Balliol College. His sister, Marie
Belloc Lowndes, a successful writer of biographies, romances and mysteries
and a prominent London society hostess, became a hospitable supporter of
Greene's literary ambitions during the 1920s. Peters also acted as the literary
agent of Alec Waugh (Evelyn's elder brother) and J. B. Priestley. But even he
could not find a publisher for Greene's distinctly quirky first novel and it was
summarily rejected by both John Lane and Heinemann. Although Peters did
not usually handle poetry, he made an exception when in November 1924
Greene completed his second collection of verses, 'Sad Cure'. He sent it to
John Lane where Priestley was then principal poetry reader. Again, rejection
followed, thereby initiating Greene's carefully nurtured and sustained dislike of
Priestley's novels and reputation.[13]

Greene's first general confession, conditional baptism and formal reception
into the Catholic Church at Nottingham Cathedral on 28 February 1926 were
largely prompted by a desire to please his future wife, Vivien. His marital intent
had been a driving force in his decision in November 1925, soon after he com-
menced work as a trainee sub-editor on *The Nottingham Journal*, to seek instruction from a Father Trollope (himself a convert) in the Catholic faith. Greene
confirms this calculated motivation in *A Sort of Life* with the frank admission
that, although Vivien was a Roman Catholic, his own religious beliefs did not
go beyond the 'sentimental hymns in the school chapel' (118). He recalls how
he decided, with characteristic evasiveness, against telling Father Trollope

specifically why he was seeking instruction or even that he was planning to marry a Catholic (120).

Greene was still determined enough on a literary career, while working briefly after graduation at the British American Tobacco Company and then at Nottingham, not only to continue drafting 'Anthony Sant' but also to begin a fresh attempt at novel writing. This time, he tried his hand at a historical romance about Spanish Carlist rebels. 'The Episode' was heavily indebted to Joseph Conrad's *Arrow of Gold* for its literary style and to Thomas Carlyle's *The Life of John Sterling* for its historical material. Completed during the summer of 1926 (by which time he had secured a post in London at *The Times*), this second attempt at novel writing was also promptly turned down, both by his literary agent in late-September 1926 and by Heinemann in late-April 1927.[14] Undaunted, while attending Mass in the following May, where for Greene prayerful moments often drifted into secular thoughts, he dreamt up an (unwritten) detective mystery, involving a murdered governess and a priest (based upon G. K. Chesterton's Father Brown) who identifies a 12-year-old girl as the culprit.[15]

While still struggling to complete 'The Episode', Greene keenly pursued various other writing opportunities. He considered compiling a life of the Elizabethan Catholic poet and martyr Robert Southwell and earnestly solicited Vivien's advice on this topic. In an early instance of his lifelong oscillation between divinely inspiring and basely sensual interests, Greene eventually opted instead for compiling a biography of the salacious Restoration rake and poet, John Wilmot, Earl of Rochester. He began work on this project in autumn 1930 but it was turned down by Heinemann and, after being put aside for decades, only found a publisher in 1974 as *Lord Rochester's Monkey*.[16] However, Greene's preliminary researches during late-1926 into Southwell's heroic death left a lasting impression on his creative imagination and stimulated a sustained interest in the heroism of Jesuit martyrology. This was later manifested in his warm reviews of Evelyn Waugh's *Edmund Campion* and Pierre Janelle's *Life of Robert Southwell* (*Spectator*, 1 November 1935), his admiration in *The Lawless Roads* for the missionary courage of the executed Mexican Father Pro, the self-sacrificing demise of the whisky priest in *The Power and the Glory* and his impassioned preface to Philip Caraman's translation from Latin of *John Gerard. The Autobiography of an Elizabethan*.[17]

Greene's poem 'First Love', a quasi-devotional meditation upon paradise inspired by his love for Vivien, won the *New Statesman* sonnet prize in September 1926. This minor literary triumph serves to confirm just how central concepts of spiritual aspiration had now become in his ambitions to establish himself as a writer.[18] Such religious influences were brought to the fore in Greene's literary creativity by Vivien and she became one of the most important influences over his development as a writer between 1925 and the early-1940s. In addition to toning down the metaphorical 'leopards' lurking in his prose, she regularly made numerous other copy-editing suggestions for emendations of vocabulary and phrasing in her husband's typescripts and proofs. Greene usually adopted her recommendations and this stylistically influential literary collaboration continued long after their formal separation.[19]

Greene's first meeting with Vivien had been prompted by her keen sense of verbal exactitude. For the February 1925 issue of *Oxford Outlook*, Greene had tried his hand at controversial journalism in a short article on 'The Average Film' in which he attacked what he regarded as the current twin obsessions with religious and sexual matters in the cinema and theatre. Such preoccupations, he argued, were now so prevalent that they were becoming seriously detrimental to the pursuit of aesthetic excellence in the arts. Depicting his own generation as prone either to going to Church to 'worship' the Virgin Mary or sniggering over bawdy stories and limericks in public houses, he deplored the diminishing effects of such banal attitudes on cinematography and the stage. This typical sample of undergraduate polemic, elicited an unexpectedly firm reply from the 19-year-old Vivien, who reprimanded Greene for his theologically inappropriate use of the word 'worship' in relation to the Virgin Mary since, she explained, from a Catholic perspective it was only possible to 'venerate' the Mother of God in a process known as 'hyperdulia'. Greene had already been impressed by Vivien's beauty during a brief visit to Blackwell's in early-March 1925 and he was delighted to find that this was the same girl when he wrote to apologize and invite her for tea in his rooms at Balliol.[20]

In *A Sort of Life* Greene recalled how in 1926, during his religious instruction by Father Trollope, his major struggle had been not with the idea of believing 'in the love of God' but 'in a God at all'. He could readily show an academic interest in the date of the Gospels and the historical evidence for the existence of Jesus Christ since he 'didn't disbelieve in Christ – I disbelieved in God'. Throughout his writing career, Greene identified strongly with the desire for conclusive proof of the presence of a higher power. He habitually regarded doubt and scepticism rather than blind faith as the natural human perspective upon matters of religious devotion – so much so, that he chose the name of Thomas, after the doubting apostle rather than Thomas Aquinas (120–1), to mark his admission into the Catholic Church.

This strong personal identification with the innate human frailties of doubt and disbelief, along with a concomitant desire for miraculous proof of a higher power, pervades Greene's early post-conversion publications. One of his most memorable short stories – written in 1929 as 'The Widow' but now known as 'The Second Death' – engages directly with two biblical miracles in its depiction of a dying man who had previously been raised from the dead and a narrator who had been given sight by a stranger whose cold touch felt like spittle on his eyelids. It overtly recalls the raisings of the widow's son (Lk. 7.11–17) and Lazarus (Jn 11.1–45) and Jesus's curing of the blind man (Jn 9.1–12). The narrator's dry scepticism – 'Miracles of that sort don't happen nowadays' (158) – rings hollow as the efficacy of miracles seems triumphantly reaffirmed by the end of the story. Whether this tale was written for (or with input from) Vivien is not known but Greene's curiosity over the potency of the miraculous seems obvious in its conclusion.

The Man Within (1929)

Despite Vivien's warning in early-1925 over confusing 'worship' with 'devotion' for the Virgin Mary, Greene's first published novel, *The Man Within*, suggests that he was still ready to exploit in his fictions the creative tension between venerating and worshipping an idealized female character. It was received with considerable acclaim and achieved impressively high sales for Heinemann in England and Doubleday Doran in the USA. It also ensured Greene's introduction into London literary life as a promising new novelist.[21] In retrospect, this level of success seems puzzling, since the novel offers a melodramatic plot and starkly wooden characters. Its wavering prose style blends powerful passages of expressionistic imagery with awkwardly mannered poetic effects. Riddled with echoes of Sir Walter Scott, R. L. Stevenson (a distant relative of Greene's mother), Joseph Conrad, Ford Madox Ford and Marjorie Bowen's *The Viper of Milan*, the novel reads as a patchwork testament to Greene's then current literary influences. In style the book is 'derivative and sentimental', Paul O'Prey suggests, 'and all attempts at creating a sense of action and excitement are spoiled by the ambitious young author's unsuccessful pretensions to high moral seriousness and depth psychology.' Similarly, Michael Shelden concludes that it is the 'apprentice work of a novelist in his twenties, who knows how to handle a rousing tale, but whose art touches no depths. Everything that is worth knowing in the book is on the surface'.

Cedric Watts focuses more constructively on what was probably the most important element of this novel to the author himself: 'This is a strange, murky, implausible novel which seems largely to be an act of psychological self-purgation by Greene.'[22] In addition to revealing strong elements of psychoanalytical influence (recalling Kenneth Richmond's treatments), *The Man Within* engages imaginatively with the author's recently espoused Catholic preoccupations. Indeed, some of the most high-flown and puzzling passages in the novel, especially those focusing upon its quasi-saintly heroine Elizabeth, can be read as a private devotional dialogue between Greene and his wife Vivien. In these passages he gives full vent to a tendency, never entirely eradicated from his fiction, towards the 'worship' of idealized female figures and, in contrast, a Manichaean denigration of alluringly sexualized and 'fallen' women.

The Man Within tells the stirring tale – in this respect, Greene makes productive use of his youthful fascination with adventure novels by Rider Haggard, Arthur Conan Doyle and John Buchan – of a group of early-nineteenth century smugglers, led by the charismatic and devilishly godlike Captain Carlyon, who are betrayed by one of their own company. This Judas figure is Francis Andrews, a sensitive Greeneian youth, who has only been allowed to join the gang because his redoubtable but now deceased father (another devilishly godlike presence) had been a hero figure to the other members. Desperate to escape from their malign influence, Andrews treacherously tips off the English customs men over where an impending delivery of contraband from France will be unloaded. As the smugglers are intercepted, one of the revenue men is killed and he flees to the Sussex Downs where he is given shelter by a calm and virtuous young woman called Elizabeth. Andrews is deeply smitten by her charismatic presence and his responses towards her (to use Vivien's terminologies) oscillate self-consciously between 'worship' and 'hyperdulia'.

Elizabeth persuades the cowardly and morally wavering Andrews to stand as a witness for the prosecution in the trial of six of the captured smugglers. Eventually, he attends the court but even this apparently honourable gesture is another Judas-like act of betrayal, this time towards Elizabeth. He is really there only at the behest of Lucy, a promiscuous woman who has agreed to have sex with him if he testifies. She, in turn, seems a devilish presence since she is willing to prostitute herself in this fashion to secure a conviction for her aged lover, Sir Henry Merriman, the prosecuting council at the assizes. Unexpectedly, the smugglers are acquitted and, after a final and moving encounter with Elizabeth at her cottage, Andrews cravenly flees just as Carlyon and some of his men burst in to take their revenge. Elizabeth heroically commits suicide (as an act of self-sacrificing martyrdom) with Andrews's knife before they can force her to inform on him.

The Man Within ends with Andrews captured by the revenue officers and, it seems, poised to snatch the knife from them to enact his own (finally honourable) demise in imitation of Elizabeth's martyrdom. Its cast-list of devilishly godlike father figures (Carlyon and Andrews's father), women who are either saint-like (Elizabeth) or devilish whores (Lucy) and the ever-vulnerable Andrews suggests that Greene was indulging in a melodramatic mixture of Manichaean and Cathar perspectives upon the horrors of the fallen world. Certainly, he shows little concern for verisimilitude or psychological depth (even the central protagonist, Andrews, is far from being a convincing character) in the caricatures that populate the unexpectedly torrid landscapes of rural Sussex in this first published novel.

In later life, Greene admitted that this melodramatic tale was the work of an inexperienced writer but he was happy for it to be reprinted in paperback in 1971. He also included it in his collected works (The Bodley Head, 1976), unlike his next two published novels *The Name of Action* and *Rumour at Nightfall*, which he continued to suppress. It seems understandable that the aging author may have retained a nostalgic fondness for his first published novel. But Greene's attitude seems to hint at more than merely sentimental nostalgia. In a striking act of self-reflective circularity and authorial closure, various elements from this 1929 novel set along the Sussex coast in the early-1800s were implicitly incorporated into Greene's last published novel, *The Captain and the Enemy*

(1988), focusing on the Nicaragua of the Sandinista guerrillas of the 1980s.[23] *The Man Within* may also have held a special significance for Greene since it was the first major work in which his new-found allegiance to Catholicism, coupled with his interest in psychoanalysis, formed a central strand in his fictional writings.

Illustrating a stylistic habit that soon became embedded in his fictions, *The Man Within* derives a wide range of its language and imagery from religious sources. The double-dealing Andrews is repeatedly denoted as a 'sort of Judas' (63, 69), as one of two 'Judases in Sussex' (84), the 'informer, traitor, Judas' (136) and 'that Judas' (150). Biblical references also intrude jarringly into Greene's descriptions, suggesting that Vivien (despite her sharp eye for secular 'leopards' in his prose) may have been far more indulgent towards her husband's scriptural excesses. Hence, we find that Andrews does not just have a sense when he is with Elizabeth of time passing too quickly but that it rushes to destruction like 'Gadarene swine' (32). Similarly, a dewpond from which some cows are drinking is bright blue from the reflected sky like an 'illuminated missal' (96). Numerous other biblical references are thrust into the narrative, such as Andrews's awkwardly oblique reference to the parable about the swept room and the 'devils which entered worse than the first' (193; see Mt. 12. 43–45 and Lk 11. 24–26), as he tries to express to Elizabeth his adoring love for her.

When Andrews first meets Elizabeth, she is under the sway of a grim, bible-reading guardian called Jenkins who, conveniently, soon dies and leaves her alone in her isolated cottage. At his funeral on a cold and misty day, Andrews loses himself in the sonorous words of the Anglican liturgy for the burial of the dead: 'And though after my skin worms destroy this body, yet in my flesh shall I see God . . . Lord, let me know mine end and the number of my days' (34). He silently admires Elizabeth's resilience until he is brought back to the present moment by the insistent words of Psalm 39.12: 'For I am a stranger with thee; and a sojourner, as all my fathers were. O spare me a little that I may recover my strength: before I go hence and be no more seen' (35) – words which poignantly encapsulate Andrews's later hiding out at Elizabeth's cottage. She also tells him how her guardian once sent a note to her school, insisting that her education should focus specifically upon scripture, so that she could read to him in the evening from the Bible and learn how to dispute 'theological points'. One evening she reads the parable of the unjust steward (Lk. 16.1–18). This triggers Jennings's guilt over his usurpation of her domestic environment, leading to his gloomy insistence – which might be taken as an epigraph for Greene's fascination with biblical language – 'you can't get over Scripture' (80–1).

When reading *The Man Within* it is also difficult to 'get over' the implicit presence of Vivien Greene, especially with reference to the novel's iconic sketching of female virtue as represented in Elizabeth. In creating such a 'sentimental complex' (Greene's description) of feminine goodness, he drew upon the rich vein of inspiration which he found in venerating and worshipping an idealized woman.[24] Certainly, while he was drafting this novel, Greene's private correspondence with Vivien also maintains this attractive mythologizing of the female beloved. It is a characteristic trope of his letters that, despite earnest attempts as an impassioned acolyte to control himself, he could not resist the rapturous contemplation of her supposed sanctity. On 27 May 1927, for example, he describes what he sees as the miraculous nature of their love, entirely due to her unsullied, saint-like virtue: 'I can believe that miracles will be done at your grave. Only you should be the patron saint of lovers & depose that nonentity St. Valentine.' In an earlier letter of 2 February 1927, he concocts another quasi-devotional fantasy of secretly visiting her bedside while she sleeps so that he can kneel in worship and kiss her gently on the lips beneath a crucifix.[25] While any verbal analysis of passionate love letters risks intruding upon a private world of significances encoded only for the benefit of two self-immersed individuals, the specific phrasing of these letters seems to have informed the insistently devotional female iconography of *The Man Within*.

W. J. West states: 'Vivien Greene . . . was the single most important person in Greene's life in his last days at Oxford and for many years afterwards'; and her significance to the genesis and drafting of *The Man Within* is undoubted.[26] Greene's idealized perspectives on his wife clearly influenced his sketching of the novel's distinctly other-worldly heroine, Elizabeth. It seems likely that her depiction was in no small measure intended as a kind of private, spiritually intense dialogue between himself and Vivien. The first edition of the novel bore the ardent printed dedication: 'For Vivienne/My Wife/In Wonder', followed by the last six lines of Thomas Hardy's love sonnet, 'Her Definition': 'As common chests encasing wares of price,/Are borne with tenderness through halls of state'. The presentation copy of the first edition given by Greene to Vivien also contains an additional manuscript dedication and original poem to her, glossing the phrase 'In Wonder' of the printed dedication:

> With all my heart
> For my eternal Love
> June 13 1929.
> Seeking to express with time-worn words
> Your wonder, mystery, delight,
> And glory, as when Spanish swords,
> Flashed for a losing fight,
> The tongue-tied Brain can utter
> No more than, in its darkening cage alone,
> The amazed Heart could mutter –
> That a light shone.[27]

Andrews first sees Elizabeth standing between 'yellow-tipped candles' (26) when he seeks refuge in her isolated cottage and she resolutely confronts him with a gun. These candles seem no more than a minor domestic detail but, in retrospect, the positioning of the young woman between two such familiar items of church devotion is striking. A few chapters later, the betrayed and murderous Carlyon comes in search of Andrews and Elizabeth bravely hides him in a cupboard. In terms reminiscent of Greene's love letters to Vivien, Andrews kneels down and watches the action through a keyhole. Elizabeth coolly saves him from certain retribution at the hands of his former devilish protector and surrogate godlike father figure. As she does so, her hitherto secular identity is miraculously transmuted in Andrews's mind into that of a potent spiritual image of female devotion. He kneels down to peer into the room beyond but 'now in heart he knelt to her. She is a saint, he thought' (61). Henceforth, Elizabeth becomes the object of Andrews's intense veneration, 'hyperdulia' and, ultimately, worship. Once the frustrated Carlyon leaves, Andrews can hardly bear to forsake the sanctuary of his cupboard as he views Elizabeth as a 'picture, as holy as a vision'. Recalling his first sight of her 'pale resolute face' between the yellow flames of two candles, he reverentially opens the cupboard door and steps back into the room, as though entering into the presence of a 'mystery' (69). When Elizabeth offers to listen to his side of the story – she is unaware of who is innocent or guilty in the enmity between Carlyon and Andrews – he feels a confessional urge to 'go down on my knees to her' (70). She calmly receives his narrative without surprise or condemnation, leading him to conclude: 'She is a saint' (75).

As the timorous Andrews hurries away from the cottage towards Lewes, now convinced by Elizabeth that he must testify as a witness for the prosecution, he remains fixated upon her gentle fortitude. He imagines her waking up and coming down the stairs into the kitchen. But then this homely perspective shifts into a more devotional one as he imagines her lighting a fire, with puffs of white smoke billowing from her chimney:

> Some the sun caught, so that they seemed like a drift of birds, wheeling and flashing their white underwings. He found in the crevice of his mind, where childhood harboured, the faint memory of a pictured saint, a young girl with a pale, set face, round whose head a flock of doves turned and twisted. (95)

This memorable image reoccurs later in the novel. When Andrews falls in with a Mr Farne at Lewes he describes this picture to him and asks if he has ever seen a 'saint surrounded with white birds' (103). In his final meeting with Elizabeth he fondly recalls how he had imagined the smoke billowing from her cottage chimney and how it had reminded him of a 'flock of white birds round a saint' (192).

The probable source of Greene's inspiration for this insistent image again focuses attention upon Vivien's importance to the genesis of *The Man Within*. In 1925 Thérèse of Lisieux (1873–1897), a young Carmelite nun of exceptional devotional zeal, was canonized. Her life story was already well known among Francophone Catholics through a collection of epistolary essays, written at the order of her prioress, and first published in 1898 as *Histoire d'une âme* (*Story of a*

Soul). To mark her canonization, in 1925 various publications in English appeared about her life and writings, including three volumes by the Catholic publisher, Burns, Oates & Co: *The Spirit of Saint Thérèse de l'Enfant Jésus*; a selection of her *Poems*; and *Saint Teresa of the Child Jesus: Four Studies*, translated by a 'Dominican of Headington'.[28] This last work is of special interest here since Vivien had been received into the Catholic Church in 1922 after receiving daily instruction from the Dominican Father Bede Jarrett (whose own mother had been a convert to Catholicism) at the Dominican Priory in Hampstead near her mother's home.[29]

Vivien's close personal association with Jarrett and the Dominicans ensured her interest in the cult and iconography of the most famous newly canonized Catholic saint of the 1920s. Her personal devotion to St Thérèse of Lisieux remained strong for the rest of her life, as is illustrated by her own prized copy of Ronald Knox's translation of her *L'Histoire d'une âme*, published by the Harvill Press in 1958 as the *Autobiography of a Saint: Thérèse of Lisieux*. Inside this volume Vivien carefully preserved until her death in 2003 various newspaper cuttings about St. Thérèse, including a copy of the photograph taken in 1886 and another taken by her sister Céline in June 1897, four months before her death.[30]

As an undergraduate historian at Oxford, Greene knew the historical publications of Jarrett (who had graduated in history from Oxford in 1907); and Vivien's friendship with him would have consolidated this interest. Greene was certainly familiar with Jarrett's *Medieval Socialism* (1913); and during his Catholic instruction he would have been required to read two of Jarrett's devotional works, *Meditations for Layfolk* (1915) and *Living Temples* (1919). Later in his career, Greene also made extensive use of Jarrett's *Social Theories in the Middle Ages* (1926) and *Medieval Socialism* as he sought to justify his strong but apparently conflicting commitments to both Catholicism and Marxism.

The best known portrait of St Thérèse of Lisieux (the 'Little Flower') is a small photograph of her in her Carmelite habit, holding a flower before a large wooden cross. This image matches well with Greene's image of Elizabeth in *The Man Within* as a 'pictured saint, a young girl with a pale, set face' (95). Since Greene had met Vivien and begun his Catholic instruction in 1925, he would have been well aware of St Thérèse's canonization in that year, an event which became of crucial importance to Catholic hagiography during the 1920s. In both France and England Catholic publishers and journalists made much of the simple purity and childlike attractiveness of Marie Françoise-Thérèse Martin (her family name). These same qualities seem to lie at the heart of Greene's depiction of his heroine, Elizabeth, in *The Man Within*. He is also likely to have seen pictures of one of the best-known images of the saint. For her canonization in May 1925 at St Peter's in Rome, the Carmelites of her convent at Lisieux produced an immense painted banner – reputedly designed by Thérèse's sister, Céline (Soeur Geneviève) – depicting the apotheosis of the saint, surrounded by a semicircle of angels (*putti*), which to the distant observer bears a striking resemblance to the wings of doves. As Greene writes in *The Man Within*, these angels resemble a 'drift of birds, wheeling and flashing their white underwings' (95). Andrews seems to draw directly upon Catholic iconography when he imagines Elizabeth as a 'pictured saint . . . round whose head a flock of doves turned and twisted' (95).[31]

The disturbing working-title of *The Man Within* had been 'Dear Sanity' and Greene seems to have sublimated several of his current sexual and psychological problems into its narrative. He had already demonstrated this tendency in late-1925 when compiling his second (unpublished) novel, 'The Episode'. He sent a draft chapter to Vivien for her editorial scrutiny, in which a character's offer of marriage is turned down by his girlfriend. She angrily considered that Greene, despite his vehement protests of innocence, was casually exploiting her initial rejection of him when he had proposed to her by the canal at Wolvercote. It is also well documented that during their courtship Greene even suggested a celibate marriage to Vivien while, at the same period, becoming a frequenter of London prostitutes, just as Andrews remains infatuated with Elizabeth's virginal purity while readily copulating with Lucy.[32]

In response to these personal dilemmas, Greene's polarized contrast in *The Man Within* between the virginally pure Elizabeth and the sensually seductive Lucy offers a meditation upon the familiar literary dichotomy of woman as either Madonna or whore. Robert Hoskins aptly suggests that as the novel progresses the two women effectively participate in a 'duel of angels for Andrews's soul'.[33] In psychological and spiritual terms Lucy, a Manichaean 'devil as well as a harlot' (167), offers physical temptation and a re-enactment of the Fall to Andrews; while Elizabeth, a Cathar-like *parfaite*, provides brief moments of sanity and self-knowledge. She also symbolizes an insistent motif of Christian hope for the possibility of redemption through her final and Christ-like act of self-sacrifice on behalf of Andrews who becomes the embodiment of fallen humanity. The concluding words of the novel take us back full circle to the devotional language of Andrews's first encounter with Elizabeth as a young girl framed by 'yellow-tipped candles' (26). As he surreptitiously reaches out for the knife to kill himself, Andrews feels a transcendent calm:

> now there were two stars or it might be two yellow candles in the night around him . . . for between the two candles there was a white set face that regarded him without pity and without disapproval, with wisdom and with sanity. (221)

Chapter 2

The Man of Letters: 1930–1935

The Name of Action (1930) and *Rumour at Nightfall* (1931)

Following the success of his first published novel, Greene sought to diversify his output as a writer. Inevitably, the literary results of the next five years were variable in both genre and quality. He was uncertain as to how best to move on stylistically from *The Man Within* and noted how his attitude changed markedly between his first and second novels: 'the first is an adventure, the second is a duty.'[1] Ultimately, his next two novels, *The Name of Action* and *Rumour at Nightfall*, proved dead ends and Greene suppressed them by refusing any republication during his lifetime (a prohibition maintained posthumously). This is problematic for modern readers since Richard Johnstone explains: 'Both novels can be seen as statements of the problem facing the twentieth-century man attracted to religious commitment; they point both to the emotional need for faith, and to the impossibility of overcoming scepticism.' Paul O'Prey endorses this view, arguing that these suppressed novels mark Greene's first sustained 'attempt to introduce Catholicism into his fictional world'. Their two protagonists, Oliver Chant and Francis Chase, reflect their author's fascination with the role of scepticism within a Catholic society:

> Both Chant and Chase are rational unbelievers who come into contact with Catholicism as yet another mysterious element of the exotic and romantic worlds into which they have strayed. They are at one and the same time attracted to and suspicious of its 'certainty'.[2]

The Name of Action, set largely in Trier, recycled material from the unpublished novel 'The Episode'. This ancient German city, close to the French and Luxembourg borders, provided Greene with a politically dangerous and geographically liminal location. After the First World War the French had sought to seize the region around Trier (the Palatinate) and had promoted a separatist movement in what became known as the 'Revolver Republic'. The area was aptly named since its first (and only) president, Herr Heinz, was soon assassinated. Although a Catholic, it was reported that Heinz had been refused the last rites and French propaganda took this denial as confirmation that local clergy were being controlled by Protestant Germany. During the long vacation of 1924 Greene volunteered his services, in murkily uncertain circumstances, to the German embassy. He was sent on a fact-finding tour of the French-occupied Rhineland around Trier, supposedly to document the repressive treatment of the native German inhabitants. British intelligence reports suggested that there were no major differences between German Protestants and Catholics in their attitude towards the French separatist movement. But at Trier Greene found a Catholic underground grouping which greatly impressed him through their heroic fortitude against oppression. The phrase, 'They are all good Catholics' (167, 169), is a repeated mantra in *The Name of Action*; and (in contrast to the puritanical dictator Demassener and his revolutionary opponent, the wily Jew Kapper) the ordinary Catholic folk of the region seem the only decent elements within the local population.[3]

Begun in March 1929 and published in October 1930, *The Name of Action* bore the dedication, 'For Vivienne', accompanied by lines from John Donne's 'The Dream', publicly confirming her role as his chief literary muse: 'Thou are so truth, that thoughts of thee suffice,/To make dreams truths; and fables histories.' In a surviving typescript, Greene added on its endpaper another affectionate tribute to her creative presence in the novel: 'Because the mountain grass/Cannot but keep the form/Where the mountain hare has lain.'[4] It seems likely that the heavily laden Catholic contexts of the novel were in no small measure intended to please Vivien. On his arrival in Trier – pointedly during the Easter period (21) – Chant has to make a secret rendezvous at a shoemaker's shop in the Jesuitenstrasse by the seminary. Although Greene refers in passing to other well known landmarks at Trier, such as the Porta Nigra Gate (21) and the church of St Gangolf (25), he makes the Jesuit seminary (16, 26, 28, 29, 43, 54), with its symbolically white walls (166), a focal centre for Chant as he gradually gains familiarity with the city. In particular, he repeatedly draws attention to the seminary's statue of the Madonna (29, 184) set high upon the walls which presides in virginal purity over the sexually decadent and disordered world of Trier.

Like *The Man Within*, there is a distinctly Manichaean quality to Greene's depiction of his characters in *The Name of Action*. Chant becomes infatuated with the dictator's hypnotically beautiful wife, Anne-Marie. Recalling Andrews's image of Elizabeth as a pale-faced saint surrounded by a halo of white doves, Chant is first seduced by a photograph of Anne-Marie (8) and imagines her as a lovely vision of 'flowers, dark hair and exciting lips' (98). His devotion, however, is sadly mistaken since Anne-Marie proves to be a coldly experienced woman, sexually frustrated by her husband's impotence. Like the whorish Lucy in *The Man Within*, she casually sleeps with Chant, not through love but, as she bluntly points out when he naively proposes marriage, merely to gratify her lustful pleasure in exerting power over men (297). Finally exposed as a devilish seducer, she schemes to become the mistress of the revolutionary Jewish leader, Kapper, as political power begins to slip away from her husband, President

Demassener. This disturbing strain of anti-semitism running through the novel creates another kind of Manichaean devil in the figure of Kapper. He is consistently associated with darkness and sexual debauchery, keeps a printing machine for black propaganda in a Hades-like cellar (37–40) and regards the Virgin Mary as the 'mother of his eternal enemy' (169).

Kapper exists as the polar opposite of the Catholic dictator Demassener and, viewed together, they reiterate Greene's continuing fascination with the idea of God and the Devil being a linked or dual entity. Demassener is sketched as an unworldly and fanatical puritan, recalling Shakespeare's Angelo in *Measure for Measure*, who hates the 'sexual debauch' (64) of Trier. He earnestly assures Chant that he sometimes feels that he is the only person who can view human society as it 'must appear to a God who is not smirched by living in the world'. In Manichaean mode, Demassener triumphantly concludes that he hates 'freedom' because it releases the 'animal in man', who needs to be bound in 'clean chains' (78). This sense of religious fanaticism is sustained throughout the novel and, in twisted parodies of devotional language, two of its most powerful scenes are laced with disturbing religious imagery.

In the first scene soon after his arrival at Trier, Chant is followed through the streets by a member of the secret police whom he finally spots as he passes between two lamps underneath a 'Virgin and Child carved in a small alcove of wall' (110). As Chant desperately tries to escape, the policeman is shot by Kapper and he slowly sinks to the ground as though 'letting himself down stiffly in a church to pray'. Horrified by this lethal intervention, Chant kneels down beside the corpse and seemingly joins the murdered man in a 'silent Communion' (106–8). The second scene takes place at the climax of the novel inside the gothic church of Our Lady, which is described as though experienced in a feverish nightmare, 'characteristic of expressionistic works, in which the vista seems the expression of an abnormal state of mind'.[5] The white face and feet of a 'gigantic hanging Christ' on a crucifix remind Chant of the loving self-sacrifice of the God of light to save mankind and, simultaneously, of the devilish God of darkness who, eagle-like, tears at the 'hearts of men with doubt, terror, mystery and . . . divine unrest' (289). As Chant pivots painfully between hope and despair, he utters a prayerful lament: '"O God . . . I wish I that I could believe in your infinity"' (291). Seeking a kind of self-sacrificing redemption, Chant finally accompanies the deposed Demassener back to England and, as they sit on the train together, dawn lights 'with an equal pallor his own and his enemy's face' (344).

Greene conceded that he had been overly influenced in *The Name of Action* by the 'point of view' technique promulgated in Percy Lubbock's *The Craft of Fiction* and by Conrad's *The Arrow of Gold*, in which the hero also becomes involved in a political conspiracy and falls under the influence of a dangerously seductive woman. The language and characters of *The Name of Action* are often overwrought and, Cedric Watts concludes: 'Like its predecessor, this novel appears . . . to be a means of psychological catharsis for its author.'[6] Although in retrospect Greene was rather too negative over its reception – he claimed that it only sold 2,000 copies while his publisher's records suggest 5,000 copies – he was still clearly an author in search of a distinctive voice as a novelist.[7]

Greene's next (and also suppressed) novel, *Rumour at Nightfall* (1931), was started in early-September 1930, revised alongside work on his biography of Rochester, and published in November 1931.[8] Again attempting to recycle materials from 'The Episode', Greene took the nineteenth-century Carlist rebellion in Spain as his historical background. The novel's torrid action focuses upon the jealous (but formerly intimate) relationship of two Protestant Englishmen. Francis Chase, an adventurous newspaper correspondent who is trusted by the outlawed rebels, is angered and confused when his romantically inclined friend, Michael Crane, unexpectedly shows up and falls in love with a beguiling Catholic woman, Eulelia Monti, with whom Chase is infatuated. Eventually, Crane marries her but is betrayed by Chase and killed by the rebels. The novel concludes melodramatically with Chase and the grieving widow consoling one another. Written primarily to satisfy the terms of a three-book contract with Heinemann, *Rumour at Nightfall* provides, despite its flaws, a fascinating insight into Greene's current preoccupations with his new found Catholicism and his determination to put it to creative purposes in his fiction.

As with *The Name of Action*, Greene's literary sources remain problematically prominent in the fabric of the novel and he particularly regretted basing his lifeless cipher of a heroine on Conrad's Doña Rita in *The Arrow of Gold*. His choice of historical setting was also unhelpful to an inexperienced novelist since he had spent only one day in Spain when he was 16 and his knowledge of the Carlist conflicts was drawn entirely from Carlyle's *Life of John Sterling* (1851).[9] Stirling, a friend of Coleridge, Wordsworth and John Stuart Mill, had written *Thoughts on the Foreign Policy of England* (1827) in support of a popular uprising in Spain. In 1830, he canvassed support for an expedition to Spain led by General Torrijos – events which became the key source for Greene's *Rumour at Nightfall*. Clearly, it was a major problem that this novel strove to offer a stirring adventure story when its author's knowledge of the relevant Spanish contexts relied entirely upon an 80-year-old English biography.

In his conversations with Marie-Françoise Allain, Greene admitted that *The Name of Action* and *Rumour at Nightfall* were 'bad' because he had failed to create enough distance 'between them and myself'.[10] This is certainly true of the latter novel since Greene forced upon it starkly formulaic echoes of his interest in psychoanalytic responses to the 'divided self', liberally blended with sporadic outbursts of Catholic iconography. Philip Stratford has traced how in *Rumour at Nightfall* Greene replaces his two previous single heroes with a 'divided mind' (Andrews and Chant) with two distinct but virtually twin heroes (Chase and Crane), 'each of whom represents one side of a nebulous total nature'. Like Greene's own pre-conversion self, they begin the novel as indifferently agnostic Protestants but then find themselves immersed in the intensely devotional Catholicism of revolutionary Spain. The novel is divided into three distinct sections, with the first and third seen through the eyes of Chase (representing, as befits a journalist, the rationally sceptical world of the Mind) and the middle part given over to his former friend Crane (representing the romantic mysticism of the Heart). They both fall in love with the elusively virtuous Eulelia Monti, the daughter of an ascetic and saintly father and an emaciated former voluptuary of a mother. Eulelia represents the world of the Soul and is also courted by the rebel leader Caveda, a secular and materialistic sensualist who represents the temptations of the Flesh and the Body. In *Rumour at Nightfall* it seems as though Greene was unwisely attempting to combine the conflicting generic forms of a Christian morality drama and an international action-adventure story.

Although *The Man Within* and *The Name of Action* are both heavily laced with Catholic scenarios and iconography, Philip Stratford has argued that *Rumour at Nightfall* should be regarded as Greene's 'first Catholic novel' since it contains his 'first attempt to find a religious basis for his emerging novelist's point of view'.[11] Certainly, the heated world of Spanish Catholicism dominates much of the action of the novel and Chase describes how an intense spirit of religious devotion directs his rebel companions who seemed to fight under the 'shadow of this sense of immortality':

> Round corners, in the shadows cast by anonymous peaks, stood wooden crosses bearing bloodstained and contorted Christs, the superstitious emblems of a race untouched by scientific knowledge. Their religion seemed to him not a consolation but a horror, the product of a deadly cold and an intolerable heat. (6)

Chase is soon instructed in the efficacy of these religious beliefs when one of the Carlist rebels, Luis Roca, is mortally wounded. As he lies dying, his leader Colonel Riego kneels alongside him with a crucifix and rosary beads, gently encouraging him to make a final confession for the 'good' of his 'soul' (8). Roca is too weak to speak but instead squeezes Riego's hand in response to a list of questions about his possible sins. At the moment of Roca's death, Riego makes a final supplicating prayer that his soldier may be saved from the 'pains of hell' and is being led by 'holy angels' to the 'home of Paradise' (10). Chase is deeply moved by the emotional power of this scene and, although he tries to dismiss the colonel's actions as mere superstition, he remains impressed by the unwavering fortitude of the rebels. As they move on, they begin to sing about their ancestors, unhappy love-affairs and 'religious songs' about the 'agony of the Cross' and the 'terror of death' (14).

Just as Oliver Chant had first been entranced by a photograph of Anne-Marie in *The Name of Action*, so in *Rumour at Nightfall* Chase becomes obsessed with a photograph of Eulelia Monti. He imagines her to be a good woman like a 'spoilt nun', whose spiritual world is made up of 'crosses and crucifixes, beads and prayers, tortures, flames, fear' (20–1). There remains, however, a persistent

Manichaean quality to Chase's attitudes towards women and, despite growing ever more infatuated with Eulelia, he still hopes to find a wife who would not be too beautiful since that 'carried with it an instinctive idea of immorality, incontinence, passion', remote from the 'begetting of children' (27). Once Crane begins to show an interest in Eulelia, Chase takes refuge in misogynistic crudity as he recognizes his friend's desire and even thinks that he might become his 'pimp' (63). Inevitably, the more romantically inclined Crane grows closer to Eulelia and she shares with him her devout father's interest in the works of Southwell and Campion, as well as her understanding of terms like 'Good and Evil, Heaven and Hell, Eternity' (194). The culminating spiritual scene of the novel takes place when they visit a church and Crane appears to undergo a quasi-mystical experience as Eulelia reaffirms her faith:

> he knew . . . if He existed at all, He existed in that church as He did not exist in the sun, in a theatre, in a crowd, at games, at an inn. He was said to be all-good, but in the sun that bred decay and made flesh rot, in any place where men were gathered for differing motives. He was qualified by evil. (211)

Once again, Manichaean qualities begin to contaminate the novel's language as Crane ponders the universality of God's presence but, ultimately, they are triumphantly swept aside through the purity of his love for Eulelia. As with Greene's devotional and idealized courtship of his wife Vivien, so Crane finds a potential for redemption in contemplating not God Himself but rather the assumed perfection of his intended spouse, Eulelia: 'If I lose you, I lose faith. I can believe in mystery with you here, in God upon the altar, in God upon the tongue. Let him marry us while I believe' (215). As he proclaims these words, Crane senses the chance to become one with the 'endless circle of God and the Mother of God'. A miraculous circle of pure white light, at first 'small as a wedding ring', then shoots through the gloom of the church: 'its orbit growing like the circle of a stone in a pool, enclosing the altar, enclosing the pillars, enclosing the priest, brushing his own face with the wind of its movement, dazzling his eyes with its light' (221).

Ultimately, Crane is betrayed and killed through the treachery of his other 'self' and former friend, Chase, whose mind resumes control over the third and final section of the novel. As he listens to bells ringing out for Benediction, Chase imagines believers kneeling at communion before the Host, devoutly acknowledging the living embodiment of the flesh and blood of God. Unlike Crane, who seems before his death to have attained a sense of oneness, via Eulelia, with God and His Mother, Chase can only cynically conclude that worshipping 'an eternal sacrifice was evil' and 'left the individual soul in loneliness' (236). Chase's renewed relationship with Eulelia offers some hope for the future in the macabre closing scene of the novel where they reverentially tend the Christ-like corpse of Crane. But any coherent religious message for the novel seems to dissolve into a series of confusing dualities created by the need to confirm Chase and Crane as a 'divided self', finally drawn together through their shared love for Eulelia and the possibility of their 'sad union' (299) – the last words of the novel.

Stamboul Train (1932)

Sales of *Rumour at Nightfall* were disappointing but its failure and that of its predecessor exerted, in retrospect, a positive effect on the direction of Greene's ambitions as a writer since he determined henceforth to dilute his dependence upon literary models (especially Conrad).[12] He also sought to temper his complex and often confusing preoccupations with psychoanalysis and religious belief. While still retaining traces of these aspects of his literary creativity, Greene's next three novels – *Stamboul Train*, *It's a Battlefield* and *England Made Me* – laid the foundations for a more distinctive personal tone. As Cedric Watts explains of *Stamboul Train*, the first of Greene's so-called 'entertainments':

> This novel was well researched and was written with a new thematic richness, diversity of characterisation, liveliness of movement and sharpness of observation. He had turned away from nostalgic literary romanticism towards contemporary cinematic realism; away from the verbosity of *The Arrow of Gold* to the mobile montage of film . . . With *Stamboul Train*, Greene reached maturity as a novelist. The callowness, dreaminess and analytic prolixity of the early works have gone. *Stamboul Train* is gripping, ruthless, powerfully atmospheric; it has a vivid gallery of characters and a dextrously interwoven thematic structure. It has the pace of a thriller, the compression and technical agility of an experimental novel, and it is, as Greene deliberately intended, superbly cinematic.

To these comments may be added Norman Sherry's observation that its structure provided Greene with ample scope to exploit as a novelist 'his true talent – his ability to observe'. Written from the outset with the hope that it might be picked up by a film company, Greene used the then popular cinematic motif of the train journey – including Von Sternberg's *Shanghai Express* (1932) and later Alfred Hitchcock's *The Lady Vanishes* (1938) – to assemble a cosmopolitan cast of characters. He was then able to play down 'the importance of creating plausible characters and plots' in favour of creating 'a satisfying thickness of texture' in his presentation of their episodic interactions. These encounters were often cast in pairs, as though they were conceived as dramatic scenes from a play or cinematic montage.[13]

Greene sought a free return-ticket for the Orient Express but the rail company turned his request down. Instead, he had to buy a third-class ticket as far as Cologne and took sandwiches made by Vivien to save using the buffet-car.

He relied for his scenic information after Cologne upon a Baedeker guidebook and memories of a fleeting visit to Istanbul in August 1929, along with repeatedly playing Honegger's 'Pacific 231' on his gramophone for inspiration. *Stamboul Train* (bearing the dedication: 'For Vivien with all my love') is the first of Greene's novels to sustain interest in a diverse range of distinctive characters, productively confined within their own microcosm by the artificially closed setting of a train journey.[14]

The two central figures in the novel are leaving the security of England for an uncertain and dangerous future abroad. Dr Paul Czinner (pronounced 'sinner'), an idealistic middle-aged Marxist from Yugoslavia who has been living in exile at Great Birchington-on-sea under the alias Richard John and teaching at a grim Berkhamsted-like school, hopes to lead an imminent revolutionary uprising back home in Belgrade. Coral Musker, a waif-like but plucky showgirl, has left her drab background in Nottingham (192) to join an English dance-troupe at Istanbul. She offers an important prototype for a familiar kind of female character in Greene's novels. She reappears, with minor variations, as Milly in *It's a Battlefield*, Loo in *England Made Me*, Anne in *A Gun for Sale*, Rose in *Brighton Rock* and Helen in *The Heart of the Matter*. Coral and Czinner find themselves travelling in the company of a motley group of archly cinematic passengers. These include a cricket-obsessed Anglican clergyman, the Reverend Opie, on his way to become chaplain at the British embassy at Budapest; Carleton Myatt, an urbane Jewish currant-trader; Josef Grünlich, a cat burglar and ruthless killer; Mabel Warren, a predatory lesbian reporter; her beautiful Jewish companion, Janet Pardoe and a mindlessly censorious English couple called Peters.

Greene began writing his 'thriller on a train' in January 1932, completed it in July and received an informal offer of publication from Charles Evans at Heinemann's on 19 August (although, thanks to a threatened libel-suit from Priestley, who felt that he was being satirized as the popular novelist Quin Savory, it was not published until early-December). Greene's diary entry for 19 August conveys his astonished relief at such news and confirms how his Catholic allegiances now provided genuine emotional support to his literary ambitions: 'O God, what a lightening of heart . . . I felt so relieved and happy that I went into the church and thanked God.'[15] While the private recording of this kind of devotional response to positive news from a publisher is understandable, the dialogues and thoughts of characters in *Stamboul Train* are also often powerfully focused on the basic human desire for a faith in some kind of higher power, whether of a secular or divine nature. Furthermore, in this novel Greene seems far more balanced in his characteristic deployment of those self-reflective religious and psychological elements which had previously informed his imaginative processes.

Stamboul Train is the most sectarian of Greene's pre-1935 novels, with a sharp focus not only upon Anglicans and Catholics but also upon their attitudes towards the archetypal outsiders of Western-European society, the Jews. Early in the novel we learn from Carleton Myatt of an earnest Jewish convert to Christianity, Mr Eckman, who has a 'chained Bible' by his lavatory to advertise his faith and whose wife sewed clothing 'for the Anglican Mission' (15). Myatt, a hard-headed but spontaneously generous Jewish businessman, gives up his warm coat and compartment to the exhausted Coral Musker who, symbolically, shrouds her innocence within a cheap 'white mackintosh' (9). In return, she eventually sacrifices her virginity to him, although he later drops her for the more attractive (and Jewish) Janet Pardoe, whose family connections will be useful to his financial affairs.

Greene clearly enjoyed creating his archetypal Anglican minister, Opie, who (prefiguring the cricket-mad Caldicott and Charters in Hitchcock's *The Lady Vanishes*) sees life essentially as a glorious cricket match. He dreams of climbing in his surplice a 'great broad flight of marble steps towards the altar of God' (24), with a cricket bat under his arm and batting-gloves hanging from his wrist. In darker vein, Greene adds to his cast of characters the sinister thief and murderer Grünlich ('Greeneish'). Described by Grahame Smith as a 'parodic double of the saint, a figure of total evil', he automatically utters 'Hail Mary, full of grace' (71) as he slips on a snow-covered roof before a break-in and then respectfully hesitates in front of a 'pink-and-white Madonna' (73), prior to seducing a middle-aged secretary, Anna, and shooting dead her employer, Herr Kolber.[16]

The dominant religious focus of *Stamboul Train* is its exploration through the dilemma of Dr Paul Czinner of the ideals of revolutionary Marxism versus the moral values of Catholicism, a dialectic which Greene was to interrogate in his fictions for the next 50 years. The ruthlessly amoral journalist, Mabel Warren, initiates the complex religious framework surrounding Greene's depiction of Czinner. Realizing that she may be close to a tremendous scoop for her paper, she seems diabolically determined to gain an interview: 'I'll get him somehow, God damn his soul' (36). This thought is followed by an expressionistic hinting at a Christ-like identity for Czinner (linking him with the potency of Christian light through a play on 'sun'/'son') and a lament for humanity trapped in a fallen world:

> A tender light flooded the compartments. It would have been possible for a moment to believe that the sun was the expression of something that loved and suffered for men. Human beings floated like fish in golden water . . . On that golden tide they rose and fell, murmured and dreamed. They were not imprisoned, for they were not during the hour of dawn, aware of their imprisonment. (37)

Mabel Warren's relentless 'seduction' of her quarry is viewed as a tabloid re-enactment of the last hours of Christ, as she hopes finally to 'nail' Czinner to the 'bill page of the paper, an exclusive crucifixion' (44).

The world-weary Czinner is depicted as an agnostic Marxist who experiences a discordant mixture of religious sensations and recollections during his train journey back home towards certain danger and possible death. Regarding his five years as a teacher at a minor English school as a kind of 'burial', he recalls having to attend chapel services in which no one believed, 'asking God with the breathing discordant multitude to dismiss him with His blessing' (60). An overheard fragment of the Reverend Opie's conversation with the murderous Grünlich – 'I have the greatest respect, of course, for the Roman Catholic Church' (90) – acts as a prologue to some twenty pages focusing upon issues of religious, psychological and political beliefs. Although this section seems a somewhat disjointing authorial interpolation into the narrative, it serves to illuminate Czinner's personal motivations as he undertakes a life-threatening journey towards the (Christ-like) self-sacrifice of political martyrdom.

The cold and fearful Czinner recalls fragmentary childhood memories as he walks along the train corridor with flakes of snow falling outside against the windows. He gratefully ponders the sacrifices made by his devoted parents so that he could qualify as a doctor. But the noble sentiments motivating these studious ambitions withered away when he found that his own people were so poor that they could not afford his prescriptions and treatments. Similarly, his parents' ardent Catholicism, once so definitively supporting for his family life, had grown as meaningless as his hard-earned medical skills. He recalls with distaste childhood religious processions:

A god who had swayed down crowded aisles under a bright moth-worn canopy, a god the size of a crown-piece enclosed in a gold framework. It was a two-faced god, a deity who comforted the poor in their distress as they raised their eyes to his coming between the pillars, and a deity who had persuaded them, for the sake of a doubtful future, to endure their pain, as they bowed their heads, while the surge of the choristers and the priests and the singing passed by. He had blown that candle out with his own breath, telling himself that God was a fiction invented by the rich to keep the poor content. (100)

Overwhelmed by despair, since he learns that the revolt which he was hoping to lead in Belgrade has already taken place and been suppressed, Czinner feels a momentary yearning for the absolution of the Catholic confessional where he could once cleanse his conscience for a 'moment's shame'. As he takes a seat opposite Opie, he blurts out: 'You are a priest?' (104), although he cannot bring himself to add the word 'Father'. As a sensitive reader of human distress, the Anglican minister gently replies, 'Not of the Roman persuasion', and explains that he is compiling an anthology of spiritual passages for the laity which he hopes the Church of England will find comparable to a 'Roman books of contemplation'. He pinpoints Czinner's dilemma in being an ardent secularist in need of temporary spiritual support with a delicately phrased reassurance: 'you may indeed be a little suspicious of religion. I aim at supplying that man's need' (105).

No longer merely cast in the stereotypical role of a cricket-mad Englishman, Opie becomes a confessor-psychoanalyst to Czinner in their train compartment (reminiscent of a Catholic confessional box). He makes explicit Greene's own fascination with the intersection of Catholicism and psychoanalysis, noting that they seem to work on 'parallel lines'. He compares the relationship between the 'confessor and the penitent' to that of the 'psycho-analyst and the patient':

> In the one case the sins are said to be forgiven and the penitent leaves the confessional with a clear mind and the intention of making a fresh start; in the other the mere expression of the patient's vices and the bringing to light of his unconscious motives in practising them are said to remove the force of the desire. The patient leaves the psycho-analyst with the power, as well as the intention, of making a fresh start.

Pointedly, Opie concludes that confessing to a psychoanalyst may even prove more useful than 'confession to the priest' (106).

Quin Savory, who has just entered the compartment, joins in the discussion and immediately casts the author's role – which he had previously defined as 'a spy' (51) – as primarily that of the 'penitent'. If the novelist bases his fiction upon his own experiences, Savory proposes, he may then be seen as making a public confession: 'This puts the public in the position of the priest and the analyst.' Opie retorts that a novel should be regarded as confessional only as far as a 'dream is a confession', concluding as an arch-Jungian: 'The Freudian censor intervenes' (119). As a popular author who simply concocts absorbing tales about a diverse cast of characters, Savory is unsure how to counter these psychoanalytical claims for authorship. Not to be outdone, however, he takes refuge in the unquestionable literary greatness of Shakespeare, wondering how he viewed the confessional: 'He was born, of course, a Roman Catholic' (107). Here the fictional debate between Czinner, Opie and Savory blends seamlessly into Greene's own thoughts since in 1951 he raised the same question about Shakespeare in his preface to Philip Caraman's translation of the autobiography of the Elizabethan Jesuit martyr, John Gerard:

> isn't there one whole area of the Elizabethan scene [Catholicism] that we miss even in Shakespeare's huge world of comedy and despair? . . . one might say that the Christians are silent . . . One might have guessed from Shakespeare's plays that there was a vast vacuum where the Faith had been.[17]

Although, on one level, Savory and Opie may be read as mischievous reflections of Greene's satiric attitude towards the English 'establishment', in this third part of the novel they are also deftly deployed to highlight the secular and spiritual tensions that ultimately render Czinner one of the most interesting and complex characters in Greene's early fictions. In the fourth part of the novel Czinner's final hours and death are recounted as a sullied, urban echo of the arrest, trial and crucifixion of Christ. The final passion of this Czinner/ sinner begins not in a pastoral environment comparable to the Garden of Gethsemane but in the grimy, metallic landscape of Subotica railway station. Recalling the soldiers who cast lots for Jesus' cloak, in the station-master's office a group of soldiers idle away time by placing bets on their card game (116). Responding to orders from the head of the secret police at Belgrade, Colonel Hartep, they arrest Czinner, Coral (who is thought to have helped Czinner) and Grünlich (whose gun has been found) for interrogation. Once Hartep and his associate, Captain Alexitch, arrive they unload a banquet of luxuries from the boot of their car, indulging themselves in a lavish lunch of champagne and delicacies (hinting at a perverse parody of the Last Supper) while Czinner and his two companions shiver without sustenance in the station's waiting room (134–5). Hartep (like Pilate) then holds a patently rigged court martial of Czinner (141–2, 145–6), ensuring that he is found guilty and sentenced to execution within three hours (150).

The resourceful crook, Grünlich, picks the lock of the waiting room but as the three of them flee in the snow, Czinner is mortally wounded and dragged by Coral into a nearby wooden shed where he slowly dies on some old grain sacks with blood trickling from his mouth (163). Close to death, he asks in German for water and she gathers a handful of snow to press to his lips (166). Momentarily revived, he realizes that the Barabbas-like Grünlich has escaped from the pursuing soldiers and wryly considers how difficult it would be for a Christian to 'reconcile that escape with his own death' (167). Although tempted to flee, Coral (now resembling Mary Magdalen, see Jn 19.25) faithfully watches over Czinner as his life slowly ebbs away. When they are finally discovered by the pursuing soldiers, one of them puts a revolver into the dead Czinner's mouth and fires a bullet through his brain, recalling the soldier who pierced the body of Jesus on the cross with a spear (174). The novel concludes by reasserting the self-interested compromises of the real world, with Coral's rescue from Subotica by Mabel Warren who wants her as a new companion (175) and Myatt's calculated invitation to Janet Pardoe to leave Mabel and stay with him (196). With sales of over 21,000 copies in the United Kingdom and 5,000 copies in the USA, following by Twentieth-Century Fox's purchase of the film rights, *Stamboul Train* confirmed Greene's now buoyant literary reputation as a commercially productive writer of fiction.[18]

Short Stories, *It's a Battlefield* (1934) and *England Made Me* (1935)

In view of this impressive level of critical and popular acclaim for a novel which Greene considered merely as an 'entertainment', it proved disappointing that his next two major fictional works, *It's a Battlefield* and *England Made Me* – regarded by their author as more serious 'novels' – were distinctly less

successful. Greene later admitted that the former was 'almost unread' with
England Made Me a close second in 'public indifference'.[19] Such problems were
also dispiriting for Greene because his shorter fictions, especially those dealing
with the polarities of life and death, were now regularly acclaimed for their
innovation and powerful visual effects. His memorably macabre 'Proof Positive', in which a local Psychical Society is addressed by a man whose visibly
dying body gradually fails his more resolute spirit, won a national ghost story
competition run by the *Manchester Guardian* in 1930. In poignant contrast,
'The End of the Party', written in 1929 and published in the *London Mercury*
(January 1931), traces the trepidations (echoing Greene's schoolboy hatred
of 'children's parties') of a young boy, Francis Martin, who is morbidly afraid
of the dark and unexpectedly dies at a friend's party.[20] As Peter, his grieving
twin brother, resolutely clutches hold of his dead fingers, the story ends within
the mind of a child too young to comprehend either the finality of human
mortality or the Christian consolations within which it is usually shrouded:

> His brain, too young to realize the full paradox, wondered with an obscure
> self-pity why it was that the pulse of his brother's fear went on and on, when
> Francis was now where he had always been told there was no more terror and
> no more darkness. (166)

Two of Greene's other shorter publications at this period offer further proof
of his imaginative range and experimental creativity. 'The Basement Room'
(1935) again focuses upon childhood perspectives and death. Its action is seen
through the eyes of a young boy, Philip, who unintentionally betrays his friend
and substitute father-figure, Baines, the butler at his family's Belgravia home.
Baines has been having an affair with a 'thin and drawn' young woman called
Emmy who (like Coral Musker) wears a 'white mackintosh' (101) and is passed
off to Philip as his 'niece'. But Philip surreptitiously sees Mrs Baines falling
over the banisters of the hall stairs in a struggle with her husband when she
returns home unexpectedly to catch him with his mistress. Recalling Francis
Andrews in *The Man Within*, Philip becomes another of Greene's youthfully
vulnerable betrayers when he innocently contradicts the claim made by Baines
(who had moved his wife's body from the hall) that she had accidentally slipped
on the stairs to the servants' basement. Republished several times and made
by Carol Reed (with Greene's screenplay) into a successful film titled *The
Fallen Idol* (1948), this moving short story encapsulates many of the most
productive elements of Greene's early-1930s prose style and potential as a
film-script writer.

By far his most experimental work at this period was *The Bear Fell Free* (1935),
recounting sexual treachery and a fatal air-flight, Greene adopted a stream-
of-consciousness fragmenting of the usual chronologies of storytelling as a
means of creating a series of stark dramatic ironies. *The Bear Fell Free* offers the
earliest sustained example of his interest as a novelist in temporal overlaps and

dream-effects, prompted by the treatise *An Experiment with Time* (1927) by the precognitive dream analyst, John William Dunne (1875–1949), whose theories also influenced John Buchan, J. B. Priestley and T. S. Eliot. Several elements of this idiosyncratic tale drew upon Greene's personal experiences. Its con-man hero, Anthony Farrell (prefiguring Anthony Farrant in *England Made Me* who, in turn, was based on Greene's unreliable eldest brother, Herbert), is tormented by a treacherous friend, Carter (echoing Greene's bullying at Berkhamsted School by a pupil called Lionel Carter). Farrant always carries with him as a good luck mascot a small teddy bear (given by an unfaithful girlfriend) which survives a fatal air-crash into the Irish Sea. This use of a bear is an obliquely self-reflective motif since Greene recalled that as a small child his favourite bedtime companions were a 'teddy bear (the most loved)' and a 'gloved bear'. Also, for many years on his overseas travels he carried a toy bear with him and there is even a photograph from one of his Cuban trips of his bear sitting on a window sill, with the inscription 'Our Ted in Havana'.[21] In this childlike tale, with its jigsaw-like patterning of disjointed sensations and dream-like experiences, only Farrant's bear survives, unsullied by the fallen world of adults, as a silent witness to a lost childhood world of innocence and loyalty.

Compiled between September 1932 and August 1933, *It's a Battlefield* (1934) is an elegantly written work of contemporary realism, 'poetic in its imagistic precision, and in its wealth of metaphor and simile'.[22] It is also a heavily politicized tract disguised as a novel, even though Greene later claimed that its subject matter had come to him in a dream. It takes as its main plot the dilemma of a communist bus-driver, Jim Drover, who has accidentally killed a policeman while defending his wife during a violent demonstration. Assuming the social-conscious role of the popular novelist (as exemplified by Priestley and Dickens), Greene had diligently researched prison conditions at Wormwood Scrubs and Wandsworth Prison and had visited the Moreland match factory at Gloucester, notorious for the exploitative conditions of its largely female workforce. These researches and his carefully layered drafting of the novel – dependent for its social ideals upon *The Intelligent Man's Guide Through World Chaos* (1932) by the political theorist and fellow Balliol graduate, G. D. H. Cole – led to Greene joining the Independent Labour Party in August 1933.[23]

If Greene was hoping to find a new role for himself as the novelist-advocate of the English working-classes, exposing the 'injustice of men's justice', then Cole's example as a political theorist would have been especially interesting.[24] Cole, who took up a fellowship at Oxford during Greene's last year there, was also a successful journalist and (with his wife Margaret) a prolific writer of detective fiction. Cole was a Fabian socialist rather than a communist and some of *It's a Battlefield's* most memorable scenes juxtapose sympathy with the grim lives of the ordinary working class against a distinctly jaundiced view of British communism during the early-1930s. Drover is cast as a representative example of how the small man invariably suffers in political disputes while his masters remain unscathed. This kind of self-interested leader is typified by the comfortably bourgeois Mr Surrogate (based, ironically, on G. D. H. Cole and the writer John Middleton Murry) and the thuggish Bennet who ruthlessly seizes power for himself at the local Communist Party meeting while remaining callously indifferent to Drover's fate.[25] Greene had joined the Oxford branch of the British Communist Party in early-1925, although this affiliation was merely to facilitate an all-expenses paid visit to its headquarters in Paris and he remained a fully paid-up member for only four weeks.[26]

Stylistically, *It's a Battlefield* is retrogressive, in that Greene lapses once more into a dependence upon Conrad's narrative methodologies, adopting an 'explicitly-registered continuity with *The Secret Agent*'.[27] The character of his Assistant Commissioner, for which he originally had great hopes, ultimately became an uneasy blending of elements drawn from Conrad's Assistant Commissioner, his own uncle, Sir William Graham Greene (formerly Secretary of the Admiralty) and an Oxfordshire friend, Colonel Turner, a retired Assistant Commissioner in the prison service.[28] To compound this problem, Greene's female characters all seem idiosyncratically sexualized without ever developing more rounded characters. Drover's weak wife Milly has sex with Jim's brother, Conrad; her sister Kay Rimmer has sex with Surrogate; and the eccentric patroness Caroline Bury (based on Lady Ottoline Morrell who, like Bury, lived at 10 Gower Street) has a platonic relationship with the Assistant Commissioner. Given the commercial success of *The Name of Action* and *Stamboul Train*, as compared to disappointing sales of *It's a Battlefield*, it seems that during the 1930s Greene's reading public desired a mixture of exciting escapist action and absorbing psychological complexity, rather than political proselytizing and pseudo-realist social commentary. Nevertheless, *It's a Battlefield* marks an important stage in Greene's development as a socially aware writer. Paul O'Prey denotes it as his 'first mature novel', emphasizing that 'the skilful way in which he handles an extremely complex plot is a considerable technical achievement'.[29]

The ending of this novel is also intriguingly downbeat. The Assistant Commissioner has survived an assassination attempt by Jim Drover's now demented brother, Conrad. He dies in the attempt and, like a disappointed lover in a Jacobean revenge drama, he seems to have been driven into madness by his sexual relationship with Milly. Although Jim finally gains a reprieve from his death sentence, he is horrified by the prospect of 18 years of incarceration and, trapped by the sin of despair, he hopes to die. His unsuccessful suicide attempt leads the prison chaplain to consider resignation since he can no longer stand the 'arbitrariness' and 'incomprehensibility' of human justice. The Commissioner gently suggests, without seeking to be blasphemous, that much the same could be said of 'divine justice', and the prison chaplain bitterly retorts: 'Perhaps. But one can't hand in a resignation to God' (199). The novel's concluding words describe a moment of 'unsought revelation' (202) for the Commissioner, but this turns out to be not spiritual enlightenment but only a temporary catharsis for him, provided by a fresh insight into evidence relating to another criminal case.

England Made Me, reiterates the continuing personal and creative influence of his wife Vivien in its dedication: 'To Vivien with ten years' love 1925–1935'. Although no more successful than its predecessor in commercial terms, it did at least refocus Greene's creative powers upon what he then did best as a novelist – the construction of an intriguing plot populated by a group of filmic characters, blended with lightly disguised reflections upon his own psyche and personal experiences. Nominally, *England Made Me* (begun in November 1933 and composed under the working title, 'Brother and Sister') traces the close (and potentially incestuous) relationship between Kate Farrant, the practical and determined mistress of Erik Krogh, a Swedish manufacturer and the wealthiest man in Europe, and her charming but feckless twin brother, Anthony, to whom she remains loyally devoted despite his faults.[30]

All three characters establish recognizable types which are liberally reused by Greene in his later fictions. The reliable and sensible Kate is a precursor to the shrewd and practical Anne Crowder in *A Gun for Sale*. Krogh (based upon the notorious Swedish match-millionaire and fraudster Ivar Kreugar) is the first of Greene's worldly successful characters, culminating in the eponymous Doctor Fischer, to be isolated by the dehumanizing potency of great wealth and power. Anthony heads a long list of dubiously charming tricksters, including Hands in 'The Other Side of the Border', Jones in *The Comedians*, Visconti in *Travels with My Aunt* and the Captain in *The Captain and the Enemy*. He is based upon an 'idealized portrait' of Greene's adventurous but notoriously unreliable eldest brother, Herbert.[31] Several other minor characters also derive from Greene's personal experiences, including Anthony's favourite prostitute, Annette (13), who is given the name of an individual whose sexual services were secretly used by Greene in London during the early years of his marriage.[32] Similarly, Loo, the provincial girl who slaps Anthony's face when he suspects her of being a virgin, is based upon an innocent English tourist who did the same to Greene after he had clumsily made just such an accusation while in Sweden on a research trip for the novel.[33]

Although *It's a Battlefield* and *England Made Me* are markedly uneven in terms of their narrative development and characterizations, each contains at least one minor character whose memorable presence grows far beyond what seems to have been originally required for their role. Both of these characters, the nondescript Soho café worker, Jules Briton, and the seedy stringer for a local newspaper, Ferdinand Minty, are defined by their ardent religious faith. We first hear a reference to Jules's name in *It's a Battlefield* as the lustful Kay idly muses on her ideal sexual partner (30); and we encounter him in person in the café where he works politely chatting in French to a French prostitute who is taking a coffee break from her shift on Lisle Street (37). For Jules, whose French father had abandoned him to be brought up alone in London by his English mother, France is a mysteriously alluring country (which he has never visited), combining two of Greene's personal preoccupations in his writings – Catholicism and sexuality: 'France meant the women in pairs trudging up Wardour Street and down again . . . Mass in the dim, badly decorated L'Eglise de Notre

Dame . . . It had the furtiveness of lust, the sombreness of religion, the gaiety of stolen cigarettes' (37).

Towards the end of the novel Jules attends a Mass to pray for Jim Drover and listens to the priest's preaching in French on the 'subject of sin', with a repetitious insistence upon '*péché*' (sin), a word which is transmuted in his mind as he thinks of Kay into '*femme*' (woman) and then '*grue*' (prostitute) (139–40). At the Consecration when the Host is raised ('*Domine, non sum dignus*'), he raises another Greeneian preoccupation – absent or problematic fathers – as he suddenly remembers that he has in his pocket an unopened letter. It is from his recently deceased father's solicitor, informing him of a paternal legacy. To celebrate this bequest, Jules borrows a car and takes Kay out for a drive to Greene's home-town of Berkhamsted (145–6) before his euphoria is dissipated by a brief and disappointing copulation (152–3).

Jules's blending of religion, sexuality and solitariness marks him out as an increasingly dark presence in the narrative action of *It's a Battlefield*. Similarly, in *England Made Me* it is the initially peripheral character of Minty who, Greene later said, 'emerged from the pre-conscious' to become the most memorable figure in the novel.[34] We first encounter this old-Harrovian journalist, 'Small, wrinkled, dusty, with a stub of cigarette stuck to his lower lip' (56), when he is trying to persuade Farrant to supply him with exclusive stories about Krogh. He clearly owes something to the eccentric journalist, Conder of *It's a Battlefield*, who leads a fictitious double life. Although known to some of his acquaintances as a lonely bachelor whose only pleasure lies in his ever-growing collection of foreign money, to others Conder pretends to be a devoted husband and father of six children. Minty's even more pathetic and isolated life is defined by the Pinkie-like trinity of solitariness, religion and misogyny. When he first meets Farrant, he recounts his frustration at having missed Krogh coming out of the British Legation because he had crossed the bridge for a 'bite and Benediction' (57). Despite his down-at-heel appearance, Minty is fanatically prudish and 'like a good Anglo-Catholic' uses the phrase, 'Holy Cnut' (68) as his only expostulation. He later tells Farrant how he always venerates on 21 August the feast-day of Jane Frances Fremiot de Chantal (1572–1641), a French saint and founder of the Order of the Visitation of Mary, since it marks the anniversary of a successful stomach operation, for which he also gives grateful thanks in his prayers to Saint Zephyrinus (d.217) (75–6). He determines every 21 August to keep his thoughts free from 'malice and uncharitableness in honour of St Zepyrinus' but in a perverse devotional stance gives full rein to his malevolence on the preceding day, the feast of St Louis, since he felt that this saint 'had never done anything to help him' (84).

During the composition of *England Made Me* Greene also put together a collection of essays, published as *The Old School* (1934), by W. H. Auden, Harold Nicolson, Elizabeth Bowen and others, about the outdated idealism and childish cruelties of school life. Minty's bitter recollections of his schooldays drew salient details from these memoirs and they emphasize the novel's insistent concern with the psychological impact of childhood and social conditioning. Minty, the irrevocably damaged schoolboy, casts himself as a hapless and unwilling lover, forced into a loathsome union with his *alma mater* since they were:

> joined by a painful, reluctant coition, a passionless coition that leaves everything to regret, nothing to love, everything to hate, but cannot destroy the idea: we are one body . . . The twisting of his arm . . . the steel nibs dug into his calf, the spilt incense and the broken sacred pictures. It had indeed been a long and hard coition for Minty. (83)

He is periodically tormented by memories of bullies vandalizing his school study and smashing his images of the 'Madonna and Child'. Such thoughts encapsulate his Manichaean loathing of all forms of human physicality, so much so that even the Incarnation is transformed into a nightmare image in his twisted mind. The thought that God Himself had 'become a man' sickens him, even more than the 'agony in the garden, the despair upon the cross' (86).

Minty only knows two places of sanctuary from the fallen, material world where he is obliged to earn a meagre living – church buildings and his distinctly monastic lodgings. He can never pass a church, even a Lutheran one, without wanting to lose himself for a moment in its gloomy sanctuary. He slips into churches 'with the caution and the dry-mouthed excitement of a secret debauchee' (91). Similarly, his dismal lodgings in Stockholm are adorned only with an old school photograph, a 'little Madonna' (112) perched on the mantelpiece and a dead spider trapped under a tooth-glass. The ordinary world exists for Minty as a cruelly inescapable 'Purgatory' and, in contrast, the grave-like solitariness of his sparse room takes on the illusory guise of a pathetic 'Paradise' (111).

Anthony is eventually murdered by one of Krogh's henchmen and Minty dutifully joins the mourners at his cremation. Greene based this scene upon his mother-in-law's cremation which he attended on 24 May 1933 because Vivien was pregnant with their first child. Greene also took the opportunity to visit afterwards 'O', one of his favourite London prostitutes.[35] At Anthony's service Minty is rendered nauseous by the Chanel perfume of a fellow mourner, a blonde woman (perhaps based on 'O') whom Anthony had casually seduced. Her Chanel fragrance triggers his pathological hatred of female sexuality as he longs for 'incense' to purge her odour and 'candles' to light in memory of Anthony, whom he now hopes is in 'some place of no pain, no failure, no sex' (202). The last words of the novel focus upon Minty's desire to escape back to the cell-like security of his lodgings with its 'missal in the cupboard, the Madonna, the spider withering under the glass, a home from home' (207). This 'sly pathetic Anglo-Catholic; a humble follower, perhaps, of Sir John Betjeman', remains an influential precursor to the grotesque and isolated anti-heroes of *A Gun for Sale* and *Brighton Rock.*[36]

Chapter 3

The Making of a Literary
Reputation: 1936–1938

Journey Without Maps (1936)

As he struggled in August 1934 to complete *England Made Me*, Greene wrote to
his brother Hugh that he would rather catch 'bubonic plague than write
another novel for a year'.[1] Seeking a change from the solitary labours of the
novelist (and perhaps also from family domesticity since his first child was
almost eight months old), Greene explained to Hugh how he had discussed
with his publisher, Charles Evans, an expenses-paid trip to Liberia. It had
become fashionable for adventurous young writers to undertake explorations
in dangerous regions, leading to the compilation of travel books and, hopefully, unusual raw material for their fictional works. Greene was impressed by
Conrad's arduous trek through the Congo Free State in 1890 and the resulting
novella, *Heart of Darkness* (1899), which he reread in June 1932.[2] More recently,
the foreign travels of Evelyn Waugh – whom he grew to admire and respect
more than any other English novelist – offered direct inspiration for his own
Liberian plans.

Waugh had travelled to British Guiana in late-1932 and described his
explorations there in his memoir, *Ninety-Two Days* (1934). He had also gone to
Abyssinia (Ethiopia) in 1930 as a journalist for *The Graphic*, and again in 1935,
leading to *Remote People* (1931) and *Waugh in Abyssinia* (1935). The latter book's
title was chosen by the publisher Tom Burns, a prime mover in Greene's travels
in Mexico during the late-1930s (leading to *The Lawless Roads* and *The Power and
the Glory*). Waugh had spent almost £500 of his own money on his African travels
in 1930, hoping thereby to boost his reputation as a foreign correspondent
and travel writer and, at the same time, to derive inspiration for future novels.
These plans proved successful and numerous incidents and characters from his
South American and African travels were incorporated into his novels, *Black
Mischief* (1932) and *A Handful of Dust* (1934).[3] Always receptive to new sources
of creative stimuli, Greene had closely observed Waugh's travel-fuelled productivity and was hoping by autumn 1934 to tap into a similar source of literary
inspiration.

Greene's excursion to Liberia was also a family-inspired venture. His patrician uncle, Sir (William) Graham Greene (1857–1950), played a shadowy but influential role in facilitating these Liberian travels. Sir Graham, a founder of British Naval Intelligence and a close friend of Winston Churchill, had probably been involved in prompting Greene's mysterious fact-finding trip to Trier in 1924. His involvements in secret-service work prefigured Greene's recruitment into MI6 in August 1941 and his subsequent posting to Sierra Leone, the setting for *The Heart of the Matter*. During the 1930s Sir Graham was a prominent member of the Christian Anti-Slavery and Aboriginal Protection Society. While planning his Liberian itinerary Greene had a productive meeting (through his uncle's agency) with Sir John Harris, the parliamentary secretary to the society. Greene was commissioned to gather up-to-date intelligence on their behalf and agreed to give a lecture to the society's members on his return to England. Rumours were rife that a black mercenary, Colonel Davis, had been kidnapping and killing natives in remote villages and that President Barclay of Liberia was exporting slaves to Fernando Po. These problems were regarded as significant enough to be discussed in the House of Lords and at the League of Nations.[4]

Despite these high-level involvements, Greene tactfully chose to present his impending travels as inspired by a high-spirited sense of adventure, coupled with an ambitious author's curiosity over one of the few remaining uncharted parts of the world. At his brother Hugh's wedding on 24 October 1934, Greene persuaded his cousin Barbara to accompany him. She later published an exhilarating account of their experiences in Liberia under the title *Land Benighted* (1938). They embarked from Liverpool in January 1935 on the *David Livingstone* and sailed to Sierra Leone, from where they entered north-western Liberia to undertake their four-week trek through the country. They also crossed briefly into French Guinea before concluding their itinerary at Grand Bassa, arriving back at Dover in April 1935. Greene's *Journey Without Maps* was published on 11 May 1936 (although it had to be withdrawn 18 months later because of a libel action and was out of print for almost a decade).[5]

Since Greene's primary mission – to find out more about the rumours of slavery in Liberia – was regarded as a secret one, the focus of the published account of his travels there required some recasting. Instead of providing a detailed critique of the current political regime and its treatment of the indigenous population, Greene often focuses in *Journey Without Maps* upon his frequently disturbed thoughts concerning his own situation. Although his narrative contains an abundance of interesting material about the natives and the largely unknown interior of Liberia, the internal landscapes of Greene's sensations as a traveller – offering at times what amounts to a psychological autobiography – remain a dominant element of this travel memoir. His choice of a prefatory quotation from the American doctor and poet Oliver Wendell Holmes hints at the attractions for Greene of travel (the more arduous the

better) as a route into self-psychoanalysis and escape from the mundane vicissitudes of everyday life:

> The life of an individual is in many respects like a child's dissected map. If
> I could live a hundred years, keeping my intelligence to the last, I feel as if
> I could put the pieces together until they made a properly connected whole.

Along with his preoccupation with the fragmented psyche, Greene's concerns
with the potency of religious belief are brought to the fore in *Journey Without
Maps* by means of a now characteristic trope in his prose style. Greene repeatedly hints at an implicit spiritual context to various scenarios by means of verbal
associations or fleeting references (like cinematic collage shots) of buildings,
images and figures of Christian relevance. The opening paragraph, for example, describes Greene's attempts in London to locate the Liberian Consul for
the purposes of obtaining a visa. Standing before an imposing black door,
he describes how he knocked and rang without success. His language then
adopts a quasi-devotional tone, since to keep ringing was 'simply an act of faith
or despair'. A passing errand boy eventually leads Greene into the vestry of
St Dunstan's Church (3), where he locates a woman who knows how to find
the Consul. Having finally obtained the necessary papers, Greene is also obliged
to swear and sign a declaration of good intent for aliens visiting Liberia. His
musings again take a theological bent as he describes himself as a 'Catholic with
an intellectual if not an emotional belief in Catholic dogma', and he confirms
how he can even rationally accept that missing Mass on Sunday is a mortal
sin. Yet the standard legalistic oath seems only to prompt in his mind a wry
scepticism towards the deep 'contradictions in human psychology' (5).

In his consideration of Liberia, Greene's receptiveness as a sceptical Catholic
to ideas of the innocence (and sometimes folly) of religiously motivated social
engineering in colonial Africa is much in evidence. He reminds his readers how
the Republic had been founded as a high-minded example for all Africa of a
self-governing Christian state. But he then qualifies this thought by recalling
how a group of early settlers in Liberia, pacifist and teetotal black Quakers from
Pennsylvania, had been massacred by Spanish slavers when they tried to defend
themselves with only the power of prayer, a distinctively Protestant gesture
'combining martyrdom with absurdity' (6). Greene does not intend here to
mock these Quakers' heroic self-sacrifice but instead offers a reminder of the
constant vulnerability of colonial Christianity within savage landscapes.

From *Journey Without Maps* onwards, passing references to English Christian
architecture and practices are often included in Greene's narratives set in
foreign locations. These descriptive touches offer soothing reminders for the
exiled author and his fictional characters of the tranquillity of distant English
landscapes, where the established church peacefully exists as a central aspect of
civilized society. On his arrival at Freetown in Sierra Leone, Greene's eye is caught
by the grandiose Anglican Cathedral of St George and a nineteenth-century

Norman-style church (25). Similarly, in a local newspaper with a reassuringly familiar title (*Daily Mail*), he reads of a fashionable society wedding at the Cathedral (27–8). Its details could have been lifted from a typical London society wedding, except for the colonial hybrid names of the bride (Miss Agatha Fidelia Shorunkeh-Sawyerr) and the groom (Mr John Buxton Ogunyorbu Logan).

The pervasive Anglo-African tone of the Christian world in Sierra Leone is confirmed when Greene encounters a local official, known only as 'Mr D.' He has been briefed to assist Greene by more senior officials, at the prompting of Greene's influential sponsors back home who had been in touch with His Majesty's Chargé d'Affaires in Monrovia. Mr. D. belonged to the Krus, a coastal tribe of sailors who are immensely proud of having escaped 'Anglicanization'. This sense of native independence, however, has not remained entirely untouched by the Christian missionaries. In Mr D.'s sparsely furnished room Greene notes crudely painted images of the Sacred Heart of Jesus (with a 'heart the colour of raw liver') and Our Lady of the Seven Swords (Lk. 2.33–5), an image of special significance to Greene since his wife's close family friend, G. K. Chesterton, had published in 1926 a collection of devotional poems, *The Queen of Seven Swords* (34).[6]

The encounter with Mr D. prompts Greene to focus on the work of the missionaries themselves, the Order of the Holy Cross, a monastic order of the American Episcopal Church based in a clearing 2 miles from the village of Bolahun in Western Liberia. On his arrival at the mission, the priests are at Benediction and he hears the familiar murmur of Latin prayers, with only his carriers' 'white eyeballs' visible in the darkness. Greene is moved to find in this republic, renowned for its 'corruption and slavery', such a haven of tranquillity created by a brave group of priests and nuns who promulgate their faith not through doctrinaire preaching but simply by expressing standards of 'gentleness' and 'honesty' matching those of the natives. Pointedly, he concludes with what becomes a central question in *The Lawless Roads* as to whether the 'crucified God' of the missionaries is in any way superior to the 'local fetish worship' (70) of the natives.

Ruminating on this question, the following chapter offers a digressive consideration of the efficacy of Christian missionary work in Africa. Titled 'Sunday at Bolahun', it opens with a distinctly filmic scenario, describing a herdsman driving his goats around 'absurdly Biblical rocks', a church bell ringing in the distance and five nuns in 'veils and white sun-helmets carrying prayer books'. Taking tea with them reminds Greene of tea in an 'English cathedral town' and he warmly commends their unwavering courage, shrouded beneath a 'gentle, devout, childlike and unselfish' (71) demeanour. His tone becomes more polemical as he notes how Christian missionaries in Africa are often misunderstood, with suggestions that they are either imperialist lackeys or 'sexually abnormal types' who try to stunt 'happy pagan people' with 'European repressions' (71–2). Provocatively viewing Christianity as a religion of Eastern origin to which 'Western pagans' have been successfully converted, he insists upon the universal validity of one prevailing God since it is fundamentally illogical to envisage a distinct God for Europe and a separate one for Africa. He also rejects what he sees as the 'new paganism', increasingly prevalent in the West due to the rise of empirical science, as a kind of social 'neurosis' that is blindly insensitive to the Christian duty to promulgate 'faith by teaching'.

Since these Episcopalian missionaries possess no influential political or commercial contacts in Liberia, Greene emphasizes how their Faith alone had provided the motivation for establishing a missionary station in such an inhospitable and dangerous environment. He also greatly admires – anticipating his approbation of the leper colony missionaries in *A Burnt Out Case* – how they are not self-absorbed ascetics but instead seek to establish a working social community with a hospital, imported supplies of vegetables and even a rough hard-court for tennis. Nor do they seek to force the natives into Western clothing or try to repress their dances and fetish worship. Essentially, they lack the power to do so since Christianity has its 'back to the wall' in Liberia and converts are few in number. Instead, the priests and nuns can only offer to the natives an 'insubstantial hope' (73) and a temporary release from some of their basic human fears. Greene concludes this chapter with the thought that Christianity in Liberia was still a 'revolutionary force' for the young, thereby voicing what became a lifelong commitment in his writings to the political and social potency of 'liberation Christianity' within Third World contexts.

The following two chapters, 'A Chief's Funeral' and 'The Liberian Devil', powerfully encapsulate Greene's responses to the dualities of missionary Christianity within native African contexts. He is taken by a black Christian schoolboy called Mark to witness the funeral ceremonies of a local chief who had died at Tailahun. His grave unselfconsciously blends Christianity with paganism, bearing: 'a rough cross stuck on the mound to propitiate the God whom the old chief had accepted on his deathbed, while in a pit close by, following a pagan rite, sat eight wives, naked except for a loin cloth'. Other women busily smear his widows with clay, making them look as though they had been exhumed 'half decomposed from the ground' (75). Two distinct religions are seemingly operating alongside one another, prompting Greene to consider how many centuries earlier in England the transcendence of Christianity over paganism must have created similar moments. Towards the end of the chief's funeral rites, a local 'devil' called Landow (really the blacksmith from Mosdambolahun), wearing a long raffia skirt and a 'wooden snouted mask', makes a dramatic entrance to lead the dancing in celebration of the new chief of the village. Strangely, his appearance stimulates Greene's memories of his own schooldays. The role of the local 'devil', he explains, might be compared to that of a headmaster endowed with 'rather more supernatural authority than Arnold of Rugby ever claimed' (77). Local bush schools regard their village devil as a kind of 'unknown head' and his terrors recall for Greene those of English public schoolboys 'between childhood and manhood' (78).

At this point in his Liberian travelogue Greene's fascination with the inter-action of Christian spirituality and native superstition leads him to consider how both elements cater for the kind of human needs and fears which are also treated by psychoanalysis in the West. Indeed, *Journey Without Maps* is permeated (and often directed) by psychoanalytical perspectives upon the working of the author's mind. In the first chapter Greene speculates on the motives for his journey, adopting the methodology of a psychoanalyst who carefully analyses each image in a dream to tease out its subconscious associa-tions. Similarly, he considers how the allure of Africa initially lay for him in its associations with a 'quality of darkness' and the 'inexplicable' (8). Retrospec-tively, his memories of Liberia seem dreamlike in apparently standing for 'something of importance to myself' (9). Viewing the nightmarish qualities of the chief's funeral at Tailahun and the dance of the devil, Landow triggers a digression upon his own childhood anxieties. These include mice in the wainscot, moths and birds (a terror inherited from his mother), all of which he still tries to avoid, just as he now avoids disturbing ideas like as 'eternal life and damnation' (84). But within the landscapes of Africa such fears are inescapable and only the methods of the psychoanalyst seem to offer any hope in attempting:

> to bring the patient back to the idea which he is repressing: a long journey backwards without maps, catching a clue here and a clue there, as I caught the names of villages from this man and that, until one has to face the general idea, the pain or the memory. This is what you have feared, Africa may be imagined as saying, you can't avoid it . . . you can't turn your back, you can't forget it, so you may as well take a long look. (84–5)

This passage of acute self-analysis becomes central to an understanding of Greene's lifelong exploitation of his writings for psychological and spiritual purposes. It makes clear that the title of *Journey Without Maps* refers not only to his geographical travels through Sierra Leone and Liberia but also to a retro-gressive journey back into his childhood memories and psyche. For Greene, all journeying (and the compilation of travelogues, novels and journalism) ultimately becomes a process of psychological self-discovery or a source of temporary relief from the anxieties of the human mind. Even his conversion in 1926 to Catholicism while working in Nottingham is cast in *Journey Without Maps* as both a spiritual and literal journeying. He describes how his most meaningful discussions with his instructor, Father Trollope, took place not within the church or presbytery but as he travelled around with him on trams, metaphorically riding into a spiritually 'new country'. He vividly recalls, for example, how he had been instructed about the Immaculate Conception as their tram 'clattered by the Post Office', and how the topic of Our Lady was dealt with as they passed the local cinema (89).

The specifics of location become of crucial importance to Greene's theologi-cal musings while in Liberia, especially when his mind repeatedly juxtaposes

African and English settings. Just before his crossing into Western Liberia, the impending dangers of his travels prompt his consideration of the ineffable remoteness of an omnipotent God. But Greene locates these thoughts not in an African context but, instead, he delves into his memories of living in Chipping Campden in Oxfordshire. He recalls there a mentally disturbed derelict, known as Charlie Sykes (formerly Seitz), who in 1933 had died from hypothermia in an unheated cottage on a 'bed of straw'. The ramblings of this sad figure raise in *Journey Without Maps* the perennial spiritual question of the quality of Divine Mercy:

> He had a grudge against God. 'There He is,' he said to me, 'up there, We think a lot about Him, but He doesn't think about us. He thinks about Himself. But we'll be up there one day and we won't let Him stay.' (59–60)

Similarly, while visiting a mission school in the Liberian Lowlands, Greene is struck by the sheer innocence of the naked black children, recalling how back in Berkhamsted a 'sense of sin lay far deeper across the altar steps of our own school chapel. Here was all the prudery and pornography one needed' (157). As he heads towards Grand Bassa, he meets Victor Prosser, an earnest Catholic headmaster of a mission school at Toweh-Ta, who has just been on a two-day march to the Catholic priest at Sanoquelleh to make his confession. He is delighted to discover that Greene is also a Catholic and enthusiastically instructs one of his youngest pupils to recite from the Catechism. As the three-year-old child dutifully works his way through rote-learned responses to questions about venial sin, purgatory and the Communion of the Saints, Greene notes that he also possesses an antiquated English reading book with engravings of Victorian ladies and gentlemen (179). This characteristic conjunction of Anglo-African religious cultures comes to an ecstatic culmination for Greene as he dreams that night of someone reciting John Milton's celebration of Divine Incarnation, 'Ode on the Morning of Christ's Nativity'. When he awakes, he comes to an enlightened understanding of the spiritual importance of missionary work, seeing it as a means of bringing the 'idea of God and heavenly hierarchies, of crystal spheres and light insufferable, into this empty pagan land' (180).

A Gun for Sale (1936)

Journey Without Maps marks a defining moment in Greene's idiosyncratic blending of spiritual and psychological concerns with his developing public identity as a creative author and journalist. It also foregrounds how confident he had become in integrating questions and doubts about religious matters into his literary narratives. Although nominally a work of travel journalism, *Journey Without Maps* seems to have successfully reactivated his creative imagination, thereby overcoming the deadening lassitude he had felt in August 1934 towards novel writing. Certainly, his account of his travels in Liberia led to three significant literary by-products: his fast-paced thriller *A Gun for Sale*, and two short stories, 'The Other Side of the Border', which he started as a new novel but eventually included in *Nineteen Stories*; and 'A Chance for Mr Lever', published in the *London Mercury* (January 1936).

This latter short story was inspired by a 'traveller for an engineering firm' (11) whom Greene had met on the cargo ship taking him out to Sierra Leone. It recounts in tragic-comic mode how an aged salesman, brought out of retirement after losing his savings in the Depression, is only able to find a sales job in Liberia. After an appalling journey through the forest he eventually locates Davidson, the local agent for a Belgian mining company, whose order he desperately requires. Lying on camp-bed in a tent and covered in black vomit, Davidson is on the point of death from yellow fever. In despair, Lever forges his signature on the necessary document which he has just drafted on the dying man's typewriter. Hardly noticing a minor mosquito bite on his ankle, he enjoys a short period of modest euphoria at having successfully concluded his arduous task. But he is now himself fatally contaminated with the yellow fever bacteria and his impending demise allows Greene to echo questions about the nature of Divine Mercy raised in *Journey Without Maps*. Even for readers who 'may possibly believe in God, a kindly god tender towards human frailty', the unremittingly harsh Liberian forest and Mr Lever's cruel fate seem to make it 'impossible to believe in any spiritual life, in anything outside the nature dying round you' (130).

While gazing upon the natural power and savagery of African landscapes early in *Journey Without Maps*, Greene makes what seems a passing aside: 'Today our world seems peculiarly susceptible to brutality. There is a touch of nostalgia in the pleasure we take in gangster novels, in characters who have . . . begun living again at a level below the cerebral' (21). But in this comment lies the genesis of his next major literary success, his dark urban thriller *A Gun for Sale* (*This Gun for Hire* in North America), which was already forming in his mind as he crossed from Sierra Leone to Liberia. During a period of creative hyperactivity in the two months following his return to England in April 1935, Greene reviewed books on West Africa, served as a judge of short stories at the annual Eisteddfod of the City of London Literary Institute, corrected the proofs of *England Made Me*, completed various short stories including *The Bear Fell Free*, 'The Basement Room' (begun on his homeward bound ship from Africa), and 'Jubilee' (its cameo-sketch of Amy, a blowsy ex-brothel madam, provides a prototype for Ida in *Brighton Rock*), and began drafting both *Journey Without Maps* and *A Gun for Sale*. Completed by the following January and published in July 1936, *A Gun for Sale* was penned as a cinematic thriller and, although sales were initially disappointing, Greene achieved his main aim when Paramount bought the film right for £2,500 (unusually before publication).[7]

A Gun for Sale proved a landmark text in Greene's development as a novelist during the late-1930s since it not only productively develops elements from his earlier entertainments but also acts as a bridge to the spiritual concerns of *Brighton Rock* and his novels of the 1940s. The fictional Nottwich, the hometown of Coral Musker in *Stamboul Train*, is revived as the depressingly tawdry location of *A Gun for Sale*. Its heroine, the showgirl Anne Crowder, is a more resolute version of Coral and her decent treatment of James Raven prefigures Rose's doggedly loyal association with Pinkie. Raven, the alienated youthful assassin with a twisted lip, provides a memorable precursor to Pinkie since they both share the mental scars of a sordid childhood and a resulting pathological hatred of humanity. Greene commented that Raven was an older Pinkie who had never 'grown up'. The Pinkies are the real Peter Pans – doomed to be juvenile for a lifetime. They have something of the fallen angel about them, a morality which once belonged to another place'.[8]

It terms of plot and characterization, *A Gun for Sale* offers a thorough trial run for *Brighton Rock*. Relying upon outlandish coincidences – Raven kidnaps the fiancée of the detective who is pursuing him and later fortuitously finds her, bizarrely, stuffed up a chimney – *A Gun for Sale* recalls the melodramatic structuring of *It's a Battlefield*. In retrospect, it taught Greene the importance of structuring *Brighton Rock* around a more credible narrative and there are some deliberate overlaps in the action of the two entertainments. For example, the account of Kite's death at a London station in *A Gun for Sale* fills out the passing references to his death in *Brighton Rock* (10), specifically noting that he died in a waiting-room at St Pancras (142). Apart from Anne and her fiancé Jim Mather, a younger and stolidly two-dimensional version of *It's a Battlefield*'s Assistant Commissioner, the rest of the characters in *A Gun for Sale* are, as Bernard Bergonzi notes, largely 'grotesques, caricatures, and humours'.[9] These include the vituperative hunchbacked Alice for whom Raven buys a rejected dress; the wealthy head of the Midland Steel Company, Sir Marcus, who heads a supposed Jewish conspiracy to profit from the impending war; and the lecherous theatre impresario, Davis (also known as Cholmondeley), who turns out to be Raven's dishonest paymaster (passing him forged banknotes) in the employ of Sir Marcus.

The narrative of *A Gun for Sale* provides an intriguing blend of international espionage, modern morality fable and scenes from English suburban life. Greene had attended in 1935 a meeting of the Royal Commission on Armaments at the Middlesex Guildhall which considered whether the manufacture of munitions should be taken out of the control of private companies. He had also recently read a biography of Sir Basil Zaharoff, a notorious private arms dealer. Exploiting this kind of information, his fictional Sir Marcus cynically hires Raven, via Davis, to kill a former friend who is now a Foreign Minister in a Balkan country and who opposes war. The assassination, he hopes, will be blamed on the Serbs, leading to an escalation of military conflicts and an increasing demand for his steel to manufacture armaments.[10] Although the narrative thread of this conspiracy is cogently maintained throughout the novel, leading to Raven's revengeful murder of both Sir Marcus and Davis, the dramatic and moral action soon tends to focus more specifically upon the three-way relationship of Raven, Anne and Mather (prefiguring that of Pinkie, Rose and Ida in *Brighton Rock*). In each novel their various interactions are cast as a kind of provincial morality tale set in, respectively, a fictional Nottwich and an only slightly less fictional Brighton.

Greene lived in Nottingham from November 1925 until March 1926 and, echoing his own experience of wintering there, *A Gun for Sale* opens during the Christmas season. Raven is introduced as a 'sour bitter screwed-up figure' walking indifferently past small festive 'Christmas trees' (1) in the windows of a suburban housing estate on his way to commit murder. He loathes the commercial trappings of Christmas and dismisses as 'junk' (10) the modest tree and crib in the German café where he keeps a room. Yet, inevitably, Raven is persistently reminded of the nativity story as he moves around Nottwich. In a religious shop close to the Catholic cathedral he gazes in fury upon a plaster Madonna and Child in the stable, along with saints' relics and devotional pictures of The Holy Family. These images trigger bitter memories of how he had been treated when he was taken into 'care' at a brutal children's home. He recalls how he waited on a bench for Christmas dinner, knowing that he would not be beaten since 'all punishments were saved for Boxing Day':

> They twisted everything; even the story in there, it was historical, it had happened, but they twisted it to their own purposes. They made him a God because they could feel fine about it all, they didn't have to consider themselves responsible for the raw deal they'd given him. (85)

Like Pinkie, the adult Raven echoes the damaged child who is 'fed the poison from boyhood drop by drop' (11). Revealing a 'horrified tenderness' towards the baby Jesus, he views the 'little bastard' as a child who will grow up to be double-crossed by Judas and defended by only a single friend when the soldiers come for him in the Garden of Gethsemane (85).

Raven's fortuitous encounter with Anne Crowder offers him the fleeting possibility of redemption from a hate-filled world consumed by his overpowering sense of original sin. Although not conventionally devout, Anne's secular decency and kindness embodies an attractively non-doctrinal approach to life. She believes in 'Fate and God and Vice and Virtue' and, unlike Raven who views the trappings of Christmas with revulsion, she is touched by images of the nativity and 'all the Christmas stuff'. Anticipating the superstitions of Ida in *Brighton Rock*, she trusts in 'unseen powers that arranging meetings' between people but tries to avoid playing 'God or the Devil's game' (50). Melodramatically exploiting this trust in higher powers drawing individuals together, Greene allows Raven to come across Anne – gagged, bound and stuffed up a chimney by Davis – and to rescue her as a kindred spirit, now like himself cruelly abused by the world. In gratitude, Anne promises Raven that she will do her best to help him. Fleeing from the police, they take refuge in a familiar

Greeneian location, a deserted railway goods-yard. Echoing Coral Musker's Magdalen-like watching over the dying Czinner in a railway shed in *Stamboul Train*, Raven takes Anne to an old wooden shed where he tries to make her comfortable (just as Coral had done for Czinner) with some old sacks (112). Despite their desolate and filthy surroundings, their conversation becomes suffused with religious language and meaning. When Anne innocently asks Raven his Christian name, he bitterly replies: 'Christian. That's a good joke, that one. Do you think anyone ever turns the other cheek these days?' (113) For Raven, a Christian in such a hostile world is merely a passive victim; and, with unconscious irony, he assures Anne of his Manichaean detestation of all women: 'I don't fall for girls. I'm saved that. You won't find me ever going soft on a skirt' (114).

Like Pinkie, his fellow Manichaean misogynist who is repeatedly drawn into theological debate by the provoking innocence of Rose, Raven's apparently idle banter with Anne strays into areas of spiritual and psychological profundity. Despite the freezing cold, they both try to sleep but Raven is jolted awake by the sound of whispering in the darkness. Anne admits that she has been praying, which provokes from Raven the unequivocal question: 'Do you believe in God?' She admits that she does not know for sure but feels that praying cannot 'do any harm' since it seems like 'crossing your fingers when you walk under a ladder'. Such an idea prompts Raven's bitter memories of endless prayers at his children's home: 'Twice a day, and before meals, too' (119). This discussion of the efficacy of prayer then leads directly into Raven's half-formed speculations upon the comparisons between psychoanalysis (or, as he says, 'psicko'), dream-analysis and confession to a priest:

> It seems your dreams mean things. I don't mean like tea-leaves or cards . . . It was like you carry a load around you; you are born with some of it because of what your father and mother were and their fathers . . . seems as if it goes right back, like it says in the Bible about the sins being visited . . . It's like confessing to a priest. Only when you've confessed you go and do it all over again . . . you tell these doctors everything, every dream you have, and afterwards you don't want to do it. But you have to tell them everything . . . And when you've told everything it's gone.

The ever-sensible Anne is duly sceptical, noting that it all sounds 'phoney' to her. She makes a casual joke about having to tell the analyst everything, even imaginary 'flying pigs' (120) – a self-reflective authorial aside since Greene used to make up dreams about pigs when he could not remember any specific ones to tell his analyst.[11]

On a more overt level of black comedy, sections of *A Gun for Sale* are dominated by two lightly-sketched caricatures: the grotesque Acky and his loyal wife Tiny. Like Minty in *England Made Me*, their twisted religiosity enables them to grow far beyond their minor roles in the novel. Acky is an unfrocked and deranged clergyman who lives in a dingy apartment house in Khyber Avenue with his coarse spouse Tiny (based upon Greene's landlady at All Saints Terrace, Nottingham), where they rent out rooms for casual sexual liaisons.[12] Raven's encounter with them begins in a suitably ecclesiastical environment, although it rapidly descends into their private suburban hell. On the run from the police and penniless, he lurks outside a church jumble sale with the intention of picking the handbags of the elderly ladies who invariably frequent such parish events. Suddenly, he notices an 'old rather dirty woman' with an expensive bag similar to one he had earlier seen Anne carrying. As the church hall doors open, he hears the vicar's prayerful welcome to the pressing throng, 'And lead us not into temptation' (86), and he uses a sixpence found in the gutter for his entrance fee. Shocked and intrigued as he identifies the bag as Anne's, he demands to know how its new owner obtained it. This woman (Tiny) flees back to her home pursued by Raven and she screams out for assistance from her husband Acky, a tall balding man with a broken nose and a 'shifty pious look' (89).

As Raven forces his way into the kitchen and draws his gun, the half-mad Acky descends into a cacophony of English obscenities and Latin devotional phrases, all delivered in his carefully modulated theological-college voice. Demented by his unending attempts to have his defrocking overturned, Acky concludes with a choice gobbet of his often-repeated ramblings: 'After all, my Lord Bishop, you too, I am sure – it your day – among the haycocks' (90–1). Just as he is about to launch into a discourse on St Augustine, Raven strikes him in the face and Tiny seeks to calm him down by telling him that a letter from the bishop has arrived. It is in their house that Raven finds Anne stuffed up a chimney and, as he hunts for her, he recalls snatches of some resonant lines from Tennyson's 'Maud' which he had previously heard on a BBC radio poetry broadcast: 'Ah, Christ! that it were possible / For one short hour to see' (93) – which continues: 'The souls we loved, that they might tell us / What and where they be'. As he rescues Anne from the chimney, Acky hits him with a poker but the ever resourceful Anne, in an act confirming her unwanted and paradoxical role as Raven's guardian angel, snatches his falling gun and covers Acky and Tiny until they make their escape. This comically demonic couple make a final appearance at the end of the novel, with Acky drafting yet another of his mad letters to the bishop while eloquently praising Tiny's loyalty to him. Touching ecstasy in their malignant devotion to one another and unaware that they are irredeemably fallen, Acky's eloquence makes Tiny 'feel kind of 'oly'. She sits lovingly beside Acky, watching him write as though she was witnessing 'some unbelievably lovely vision passing through the room'. The scene closes with these 'two old vicious faces' gazing upon each other with the 'complete belief, the awe and mutual suffering of a great love, while they affirmed their eternal union' (177).

The pursuit of Raven works towards its inevitable conclusion with the hectic pace of a thriller and the digressive structure of a dramatic tragedy. Ultimately, no salvation is possible for him because of his unwavering self-image as a brutalized scapegoat for the sins of his narrow, tawdry world. As the child of a hanged criminal and a suicidal mother, Raven sees himself as 'made by hatred', constantly betrayed by various Judas figures in his life and excluded by his physical deformity from the warmth of human society. Although Anne's decency and murmured prayers begin to melt the 'dagger of ice' (62) within his heart while they hide in the railway shed, even this glimmering of hope is transitory. Nor do established church practices offer him any permanent respite from a sense of his own damnation. He spends a night sleeping in the Roman Catholic Cathedral of St Mark's (69), but this sanctuary provides him with only a momentary sense of peace before he renders himself up again for pursuit by the police on the streets of Nottwich.

Raven's understanding of life is defined by cruelty, indifference and his sense of the utter nihilism of mortal extinction, although the enlightening image of Anne – like that of the saintly Elizabeth in the mind of Andrews in *The Man Within* – still occasionally soothes his darkest thoughts. As he prepares to shoot Sir Marcus, he has a momentary flashback to when Anne had prayed in the 'dark cold shed'. This prompts him to demand of his impassive victim, whose age seems to have taken him beyond fear: 'Don't you want to pray? You're a Jew, aren't you? Better people than you,' he said, 'believe in a God' (161–2). Having killed Sir Marcus, he points the gun at Davis and pulls the trigger twice, as though he is murdering the 'whole world . . . And so he was. For a man's world is his life and he was shooting that' (164). While Davis slowly bleeds to death, Raven's mind is filled with grim images of what he understands best – human mortality. He recalls his mother's suicide, Kite's murder and shooting the minister and his aged secretary at the beginning of the novel. Then, as these thoughts overwhelm him with alienation and despair, he remembers how he had even once tried confessing to a priest. In perverse contrast to his morbid state of mind, the local church bells suddenly break into a joyous Christmas celebration but for Raven they only confirm his absolute spiritual isolation: 'There was no one outside your own brain whom you could trust: not a doctor, not a priest, not a woman' (164). Unlike Pinkie, Raven is so alone in his despair that he cannot even conceive of an eternal Hell. His final oblivion comes as an 'unbearable pain', as though he was delivering his disappearance into nothingness like a woman in childbirth: 'At last it came out of him and he followed his only child into a vast desolation' (166).

Magazines and *Brighton Rock* (1938)

Between the publication of *A Gun for Sale* in July 1936 and *Brighton Rock* in July 1938, Greene was kept busy with his regular film reviews for the *Spectator* (published between 1935 and 1940). These reviews, ranging from the light-hearted to the serious, often focused on films with religious themes or settings.

One review (30 August 1935) derided Paramount's *The Crusades*, which despite its subject had 'nothing Romish' about it (18) and showed the marriage of Richard Coeur-de-Lion performed in English according to the Anglican service. Greene was more impressed (4 December 1936) by *The Green Pastures*, based upon a Pulitzer Prize-winning play with scenes from the Bible presented by an all black cast, which he considered as 'good a religious play' (122) as was likely to be penned nowadays by a New York writer. *The Garden of Allah* was deservedly mocked (25 December 1936), with Charles Boyer as a renegade trappist monk and Marlene Dietrich as an orphaned heiress who meet in a Moroccan dance hall and are eventually married by a Catholic priest in an Anglican service. In contrast, Greene was deeply moved (24 June 1938) by the revival of W. D. Griffith's 1913 film, *From the Manger to the Cross*, filmed on location in Egypt and the Holy Land and re-released with a sound narrative. He was impressed by its powerful physical directness, a quality which was to prove central to his representation of Mexican Catholicism in *The Power and the Glory*:

> as in Spanish churches, you are allowed no escape at all from physical suffering; Christ is a man beaten up, like a Nazi prisoner in the Brown House. The physical horror is never far away and always well conveyed – whether it is the Massacre of the Innocents, dark passages and patches of brilliant sunlight and the sudden intrusion of spears in the old city, or the raising of Lazarus from the tomb. (194)

Much of Greene's time at this period was also consumed by his editorship of Chatto & Windus's new weekly magazine, *Night and Day* (published between July and December 1937), modelled on the *New Yorker* and titled in imitation of an urbane Cole Porter song. It had an illustrious range of regular reviewers, including Evelyn Waugh (books), Elizabeth Bowen (theatre), Herbert Read (detective stories) and Osbert Lancaster (arts). It also offered short articles by William Empson, John Betjeman, Cyril Connolly and Stevie Smith, and a generous smattering of idiosyncratic contributions, such as William Plomer on all-in wrestling and Louis MacNeice on the Kennel Club. Despite the intellectual distinction of its writers, the magazine was always in financial difficulties and its demise was rendered inevitable by a lawsuit launched by Twentieth-Century Fox and the child-star Shirley Temple. In a review of the film *Wee Willie Winkie*, loosely based on a Kipling story and directed by John Ford, Greene had joked about the allure of Miss Temple's 'dimpled depravity' to middle-aged men and clergymen. As he drafted his review, Greene probably had in mind his own deranged clergyman Acky, whose endless letters to his Bishop always proposed that a 'little carnality may be forgiven even to a man of my cloth' (176). The lawsuit proved disastrous since punitive damages of £3,500 were awarded against the magazine in March 1938, with Greene personally having to pay £600.[13]

Following the collapse of *Night and Day*, Greene was glad in late-January 1938 to be leaving England on a long-planned trip to Mexico, wearily confessing to his brother Hugh in a letter that he wanted to escape 'this bloody country'. A few days before his departure, he submitted to his publisher a complete draft of his next novel, *Brighton Rock*, intended as another cinematically adaptable prose 'entertainment' after the lucrative purchase of *A Gun for Sale* by Paramount.[14] This new work, however, turned out to be much more than a would-be film script. While certainly a first-rate thriller, it also marks the culmination of many of Greene's paradoxical thoughts during the ten years since his conversion to Catholicism about the malignant potency of the fallen world, the often mundane guises of good and evil and the ineffable nature of Divine Mercy.

Offering a moral fable of sin and damnation, *Brighton Rock* explores the disturbing theological paradox of the 'virtue of evil', suggesting that even a creature as callous as Pinkie may not be irrevocably separated from Christian concepts of goodness and the possibility of Divine redemption. The virginal Pinkie is a 17-year-old cradle-Catholic and former choirboy who through his warped beliefs, containing elements of Manichaeism and Satanism, remains tragically aware of the omnipresence of a vengeful Old-Testament God. Through his acute sensibility of evil and his belief in the existence of an eternal Hell, Pinkie dominates the novel and is variously cast as a fallen angel, a diabolical apostle and a priest manqué who feels genuine nostalgia for the Latin Mass and the Catholic choir of his youth. Through the paradoxical perversity of his beliefs, Pinkie endows the novel with a haunting religious dimension and, as Cedric Watts suggests, 'Greene seems to be conducting a taxing literary experiment: to see how far the reader's pity can be won for a person who seems to be irredeemably evil and monstrously callous.'[15]

Brighton Rock begins with one of Greene's most memorable opening lines: 'Hale knew, before he had been in Brighton three hours, that they meant to murder him' (3), echoing the laconic first words of *A Gun for Sale*: 'Murder didn't mean much to Raven' (1). As Charles Hale hides away in a saloon bar and admires the blowsy charms of Ida (known as Lily by her male admirers in the public bar), he is accosted by Pinkie who calls him Fred. He attempts to make casual conversation by saying that she seems a 'cheery soul' but receives a sharp and oddly theological riposte: 'You've no cause to talk about souls,' as Pinkie's hatred focuses on Hale. The most menacing aspect of this sense of malevolence lies in Pinkie's soulless, grey eyes, like an old man's in which 'human feeling has died' (6), echoing Sir Marcus's inability to show fear in a *Gun for Sale* as Raven is about to shoot him.

Soon afterwards, as Pinkie wanders like Mephistopheles through the amusement arcades of the Palace of Pleasure, his 'slatey eyes' seemed 'touched with the annihilating eternity from which he had come and to which he went'. He pauses to buy six shots at the shooting-booth and his devilish vision seems to bathe even these mundane surroundings with a nightmarish sense of perverted spirituality. As he glances up at the shelves of cheap dolls offered as fairground prizes, their eyes gaze down on him with the glassy innocence of 'Virgins in a church repository', prompting a parody of prayerful thought in his mind,

'Hail Mary . . . in the hour of our death' (20), as he pulls the trigger. Having won a doll with six bulls-eyes, he walks away from the booth with his fingers reeking of gunpowder and holding by the hair the 'Mother of God'. While he waits in a tea room for Cubitt and Dallow, he gives the doll away to a nondescript waitress with the blasphemous aside: 'Stick it up in your room and pray' (21).

Unlike the dull policeman, Jim Mather, who doggedly follows Raven in *A Gun for Sale*, Pinkie is pursued by one of Greene's most vibrant female creations. Ida's physical descriptions echo the allure of the film star, Mae West, whom Greene describes as a 'big-busted carnivorous creature' in his 1936 review of 'Klondyke Annie' for the *Spectator* (22 May 1936). The scene in which Hale watches Ida from the saloon bar of a pub was directly inspired by this film. In his review Greene notes how Mae's character naturally belonged to the smoky, alcoholic world of the private bar, decorated with 'advertisements for Guinness' and surrounded by a small group of 'middle-aged bowler-hatted businessmen'.[16] Ida's character is given considerably greater moral depth than her comic counterpart by her kind heart and sense of fair play. Like Anne Crowder in *A Gun for Sale*, Ida holds no firm Christian beliefs and is an avowed secularist. But the essential decency of their respective characters becomes a useful focus for Greene's theological debates. After Hale suffers a fatal heart attack (81), Ida is saddened that his cremation will be a bleak occasion with no family members present and she determines to attend the secular chapel where the commemorations are readily adaptable to whatever beliefs may have been held by the deceased. With no personal knowledge of Hale, the officiating clergyman simply gives his standard ecumenical address. Its diffusely abstract concepts seem to parody Greene's youthful memories of Kenneth Richmond's distinctive brand of Jungian dream analysis, with its bland emphasis upon guiding the personal unconscious into a union with humanity's mythological collective unconscious:

> Our belief in heaven . . . is not qualified by our disbelief in the old medieval hell . . . we believe that this our brother is already at one with the One . . . He has attained unity. We do not know what that One is with whom (or with which) he is now at one . . . Truth is beauty and there is more beauty for us . . . in the certainty that our brother is at this moment reabsorbed in the universal spirit. (34)

In contrast to this sanitized perspective upon the afterlife, Ida embodies the rationalist idea that life is for living to the full since nothing follows it. With her innate sense of decency replacing any doctrinal concepts of sin or virtue, she is untroubled in her casual rejection of Heaven and Hell. Instead, her impressionable superstitions lead her into the shadowy world of 'ghosts, ouija boards, tables which rapped and little inept voices speaking plaintively of flowers'. She reassures herself with a specifically anti-Catholic thought: 'Let Papists treat death with flippancy: life wasn't so important perhaps to them as what came after: but to her death was the end of everything' (35). Greene often pokes fun at Ida by, for example, placing a copy of Priestley's despised *The Good Companions* on her bookshelf (41, 176). Yet, despite her obvious limitations, Ida becomes a powerful moral centre for the novel since she believes, unambiguously, in 'right and wrong' (43). This personal mantra frames and motivates her pursuit of Pinkie and she reiterates her confident distinctions between 'Right and Wrong' (217) as she attempts to persuade Rose of Pinkie's irredeemable malevolence.

Although the central moral challenge in *Brighton Rock* is between Ida (as the innate goodness of the Flesh) and Pinkie (as the irredeemable malevolence of the Devil), it is the naive figure of Rose (as the potency of innocence) who most powerfully animates an understanding of Pinkie's perversely loyal commitment to sin and damnation. She also reiterates Greene's fondness for utilizing the 'woman as victim' motive in his early fiction, as previously exemplified in Elizabeth (*The Man Within*) and the chorus girls, Coral (*Stamboul Train*) and Anne (*A Gun for Sale*). But unlike these predecessors, who in varying ways show fortitude and resistance to personal threats engendered by their obviously flawed male protagonists, Rose passively, almost sacrificially, acquiesces in the face of Pinkie's diabolical temptations. It is as though the earlier female characters only had to face dangers brought to them by common humanity but Rose is drawn into a degrading world by a 'fallen angel' who believes himself beyond redemption. Their relationship is defined by Rose's unquestioning acceptance of Pinkie's cruelty. As he viciously pinches her skin, she winces with tears of 'pride and pain', pleading with him to carry on his torture, 'If you like doing that' (54). Even when he casually takes hold of her wrist as they plan a trip to the country on her afternoon off, he cannot resist telling her: 'I could break your arm' (91). Pinkie habitually treats Rose as he later treats a buzzing leather-jacket fly, idly pulling its legs off one by one as it still vibrates: 'He felt no pity at all; he wasn't old enough for pity' (100).

Coupled with this psychopathic inability to empathize with the sufferings of others is Pinkie's pathological distaste for female flesh, a characteristic fleshed out from Minty's closet loathing of femininity in *England Made Me*. Still haunted by childhood memories of his parents' frightening weekly congress witnessed from his single bed (95) and his mother's 'horrifying sound of pleasurable pain' (203), Pinkie's Manichaean views of humanity are crippled by his 'soured virginity' (93). A couple innocently dancing together become in his eyes 'two-backed beasts' (52); and the sight of another couple, leaning against each other by a fence, 'pricked him with nausea and cruelty' (117). Much to his own distaste, he is occasionally tormented, like Milton's Satan first catching sight of the sensual Eve in the Garden of Eden, by a nascent lust at the sight of female flesh. Soon after meeting Rose, he catches a glance of her bare thigh above her stocking and 'a prick of sexual desire disturbed him like a sickness' (97). Later he gazes 'with scared lust' on Spicer's girl, Sylvie, even though she repulses him by her willingness to copulate in the back of a car. He loathes the idea of physical intimacy and feels that it would be 'worth murdering a world' (97) to avoid such liaisons. Ultimately, however, Pinkie finds himself forced into a civil marriage and sexual congress with Rose to ensure her inability to testify as a witness against him.

It is this perverse and anti-sacramental union between the childlike gangster and his café-waitress bride that provokes the most overt theological discussions in *Brighton Rock*. Soon after they first meet, Pinkie demands of Rose: 'You a Roman?' and he proudly tells her that he was once a choirboy as he sings softly in his 'spoilt boy's voice': '"Agnus dei qui tollis peccata mundi, dona nobis pacem"' (54). This unexpected outburst of devotional music pervades his mind with memories of a lost world of incense, surplices and prayerful incantations, prompting him to ask Rose if she attends Mass even though he no longer does himself. She hopes that he still believes and he bitterly replies: 'Of course it's true . . . Of course there's Hell, Flames and damnation . . . torments.' Her anxious insistence that there is a 'Heaven too' merely provokes the bathetic reply, 'maybe' (54–5), as though Pinkie is a dark angel who finds it too painful even to contemplate momentarily the lost world of Paradise. As the action develops, he becomes more overtly devilish. When the police inspector advises him to leave Brighton since he cannot hope to take over Colleoni's rackets, Pinkie storms out of his office with 'poison in his veins'. He trails 'clouds of his own glory after him: hell lay about him in his infancy' (70), in a perverse parody of Wordsworth's inspiring 'Ode: Intimations of Immortality': 'But trailing clouds of glory do we come / From God who is our home: / Heaven lies about us in our infancy' (65–7).

Pinkie and Rose both originate from the Catholic ghetto around the Carlton Hill area of Brighton, with Rose's childhood home located in Nelson Place and Pinkie's, ironically, in Paradise Piece. Rose comments that such a background ensures that you believe in 'things. Like Hell', while Pinkie cynically reassures her that you don't need to pay any attention to religion or Hell until you are about to die. Inspired by another recollection of his childhood Catholic indoctrination, he quotes from William Camden's axiom about Divine Mercy: 'Between the stirrup and the ground, he something sought and something found,' although, like Marlowe's Doctor Faustus, repentance always seems just beyond Pinkie's spiritual grasp. When he is slashed by Colleoni's mob, he desperately tries to pray as he flees but 'you couldn't be saved if you didn't repent and he hadn't time' (115). The Faustian context of Pinkie's degeneracy is again made explicit when he visits on a Sunday the seedy residence of the ex-public schoolboy, Mr Prewitt. Pinkie finds him in a state of spiritual despair, with his loathsome wife hovering around like a decrepit succubus: 'Mr Prewitt said, "You know what Mephistopheles said to Faustus when he asked where Hell was?" He said, "Why, this is Hell, nor are we out of it"' (228).

Greene tends to depersonalize Pinkie by referring to him only as the 'Boy' – 'The poison twisted in the Boy's veins' (91) – when emphasizing his devilish

malignancy. Even so, he remains haunted by his 'angelic' childhood past, with
the words of the *Agnus Dei* (105) again echoing through his mind as he plots
against Colleoni in his tawdry lodgings. When he is slashed by Colleoni's men,
he takes refuge in the cellar of the café where Rose works. As she watches over
Pinkie 'with devotion' and tends his wounds, they begin to discuss 'mortal sin'
like two spoilt, depraved children. Desperate to please Pinkie, the 16-year-old
Rose claims to have committed a mortal sin when she was twelve. In response to
his admission that he hasn't attended Mass for years, she insists that she would
'rather burn' (121) with him than be like Ida and other women. When the café
manageress flushes them out of the cellar, she refers to Rose only as 'Child' and
with disgust tells them that they are 'too young for this sort of thing' (122).

The image of Pinkie as a depraved child set upon debauching Rose's childlike innocence persists as he plots their marriage. When Prewitt enquires
whether Pinkie wants a church ceremony, Pinkie angrily rejects the suggestion
since he does not view it as a 'real marriage . . . Not real like when the priest says
it'. Prewitt ironically comments that his 'religious feelings do you credit' (125).
Perversely, Pinkie's devious scheme to ensure Rose's silence through a registry
office marriage only serves to aggravate more haunting flashbacks to his lost
Catholic childhood. As he lies on his bed recalling Spicer's slashing at the race-
course, the words 'Dona nobis pacem' inexplicably come into his mind and he
is left with a 'faint nostalgia', as though for something 'lost or forgotten or
rejected' (127). While waiting at the Registry Office Pinkie confides to Dallow
that as a child he had wanted to be a priest since they 'know what's what' and
are able to 'keep away' from sex (181). Dallow asks if he is still a 'Roman' and,
confirming his fitness for this perverted parody of a marital union, Pinkie
recites the first commandment of the diabolical catechist: 'Credo in unum
Satanum' (182). Even the fact that no birth certificate can be found for him
symbolizes his tragic exclusion from the world of common humanity. But it at
least allows Prewitt to add a couple of years to his age to facilitate his civil marriage with Rose. She arrives late, having gone to the church to make her confession but then, thinking that there is no longer any point, with a mixture of
pride and fear she tells Pinkie: 'We're going to do a mortal sin.' Confirming
his own Faustian identity, Pinkie bitterly concludes that it will be no point going
'to confession ever again – as long as we're both alive' (183).

The short, grim ceremony in the Registry Office insistently reminds Pinkie of
the fallen nature of their union. The registrar conducts himself with immense
dignity, as though he himself was on the 'fringe of the priestly office'. But Pinkie
angrily dismisses his enquiry about not having a ring by insisting that they don't
need one because this 'isn't a church'. As the ceremony concludes with the
signing of the register, Pinkie views this moment as though it marks the consummation of his own now indissoluble union with Satan and the forces of
evil. As Rose signs, he senses that he has traded his own 'temporal safety' for
their 'two immortalities of pain'. Borne up by a 'kind of gloomy hilarity and
pride' he finally sees himself as an adult mortal sinner for whom the 'angels

wept' (185–6). After the ceremony they are brusquely refused a room at the Cosmopolitan (Colleoni's usual haunt) and Rose pleads with Pinkie to make as a love-token a gramophone disc of his voice in a promenade recording booth. Rejecting the expected endearments of a newly wed, Pinkie venomously whispers into the equipment: 'God damn you, you little bitch, why can't you go back home for ever and let me be?' (193). Afterwards, they go together down to the covered walkway under the pier and Pinkie, now confirmed in his fallen role, regards his physical proximity to Rose as 'a kind of sensuality: the coupling of good and evil'.

As they proceed down the long tunnel under the parade, the tackiest section of Brighton's amusements, it is as though a devil is leading Rose on a personalized tour of this grotesque urban underworld. Still unaware of the marital and eternal hell into which she has been lured, Rose cheerfully requests a stick of Brighton rock which Pinkie's twisted mind envisages as a kind of marital communion host:

> Again he grinned, only the devil, he thought, could have made her answer that. She was good, but he'd got her like you got God in the Eucharist – in the guts. God couldn't escape the evil mouth which chose to eat its own damnation. (194)

Since they are unable to find a hotel, they return for the night to Pinkie's dismal abode. The physical consummation of their marriage is tinged with Pinkie's preoccupation with mortal sin and death. As Rose takes off her hat and mackintosh, he sees it as the beginning of the 'ritual of mortal sin' since people damn each other through their pursuit of sex. As he unwillingly forces himself upon her, his only blandishment is to remind her that their coupling is a 'mortal sin'. When their lips meet, he imagines himself as a devil sucking the 'innocence' out of her and trying to 'taste God in the mouth'. Paradoxically, their copulation brings him ease from the fear of damnation and a 'sudden and unshriven death' which he had felt as he fled wounded from his slashing at the racetrack. Now, since he knows himself to be 'damned already' (198), there seems nothing else left to fear in life and he feels an 'invincible energy' (199) and the 'spirit of cruel mischief' (200) vitalizing his soul. Through his sense of evil, he now believes that his registry office union is as 'irrevocable as a sacrament' (203) and that death alone can free him from Rose.

The major challenge of the spiritual allegory of *Brighton Rock* now becomes the redemption of Rose with Ida, 'like the chariot in a triumph' (241), cast as her potential redeemer. Ida consistently emphasizes the importance of knowing the difference between right and wrong but Rose remains indifferent to her entreaties since her tastes are now in thrall to 'stronger foods – Good and Evil' (217). The idea that she might become pregnant suddenly dawns on her in a 'sense of Glory', as she imagines her children and grandchildren as an 'army of friends for Pinkie'. She ponders the sheer magnitude of their first sexual congress and delights in the thought that they will all be damned together and that union was now an 'eternal act' (218). But in contrast to Rose's delusory acceptance of her fallen state, Pinkie's malevolent mind is still plagued by occasional thoughts of redemption. As he begins to plan how to rid himself of Rose on a drive into the country, he softly intones to himself, 'Dona nobis pacem' (248). He derives a grim consolation from the idea that as he eventually approaches his own death he will still be able to confess to a priest and be shriven. But, for the present, the concept of redemption remains to him little more than a shapeless promise: 'Heaven was a word: hell was something he could trust' (248). When Rose feels terror at his proposed joint-suicide pact and tries to pray quietly to the Virgin Mary, her sense of being in a state of mortal sin silences her.[17] Nevertheless, when they encounter Piker, Pinkie's school contemporary, working as a waiter in a roadside hotel, he cannot resist enquiring whether Piker is still a practising 'Roman' (260).

These polarities in their respective attitudes towards damnation and redemption remain constant right up to the moment when Rose is meant to shoot herself with a gun provided by Pinkie. She fears that if she does not kill herself and Pinkie does, then she will be unable to follow him into damnation. She seems to hear her 'guardian angel speaking to her' – but it is a devilish one who preaches that the 'evil act was the honest act, the bold and the faithful' (263). As she again raises the gun to her head, she is saved from damnation only by the intervention of three secular agents of Divine Mercy – Ida, Dallow and a policeman. With Rose now saved from her fall, the bottle of vitriol held above Pinkie's head breaks and, as the humanity is burnt away from his face, his end is cast as though in a morality play. Pinkie, a damned soul because of his determination to kill Rose, is inexorably drawn down into the eternal flames of hellish oblivion: 'it was as if the flames had literally got him and he shrank . . . as if he'd been withdrawn suddenly by a hand out of any existence – past or present, whipped away into zero – nothing' (264).

The bowdlerized ending forced by the censors upon John Boulting's otherwise impressive 1947 film-version of *Brighton Rock* has tended to dilute the theological and dramatic impact of Greene's written ending. In the concluding scene of the novel, where Rose is cloistered in the confessional box with an aged priest, she defiantly insists that she only repents for not having killed herself so that she could accompany Pinkie into his eternal torment. She rejects absolution and insists that she wants to be 'like him – damned' (267). In reply, the priest tells her about a Frenchman – the theologian and philosopher Charles Péguy (1873–1914) – who held similar views. Although he was reputed a 'good man, a holy man' he couldn't bear the idea of others being damned and so determined that he would suffer damnation with them. And so he never married his wife and excluded himself from the sacraments. Even though he died in what would ordinarily be determined as a state of moral sin, some considered him to be nothing less than a 'saint'. The priest concludes from this example that nobody can rationalize the 'appalling . . . strangeness of the mercy of God' and that the Church never demands that we should consider any soul absolutely 'cut off from mercy' (268).

The priest advises Rose, 'Corruptio optimis est pessima' ('the corruption of the best is the worst'), but this axiom applies more to her own state rather than that of her now deceased seducer. Like Péguy who thought that he loved his fellow humans too much to see any of them eternally damned, Rose aspires to damnation not through an embracing of evil but though the sheer intensity of her love for Pinkie. Hence, it remains possible for her to be shriven and, although the priest cannot offer her immediate absolution in her distraught state of mind, he asks her to return on the following day when an absolute confession would allow the forgiveness of her sins. But Pinkie's eternal state at the end of the novel is an entirely different matter. While Greene is careful to suggest through the priest's words that no human mind can rationalize the workings of Divine Mercy, it is important to remember that *Brighton Rock* was composed as a literary 'entertainment' and potential film-script rather than as a strictly conformist tract of Catholic theology.

In this sense, it is possible to see the novel's ending as dramatically polarized between the redemption of Rose and the confirmation of Pinkie's eternal damnation. Their possible child, of course, remains entirely innocent of the sins of his father and the priest suggests that Rose and her infant might well 'pray for his father'. But the likelihood of such prayers ultimately making Pinkie a 'saint' is negated by the looming significance of the gramophone recording of Pinkie's voice. Thinking that the 'worst horror' is now over, Rose takes consolation in the thought that Pinkie, like God, 'had existed and would always exist'. With renewed hope, she hurries home to listen to his assuming loving words, believing that if Pinkie had shown her genuine love then he would not necessarily be eternally damned. But, unlike Rose who hastens through the June sunlight 'towards the worst horror of all' (269), the reader already knows Pinkie's recorded words of absolute malevolence. Even after death, Pinkie's hatred lives on through modern technology and still remains capable of seducing Rose into the sin of absolute despair.

Chapter 4

Missionary Zeal and the Established Writer: 1939–1943

Mexican Travels (1938)

The Mexican Catholic martyr, Miguel Augustín Pro-Juárez (b.1891), was executed by firing squad on 23 November 1927 at Mexico City. He had entered the Society of Jesus in 1911 but the anti-Catholic persecutions of President Venustiano Carranza obliged him in 1914 to flee to California. After studies in Spain and Nicaragua, he was ordained in August 1925 at Enghien, Belgium. Although the anti-Catholicism of Carranza was sustained by President Alvaro Obregón (1920–1924) and his successor Plutarco Calles, Father Pro returned to Mexico in 1926. He managed for 15 months, travelling under various disguises, to conduct his ministry before being apprehended by the government authorities. He and his brother, also a priest, were falsely accused of complicity in an attempted assassination of the president and condemned to death. Standing before the firing squad with his arms stretched out as though on a cross, Father Pro forgave those who were about to kill him and died with the cry: '*Viva Cristo Rey*' (Long Live Christ the King). The government ordered photographs to be taken at his execution so that they could be disseminated as a warning to other Catholics in Mexico. This propagandist plan backfired since the photographs – the first such record of an actual moment of martyrdom – were soon venerated as holy objects, commemorating Pro's heroic missionary zeal.

Vivien first drew her husband's attention to the heroic sacrifice of Father Pro and Greene confirmed to her in late-November 1927 that he had carefully read the 'article on the Mexican martyrs'.[1] Although there is no evidence that he considered travelling to Mexico during the late-1920s, the publication of *Journey Without Maps* on 11 May 1936 endowed him, virtually overnight, with the reputation of an adventurous writer, willing to undergo physical hardship in pursuit of interesting material. No doubt hoping to cash in on this success, Greene wrote on 24 May 1936 to his brother Hugh that he hoped to be leaving for Mexico: 'negotiations are on hand for a book on the Mexican Revolution and the Catholic Church.'[2]

These discussions were with Sheed and Ward, the firm that in 1935 had published Evelyn Waugh's *Edmund Campion*; and by July Greene's agent was hopeful of securing from them a £500 advance and a book contract. Greene had written an enthusiastic review of Waugh's biography for the November 1935 issue of the *Spectator* which was reprinted as a preface to later editions of *Edmund Campion*. This biography exercised a powerful influence over Greene's views of Catholicism during the late-1930s. It also seems that Waugh and Greene were willingly drawn at this period into a deftly orchestrated literary campaign on behalf of the Jesuits. Waugh had first received Catholic instruction from Father Martin D'Arcy, S.J., and was received into the Church on 29 September 1930. When Waugh offered in 1934 to write a biography of Pope Gregory XIII (a vocal opponent of Elizabeth I's anti-Catholicism), with the proceeds going towards the building of a new Jesuit house at Oxford, Father D'Arcy suggested Campion's life as preferable subject matter. Waugh duly produced his best-selling biography, combining a meticulous use of historical sources with a potent contribution to Jesuit hagiography.

For Waugh, the essence of Campion's achievement lay in his heroic commitment to the inevitable culmination of his mission – a resolutely embraced martyrdom which would serve as an inspiring example to other missionary priests. In his final chapter, starkly titled 'Martyr', Waugh recounts the horrific agonies of Campion's torture, hanging and mutilation as both a reverential imitation of Christ's Passion and a means of ensuring the inspiration of others to continue his work. When Campion's disembowelled entrails are thrown into a cauldron of boiling water, an onlooker is splashed by a spot of his blood. This is the future Jesuit martyr, Henry Walpole, and Waugh explains:

> In that moment he was caught into a new life; he crossed the sea, became a priest, and, thirteen years later, after very terrible sufferings, died the same death as Campion's on the gallows at York.
> And so the work of Campion continued; so it continues. He was one of a host of martyrs, each, in their several ways, gallant and venerable . . . to each succeeding generation, Campion's fame has burned with unique warmth and brilliance. (167)

Greene picks up on this anointing of Walpole with a 'spot of blood from Campion's entrails' in his *Spectator* review to emphasize how Catholic martyrdom effectively creates a 'continuity of culture'. He is also struck by that peculiar blending of extreme heroism and playfulness, characteristic of young men about to cross psychological and geographical frontiers into dangerous territories. The missionaries from Douai crossed the Channel with the 'same enthusiasm, the same rather childish release of spirits in practical jokes' as recruits at the beginning of the First World War, although for the missionaries there was no hope of temporary home leave: 'They had simply to stay in the line until death' (3).

Although Sheed and Ward eventually decided against Greene's Mexican project, he secured the interest of the Jesuit-educated Tom Burns at Longman and on 29 January 1938 he and Vivien embarked on the 'Normandie' for New York. From there they headed south to Washington, where Greene met at Georgetown University Father Wilfred Parsons, S.J., whose *Mexican Martyrdom* (1936) provided an eloquent record of the systematic repression of the Catholic Church in Mexico. Greene consulted some other recent works on the subject, including Francis McCullagh's *Red Mexico* and F. C. Kelly's *Blood-Drenched Altars*, but it was Father Parsons's work which exerted the strongest influence over his creative thoughts while in Mexico. Parsons traced the activities of the Jesuits in Mexico from their arrival in 1569 to their establishment of some thirty-two colleges by 1767. But the persecutions of the 1920s formed the central focus of his polemic when the 'priests and people suffered . . . a silent epic' (27), resulting by 1928 in the execution by firing-squad of about 100 priests. Parsons compiled a grim catalogue of the atrocities performed on these priests by their captors, recalling the obscene brutalities meted out to the Elizabethan Jesuit martyrs. He also provided Greene with a model for his idealistic lieutenant in *The Power and the Glory* in his account of the hunting down of an Augustinian priest, Father Elias Nieves, by a pursuing captain who was 'sea-green incorruptible' (30). This real-life captain and the fictional lieutenant are strikingly similar in that they are motivated by their idealistic communism to improve the lot of their poor compatriots, and they show genuine compassion for their priestly victims. They both try to persuade their prisoners to recant and ensure that at the moment of execution they are mercifully dispatched by a single shot from their revolvers. The fourth chapter of Parsons' book (41–53) is devoted to the commemoration of Father Pro's martyrdom. Potently, he recounts how at the end of the day when Pro was executed, prayers were led in secret at his family home by a 'Jesuit priest, defying the law in cassock and surplice'. This priest reappears in the concluding scene of *The Power and the Glory* when, following the whisky priest's execution, the next, unnamed missionary quietly arrives at the door of the young boy and his pious mother.[3]

After they reached New Orleans, Vivien was sent home on a Dutch cargo boat and Greene pressed on south alone, as vividly described in *The Lawless Roads*. After passing through San Antonio in Texas and the border town of Laredo, he traversed a broad sweep through Mexico, taking in Monterrey, Mexico City (where Trotsky was living in exile), Vera Cruz, Frontera and Palenque before curving back towards Mexico City, via Las Casas, Tuxfla and Oaxaca. He even found some spare moments to pen a short story, 'Across the Border' for the *Strand* magazine and a travelogue, 'A Postcard from San Antonio' for the *Spectator* (but both were rejected). Physically and mentally drained by his experiences in Mexico, Greene arrived back in England on 25 May 1938 and in his account (which foreshortens the chronology) he describes finding preparations in full swing for the now inevitable war, with trenches being dug in London and anti-aircraft guns set up on Clapham Common (events relating in actuality to the following September). For the next five years, his creative energies were strongly focused upon man's infinite capacities for violence and self-destruction in Western Europe (*The Confidential Agent* and *The Ministry of Fear*) and Mexico (*The Lawless Roads* and *The Power and the Glory*).

The Lawless Roads (1939)

Greene was commissioned by Tom Burns to write a book on 'The Position of the Church in Mexico' and the first instalments of what became *The Lawless Roads* appeared in the Catholic periodical the *Tablet* on 14 May, 2 July, 13 August and 31 December 1938.[4] Between February and April 1939 he was preoccupied with the proofs for the book's English and North American editions (where it was titled *Another Mexico*). Nominally a work of documentary travel writing, *The Lawless Roads* adopts the self-reflective literary techniques utilized by Greene in *Journey Without Maps*, in which the author's psychological perceptions are consistently filtered through his traveller's descriptions of the alien Mexican landscapes. Borrowing his title from the poet Edwin Muir ('And without fear the lawless roads/Ran wrong through all the land'), Greene associated his book with the mounting international anxieties of the late-1930s by choosing Cardinal Newman's apocalyptic warning to godless societies as one of his epigraphs:

> either there is no Creator, or this living society of men is in a true sense discarded from His presence . . . *if* there be a God, *since* there is a God, the human race is implicated in some terrible aboriginal calamity.

In a meditative prologue to *The Lawless Roads*, divided into two distinct sections, Greene makes explicit the central duality of his approach to his Mexican subject matter. In the first section, 'The Anarchists', he reminisces over the trepidations of his school-life at Berkhamsted. In the second, 'The Faith', he sets the historical scene for the martyrdom of Father Pro and the state's attempts to secularize the traditionally Catholic Mexican society. The prologue opens in confessional mode, as he recalls lying on a croquet lawn at Berkhamsted when aged about thirteen. Luxuriating in the memory of a melancholy happiness, while in the distance the school orchestra plays Mendelssohn, Greene realizes that he was then living simultaneously in two 'countries' separated by a green baize door, marking the transition from school premises into his father's private lodgings as headmaster. On the latter side was the calmly ordered world of suburban English family life and on the former the unmerciful world of the schoolrooms, leaving him continuously torn between 'different ties of hate and love' (13). He recalls two disliked teachers and the 'appalling cruelties' of a hated schoolboy called Collifax who tormented him with dividers. He muses how for his classmates, 'Hell lay about them in their infancy,' echoing the twisted parody of Wordworth's line applied to Pinkie in *Brighton Rock*.

Lying on the croquet lawn in the darkness, the schoolboy Greene experiences a powerful sense of spiritual enlightenment which he had never found within the school chapel with its huge brass lectern-eagle and interminable organ voluntaries.

> It was an hour of release – and also an hour of prayer. One became aware of God with an intensity . . . faith was almost great enough to move mountains . . . And so faith came to one – shapelessly, without dogma, a presence above a croquet lawn, something associated with violence, cruelty, evil across the way. I began to believe in heaven because I believed in hell, but for a long while it was only hell I could picture with a certain intimacy. (14)

Greene's mind then shifts back to his brief residence at Nottingham in 1926, where he first explored the mysteries of the Catholic faith and how this instruction gradually began to 'populate heaven' in his imagination. The inanimate remoteness of the lectern-eagle of his Anglican school chapel was replaced by the emotional potency of the 'Mother of God' and he began to have a glimmering sense of the 'appalling mysteries of love moving through a ravaged world', as he studied the writings of the Curé d'Ars and Charles Péguy who challenged 'God in the cause of the damned' (15). He also ponders the arduous nature of his forthcoming travels to Mexico, recalling the despairing words from Marlowe's *Dr Faustus* quoted by Prewitt in *Brighton Rock*: 'Did I really expect to find there what I hadn't found here? "Why, this is hell," Mephistopheles told Faustus, "nor am I out of it"' (17).

In the second section of the prologue, Greene summarizes the story of Father Miguel Pro. He forges a strong connection between Mexico and England of the Elizabethan Jesuit martyrs, noting how Pro came back from an overseas seminary to his own land just as Campion left Douai to return to England. He describes Pro's civilian disguises as matching Campion's 'doublet and hose' and assesses President Calles's Catholic persecutions as more fierce than anytime 'since the reign of Elizabeth' (19). In the face of this oppression, Father Pro still manages to give the Sacrament to 900, 1,300 and 1,500 people on three successive First Fridays before he and his brother, Humberto, are finally apprehended. Pro was condemned to death in a mock show trail and the popularity of the photographs of his martyrdom serves only to confirm the error of Calles's anti-religious policies. 'For Mexico remained Catholic', Greene notes, as his own mind turns towards the impending war in Western Europe. Only the ruling-class, the 'politicians and pistoleros' were anti-Catholic: 'It was a war – they admitted it – for the soul of the Indian' (20). The prologue then draws to a close, focusing again on the mind of the schoolboy lying on the croquet lawn at Berkhamsted as a clock strikes: 'God was there and might intervene before the music ended' (21).

At the heart of Greene's admiration for the Catholic ethos of Mexico lies his anger at the stark contrast between the self-interested motives of politicians and the material needs of their impoverished people. While still in Texas at the beginning of his journey, he attends Mass at the Catholic cathedral of San Antonio (27). There he first hears about 'Catholic Action' when a Mexican priest, Father Lopez, organized a strike among exploited pecan-nut workers in southern Texas which was then taken over by communists. This was the first example Greene had found of 'genuine Catholic Action' over social issues. He admires the 'old, fiery, half-blind Archbishop' who so bravely seeks to enforce 'papal encyclicals' (28) condemning capitalism just as much as communism. Catholicism, he concludes, needed to 'rediscover the technique of revolution' (29), an idea that was to remain strong in Greene's mind for the next five decades.

In the border town of Laredo he whiles away time by rereading Trollope's *Barchester Towers* but, as he immerses himself in its quintessentially English landscapes, he is still reminded of the universality of the struggle between good and evil: 'The world . . . is engaged everywhere in the same subterranean struggle . . . between the two eternities of pain and – God knows the opposite of pain' (33). Western Europe and Latin America form a reoccurring duality in his mind, as he compares the First World War battlefields of Belgium with the contemporary political conflicts of Russia, Spain and Mexico. So many years have passed since the Elizabethan persecutions of Campion and his fellow Jesuits that the stark immediacy of the grave of Father Pro and the ruined churches of Tabasco serve as a valuable reminder of the unending global struggle between 'faith' and 'anarchy'. Barchester and Laredo become polarized landscapes comparable to the two sides of the green baize door at Berkhamsted School. As Greene attempts to concentrate on Mr Arabin's High Church Anglicanism and breakfast at the archdeacon's, a hallucinatory blending of Laredo and Barchester takes place. The two contrasting environments of Mexico and England finally merge into one unified microcosm of the fallen human condition. The self-sacrifice of Father Pro (killed like Campion, the authorities claimed, for his 'treason' rather than his 'religion') takes Greene back in time to an England before the Elizabethan persecutions with Pro echoing the 'psychology of Thomas of Canterbury, who also was in love with the good death' (34).

Greene's descriptions of Catholic devotions in Mexico blend familiar Christian rituals with grim reminders of the sufferings of the faithful. Attending eight o'clock Mass in the cathedral at Monterrey, he watches three young girls making the Stations of the Cross, 'giggling and chattering from agony to agony' (39). When the priest holds up the Host at the Consecration he imagines how the same moment would have looked in the catacombs during the Roman persecutions of Christians. As an endless line of faithful devotees, compared to labourers on the road to Calvary, files along the walls bearing the Stations of the Cross, he senses a 'real religion' (41) in their 'continuous traffic of piety'. Similarly, when he returns to the cathedral on Ash Wednesday, the congregation is so large that it takes him 15 minutes to reach the priest for his ashes. After then witnessing the curiously operatic duel of a Mexican cockfight, pain 'in miniature', and death on a 'very small scale' (47), he takes refuge in the Templo del Carmen to hear Benediction, with its familiar Latin phrases, as a means of temporarily transporting himself back home.

Delving into the history of Catholic Mexico, Greene evokes another reminder of the Elizabethan martyrs when he visits the Monastery of San Augustin Acolman, founded by the survivors of an early-sixteenth century Augustinian mission. Nearby, he also views the Temple of Quetzalcoatl and the ancient native pyramids of Teotihuacán, where human sacrifices were assumed to have taken place. Such stark contrasts leave him wondering at the 'appalling strangeness' of this place which 'should have been over the world's edge' (82). Turning back again from pagan to Christian, he visits the shrine to the Virgin of Guadalupe, which even at the height of the persecutions had remained open. Like Joan of Arc in France, Greene suggests, she became identified not just with faith but also with the country itself: 'she was a patriotic symbol even to the faithless' (88). Understandably, after leaving Mexico City and passing through Orizaba, which he compares to Galilee 'between the Crucifixion and the Resurrection – all the enthusiasm had been spent' (95) – Greene arrives in Veracruz. There he hopes to rest and read more Trollope, acknowledging how Mr Arabin seems to offer him a sense of sanity in this troubled country (101).

On of the most curious Anglo-Mexican linkages for Greene in *The Lawless Roads* occurs at Villahermosa where the chief of police casually informs him that he has come 'home' since 'everyone in Villahermosa is called Greene – or Graham' (115), even though they are not English but Mexicans. European names proliferate in the history of colonial South America but – as he encounters various Señoritas Greenes, Mr De Witt Greene, a seedy Mexican Greene with a gun and a young dentist called Graham – this oddity of nomenclature fosters Greene's growing sense of vulnerability over preserving his own individuality as an 'unabsorbed Greene' (118) in this threatening world. As the martyrdoms of Campion and Pro now mingle interchangeably and the Greenes of Villahermosa threaten to absorb a disorientated Greene from Berkhamsted, even the boundaries of individual identity seem to have become nightmarishly confused in Mexico.

The Greenes of Villahermosa illustrate how in the *The Lawless Roads* there is an insistent movement from the specific to the universal, rendering the religious persecutions of Mexico directly relevant not only to the history of anti-Catholicism in England but also to the contemporary dilemmas of Western Europe. For a book published in 1939, a prophetic message lies in its epilogue as Greene describes his embarkation in mid-1938 at Veracruz for Havana and then the Atlantic crossing to Lisbon. Through newspaper and radio reports, the Spanish Civil War casts its shadow across the 'South Atlantic and the Gulf' (215). Greene was travelling as a third-class passenger on a German liner and its multinational passenger list encapsulates the universal human propensity towards idealism and persecution found anywhere in the world. The dangerous border soon to be crossed is now not that between Texas and Mexico but rather that between Christian Western Europe and the rising tide of National Socialism in Germany. Greene observes among his fellow voyagers a 'German stewardess' and a 'German ex-officer' (218) and two other German passengers serve to elucidate the concluding message of *The Lawless Roads*.

The first is a young German farmer from Chiapas who 'hated Christianity' and instead venerates General Erich Ludendorff (1865–1937), a leader of German military strategy during the First World War. Recently deceased, Ludendorff had been cynically exploited by the Nazi Party as a respected national hero whose advocacy of *Der Totale Kreig* (Total War) proved useful to Hitler's expansionist plans. In debating the confrontation of Catholicism and Fascism in General Franco's Spain and Hitler's Germany, he insists in confidently ungrammatical English:

> The Christians have only winned because they have killed all not Christian. Once we had nothing to give people, only Religion. Now we give the Nation. But we are not atheists like the Reds. We have a God, one God . . . A Force, We do not pretend to know what he is. A Principle. (217)

Greene notes how the Mexican volunteers for the Spanish Civil War listen politely to this intolerant voice of the new fascist Germany and the young farmer's fanaticism prophesies the threat of European horrors to come. A gently insistent voice of opposition comes from another German passenger called Kruger who had been falsely imprisoned in Chiapas. He makes no secret of his low opinion of National Socialism and throughout the voyage towards Europe a remarkable sense of 'goodness surrounded him' (219). It turns out that he had fled Germany in 1913 because of the impending war but, in a potentially tragic irony, he now finds himself in 1938 being repatriated back to Hamburg and prison. Kruger seems missionary-like in his unwavering courage as he heads, like Campion and Pro returning to their homelands, towards the now hostile country of his birth. He quietly affirms his fortitude and there is a quasi-spiritual ring to his touching ambition one day to return and live in peace near the River Amazon. He assures his listeners that he knows of an Edenic land there where people can live together 'on nothing, without violence or hate', where fresh water and food are always abundant and 'there was nothing to worry about any more for ever' (220).

As they come within a day's sailing of Lisbon, Greene and his fellow travellers hope that they can finally leave behind them the violent world of Mexico. But now they have to face up to the political and military dangers confronting Western Europe. Back in London, Greene is troubled by the proliferation of A.R.P. posters, trenches and anti-aircraft guns. He also senses that the sheer intensity of the religious struggle in Mexico renders his attendance at Mass in Chelsea 'curiously fictitious'. *The Lawless Roads* concludes with the perversely reassuring thought that the now inevitable threat of Nazi Germany and its

expected air raids will soon bring to London a similar intensification of sensations: 'Violence came nearer – Mexico is a state of mind' (224).

The Confidential Agent (1939)

In *Ways of Escape* Greene recalled how the volunteers for Franco on his German
ship back from Mexico 'began a train of ideas' which culminated in *The Confidential Agent* (82). He admitted that this commercially minded thriller was
written in haste because war was imminent and he wanted to earn some quick
money. Begun in March 1939, it was completed within six weeks and published
in the following September. Relying on regular doses of Benzedrine, he drafted
The Confidential Agent in the mornings and *The Power and the Glory* in the after-
noons. It sold 5,000 copies in the United Kingdom and the film rights were
purchased by Warner Brothers. Aptly described by Roger Sharrock as a 'strangely
phantasmagoric thriller', Greene later suggested that *The Confidential Agent*
read as though he had been 'ghosting' it for one of his favourite writers, the
Catholic convert Ford Madox Ford (formerly Ford Hermann Hueffer). Greene
greatly admired his four novels, known collectively as *Parade's End* (1924–1928),
based upon his wartime experiences as an English soldier of German extraction
in the trenches at the Somme and Ypres. He was also impressed by his explorations as a novelist of mental multiplicity and stream of consciousness. The
characters of 'D.', a widowed professor of medieval French literature, and the
Jewish Forbes (Furtstein) in *The Confidential Agent* were modelled as typical
Ford characters. Some of Ford's publications, including *Provence* (1935) and
Great Trade Route (1937), followed a model similar to Greene's *Journey Without
Maps* and *The Lawless Roads* in offering a rich mixture of travel writing, personal
musings and social criticism. Greene's admiration for Ford's work was lasting
and during the early-1960s he edited four of Ford's novels for The Bodley
Head.[5]

   Although derivative, written under the stimulus of drugs and fantastically
plotted, *The Confidential Agent* offers a landmark in the politicization of Greene's
approaches to the social function of religious belief. The clash during the
Spanish Civil War (1936–1939) between the anti-clerical Republicans and
Franco's Fascists (supported by the Catholic hierarchy) provides the inspiration
for the political background to this largely secular novel. Greene had been
commissioned by the BBC to travel to Bilbao, then under siege from the
Fascists, but he was unable to board a flight beyond Toulouse. Instead, his
disreputable brother Herbert had reached Spain and may have acted as a spy
for the Fascists, although, typically, in his book *Secret Agent in Spain* (1937), he
claimed to have supported the Republicans (while also supposedly developing
links with Japanese Intelligence). Torn between the two opposing sides, Greene
eventually decided to support the Republican Basques of northern Spain whose
priests fought with them, echoing the revolutionary Catholicism which he had
so admired in the 'Catholic Action' of Father Lopez during his Mexican travels.

As he later explained, his sympathies were more readily 'engaged by the Catholic struggle against Franco' than by the 'competing sectarians in Madrid'.[6]

The Confidential Agent opens with the world-weary 'D.' secretly travelling from the continent by ferry to Dover as an agent of a government which may be equated with the Republicans, even though Spain is never mentioned in the novel. Like Campion and Pro returning to their homelands, he has 'no sense of safety' while on board the ferry since 'Danger was part of him.' But, unlike the Jesuit martyrs, 'D.' comes from an unnamed continental environment in which religion has been stripped out from society and where a friend was denounced for having a 'holy medal' (4) under his shirt. As the plot progresses, he is outwitted by another agent, the urbanely aristocratic 'L.', who serves a general (reminiscent of Franco). One of the novel's most effective structural devices is its division into two sequential parts. In the first, the passive 'D.' assumes the role of 'The Hunted', a man like Andrews in *The Man Within*, living in constant fear of capture by his pursuers. 'D.' seems a timorous version of Dr Czinner in *Stamboul Train*. Although he fails entirely in his mission to obtain a supply of coal, he thwarts the similar intentions of his opponents. In the second part of the novel, having been vitalized into a revenging pursuer by the murder of an innocent child, he becomes 'The Hunter' – a reversal of fortune later reused in *The Ministry of Fear* and *Our Man in Havana* – thereby enabling Greene to 'create something legendary out the a contemporary thriller'.[7]

'D.' is alone in the world and emotionally numbed by the accidental shooting of his wife by fascists. He no longer believes in a benign God and considers himself beyond all feeling as he moves through a dismally secular world. After arriving in England, he is befriended by the Honourable Rose Cullen. She turns out to be the spirited and warm-hearted daughter of Lord Benditch an industrialist and mine-owner who, in the first of several coincidences, proves to be the key figure for 'D.' in his coal negotiations. While staying at a seedy hotel, he entrusts his identity papers to a serving girl, Else Crole, who is brutally killed when she loyally refuses to betray him to her mannish manageress. Finally aroused by this senseless tragedy, he takes upon himself, like Ida in *Brighton Rock*, the role of avenger. A. A. DeVitis explains how his vengeful pursuit is deployed to reintroduce a religious sense into this thriller:

> so long as he adheres to the world's dictum regarding right and wrong, he can allow himself the luxury of revenge, an eye for an eye, a tooth for a tooth. There is no God, so vengeance is D.'s. . . . The secular attitude . . . in the entertainments . . . is the chief focus through which Greene develops his characters and his action. And yet by subduing the religious center, Greene does not minimize the religious sense. Ultimately, in all his writings – entertainments, novels, stories, plays – the final point of reference is God.[8]

Even when the sense of a religious world seems negligible or absent in this novel, hints of its power remain detectable within the action and dialogue. For example, 'D.' and Rose hire a car but a puncture forces them into a wayside hotel where he encounters 'L.' and they fall into conversation about their polarized political allegiances. 'L.' is aware that 'D.' had discovered a previously unknown Berne manuscript of the verse romance, 'The Song of Roland', the oldest surviving major work of French literature. Greene's choice of this text is far from random since it tells how in 788 Charlemagne's retreating Franks, after a Christian campaign against the Muslim Saracens in Spain, were attacked by the Basques. This echoes the current clash in Spain between the Church and secularism and Greene's siding with the Catholic Basques. 'D.' is surprised to learn that the aristocratic 'L.', despite his lofty indifference to personal spirituality, had prized among his now destroyed artistic collections an early manuscript of the 'City of God' by that devotee and then ardent opponent of Manichaeism, St Augustine of Hippo. This academic revelation, echoing Greene's preoccupation with the Manichaean heresy, prompts 'D.' to consider how sterile the world would become if religious objects were all reduced merely to the status of museum objects, 'labelled "Not to be touched"'. Faith would be replaced by superstitions and an antiquarian fascination with 'Gregorian chants' and 'picturesque ceremonies'. There would be great libraries but 'no new books' and miraculous images which 'bled or waggled their heads on certain days would be preserved for the quaintness'. Inevitably, 'D.' longs for the 'distrust, the barbarity, the betrayals' of a religious world: 'The Dark Ages, after all, had been his 'period' (30).

Lying exhausted on his hotel bed, 'D.' ponders the relevance of Roland's struggles to contemporary Western European politics and its relentless secularism. He imagines the 'whole chivalry of Europe' coming to Roland's aid and a resulting unification of disparate religious creeds:

> Men were united by a common belief. Even a heretic would be on the side of Christendom against the Moors; they might differ about the persons of the Trinity, but on the main issue they were like rock. Now there were so many varieties of economic materialism, so many initial letters. (62)

It becomes of central significance that the Berne manuscript of 'The Song of Roland' offers an alternative version of the story. In this text Roland's loyal companion Oliver, instead of accidentally killing him with a random blow, deliberately strikes down the 'big boasting courageous fool' who had refused to blow his horn to summon reinforcements from Charlemagne because he was more preoccupied with his own 'glory' than with the triumph of his 'faith' (70). But this version had been suppressed by the medieval nobles who, like current political leaders and businessmen such as Lord Benditch, were driven by personal ambitions and fanatical ideologies, rendering them unable to face up to a shared belief that could have saved countless lives consumed in military conflicts, including that still raging in 1930s Spain.

Although he professes no faith or interest in formal religion, 'D.' represents the vigour of intellectual honesty and the innate decency of humanity. *The*

Confidential Agent proposes that while all men are fallen creatures and must dwell in a permanently hostile world, some men (and some women like Rose Cullen and Else Crole) are less fallen than their more powerful superiors. Without needing the crutch of organized religion, 'D.' adheres to the concept that a healthy society must be based upon individual morality and honesty. As he explains to Rose, it is necessary to live by some decent standard of behaviour, 'Otherwise nothing matters at all' (67). Once Else has been murdered by her manageress, who seems like a 'devil' (87), 'D.' embraces a passionate desire for justice instead of a stoical acceptance of human frailty. As he gazes on her lifeless body, he wonders if a belief in God would have allowed him to consider Else 'saved from much misery' and to leave all 'punishment to God'. But he has to admit that he personally lacks such faith and that unless 'people received their deserts, the world to him was chaos, he was faced with despair' (138).

Despite such dark thoughts, *The Confidential Agent* does not ultimately conclude that secular justice alone is sufficient for a vital society since the authority of God, who remains frustratingly remote to 'D.', continues to pervade the intellectual framework of the novel. 'D.' begrudgingly admits to Rose that if he could believe in a 'god it would be simpler' (67). Similarly, when he meets Forbes (the Jew, Furtstein), he enviously imagines him as a figure from the Old Testament, with its strangely reassuring balance of violence and justice: 'Very far back in the past was the desert, the dead salt sea, the desolate mountains and the violence on the road from Jericho. He had a basis of belief' (111). A short time later, when he discovers Else's lifeless body, he acknowledges that some 'people might pray' in such a situation but he can only take refuge from its horror 'in action' (136).

When 'D.' is planning his botched murder of the traitor 'K.', he brings him to a basement flat of a woman called Glover. (The novel is dedicated to 'Dorothy Craigie', the pen-name of Greene's then mistress, Dorothy Glover.) There he finds among her meagre possessions the small library of a 'pious woman' (163). As 'D.' threatens 'K.' with a gun, he accidentally knocks a book of devotional verse off the shelf and it falls open at the lines: 'God is in the sunlight, / Where the butterflies roam, / God is in the candlelight, / Waiting in your home.' This simple verse provokes a profound response in 'D.', as he realizes that because he cannot 'believe in God' he ultimately has 'no home' (169). Rose then fortuitously arrives at the flat to discover that 'K.', who had a weak heart, has died from the shock of 'D.' firing the gun at him. They lay him out on the divan with the 'pious book' (144) near his ear and plan their escape. As 'D.' finally embraces her (in what Greene later regarded as an overstrained romantic ending), he makes explicit a link between a loss of religious faith and a loss of sexual desire (a conjunction later reiterated in 'A Visit to Morin' and *The End of the Affair*): 'He couldn't feel desire. It was as if he had made himself a eunuch for his people's sake . . . The act of desire remained an act of faith, and he had lost his faith' (174).

'D.' eventually makes his escape alone and, waiting on a dark Sunday morning for his train, he remains troubled by the absence of a consoling Divinity. He undergoes no miraculous conversion but instead takes solace in Rose's plaintive words that they are merely unlucky: 'We don't believe in God. So it's no use praying . . . As it is, I can only keep my fingers crossed' (186). When, unexpectedly, she meets up with him on the ferry back to the continent, he has already found some consolation in the idea that the likes of Else and 'K.' are now beyond earthly sufferings caused by solitude and suspicion. In keeping with his melancholy sense of mortality, Rose promises to love the aged 'D.' only as long as he is alive, and then she will happily return him to his dead wife. Greene seems to conclude the novel with the unorthodox idea that by redis-covering his physical desire for a woman, 'D.' may ultimately also open himself up to the processes of faith and religious belief.

The Power and the Glory (1940)

Begun alongside *The Confidential Agent* in March 1939, this novel was largely completed by September, although to delay his military draft Greene claimed to the authorities that he needed until June 1940 to finish it. His request was granted and he used this extra time to pursue other literary projects, some of which had a strongly religious focus. He proposed to his agent an anthology illustrative of historical and contemporary Catholic concerns with, for example, one of Crashaw's verses followed by a murderer's statement (similar to that included in *The Lawless Roads*) and a passage from St Augustine's City of God (recalling its relevance to *The Confidential Agent*) alongside a coroner's report on a suicide case. He hoped thereby to depict the modern world as 'full of horror, grotesqueness, courage, meanness, spirituality', with the 'shadow of the City of God' falling across the whole selection. This idea was rejected and Tom Burns's alternative suggestion that he should write about the Belgian leper missionary, Father Joseph Damien, also never came to fruition (although it later stimulated the genesis of *A Burnt Out Case*). Greene continued to churn out book and film reviews for the *Spectator* and to write some short fictional pieces, including a disturbing horror story rich in abnormal psychology, 'A Little Place Off the Edgware Road', offering a grim reinterpretation of 'death in life' and the Resurrection. A depressive called Craven is haunted by a recurrent nightmare, imagining that bodies cannot decay after death as they remain 'ready to rise again' (66), only to find himself sitting in the darkness of a local cinema next to a still-talking murdered man whose throat had been cut.[9]

The Power and the Glory's publication on 4 March 1940 stands as the single most important landmark in Greene's reputation as a Catholic novelist, even though sales in England were slow. The escalation of the Second World War curtailed both the novel's publicity campaign and British public taste for fictions set in far away environments. Sales in France, stimulated by a generous preface from François Mauriac, eventually proved more substantial than in England. In *Ways of Escape* Greene commented that *The Power and the Glory* was the only novel he had ever tried to write to a 'thesis' (85) and its structure is indeed systematically defined. The first section of its fable-like narrative involves a miscellany of characters who encounter the priest as he tries to evade capture. These include the amnesiac dentist Mr Tench, the precocious child Coral Fellows and the boy Luis whose devout mother tells stories of the heroic life and martyrdom of a Father Juan (recalling Father Pro). To foster a timeless and allegorical quality, both the priest and his pursuer, the idealistic atheist lieutenant, remain nameless. This echoes Greene's use of 'D.' and 'L.' in *The Confidential Agent*, as he sought to endow a 'legendary' quality to their opposition.

The second section of the novel recounts the priest's flight from the authorities and introduces the Judas-like *mestizo* who will eventually betray him. The priest spends a night in a filthy and overcrowded prison cell, a hellish microcosm of the fallen world. Here he is surrounded by absolute darkness, the groans of fellow prisoners, the stench of an overflowing toilet-bucket and even the sounds of a copulating couple. Paradoxically, these experiences teach him – as an example of Charles Péguy's 'sinner at the heart of Christianity' – the essential human interconnectedness of beauty and suffering, hope and despair and, above all, the possibility for even a flawed man like himself of finding Divine inspiration within the fallen world: 'This place was very like the world: overcrowded with lust and crime and unhappy love, it stank to heaven; but he realized that after all it was possible to find peace there' (123).

The third section begins with an Eden-like pastoral interlude when the Lehrs, a gentle Lutheran brother and sister, nurse the priest back to health on their idyllic estate. But he is also lulled into a false sense of complacency by their kindness which, paradoxically, finally persuades him to accept that his 'martyrdom' is unavoidable. As A. A. DeVitis explains:

> At this point the motif of flight and pursuit is reversed so that the priest may become the aggressor and the champion of his convictions. Through the priest Greene deploys his major concern: the grace of God exerted on the soul of a man whose weakness is, paradoxically, the symbol of his strength. The figure of the priest allows Greene to work within the anatomy of sainthood.[10]

Although his body is rested and healed during his time with the Lehrs, the priest's sense of his own spiritual worth rapidly declines. He begins to haggle with the poverty-stricken natives over the price of a baptism and is tempted back into his alcoholism by a devilish brandy seller: 'He drank the brandy down like damnation' (166). His lowest moment comes when, as he struggles to say

Mass for the local natives, his mind is tormented by despairing, dream-like fantasies as, like Pinkie, he feels that he carries 'Hell about with him':

> He remembered a dream he had had of a big grassy arena lined with the statues of saints – but the saints were alive, they turned their eyes this way and that, waiting for something. He waited, too, with an awful expectancy. Bearded Peters and Pauls, with Bibles pressed to their breasts, watched some entrance behind his back he couldn't see – it had the menace of a beast. Then a marimba began to play, tinkly and repetitive, a firework exploded, and Christ danced into the arena – danced and postured with a bleeding painted face, up and down, up and down, grimacing like a prostitute, smiling and suggestive. He woke with the sense of complete despair. (173)

Rose and Pinkie together had represented the duality of Greene's configuration of good and evil but in this passage both moral extremes are encapsulated within a single flawed human being. As Greene pertinently commented in his essay, 'Frederick Rolfe: Edwardian Inferno': 'The greatest saints have been men with more than a normal capacity for evil, and the most vicious men have sometimes narrowly evaded sanctity' (131).

Greene regarded *The Power and the Glory* essentially as a seventeenth-century tragedy in which 'the actors symbolize a virtue or a vice'.[11] But in this drama the expected polarities between religious and secular elements are pointedly reversed. The whisky priest is a timorous drunkard who tries to evade his vocational responsibilities. On an allegorical level, the novel can be read as the story of his unsuccessful attempts to avoid sainthood. He is persistently guilty of pride and despair and he belongs to the world of the flesh, even having sired an illegitimate daughter, Brigitta. In contrast, his secular, church-hating counterpart, the lieutenant, possesses many of the desirable attributes of a missionary priest. He is temperate, celibate and inspired to a socialist vocation through his idealistic principles. He maintains high standards of personal purity and truthfulness and regards himself as the loyal servant of his own people. Pointedly, his frugal and unadorned lodgings resemble a 'prison or a monastic cell' (19).

Our first encounter with the lieutenant comes as he is fining petty criminals, including a man brought before him (recalling a similar case in *The Confidential Agent*), for having a holy medal 'under his shirt' (15). The lieutenant fines him five pesos, the usual price of a Mass, before focusing on his pursuit of the whisky priest. He bitterly recalls the 'smell of incense in the churches of his boyhood, the candles and the laciness and the self-esteem' (17) of the pompous priests respected by his parents' generation. With the lieutenant's anti-clerical mindset firmly established, the priest's first encounter with him comes when he has just said Mass at a local village. A worshipper whispers to him that the police are on their way and the dramatic tension escalates as the priest hastens through the Mass. Finally reaching the Consecration: '*Hoc est enim Corpus Meum*', the priest and his congregation breathe a communal sigh of relief. With the Mass safely concluded, Maria (the mother of his malevolent-looking child Brigitta) bundles him away with a raw onion to hide the smell of the communion wine on his breath. The lieutenant systematically interrogates the villagers and the priest is momentarily tempted to throw himself before the lieutenant. Another man is finally taken as a hostage and the villagers, now wanting to be rid of him, tell the priest to head north and cross over the border into an area where churches are still tolerated. Maria savagely derides him as a 'whisky priest' and mocks his tremulous offer to sacrifice himself to protect the villagers: 'What kind of a martyr do you think you'll be?' (76). As he leaves the hut, he is aware of 'faith dying out between the bed and the door – the Mass would soon mean no more to anyone than a black cat crossing the path' (77).

On the day of his imprisonment the priest encounters the lieutenant for a second time. He is mistaken for a drunk and given the offer of a fine, again 5 pesos, which he cannot pay since he only has 25 centavos. Now knowing that he was approaching the 'beginning of the end' (116), he is thrust into the dark cell for the night where he confesses his true identity to his fellow inmates and acknowledges that he is no more than a 'whisky priest' (133) with an illegitimate child. When he is freed the next morning, he stands next to a wanted poster of himself but, still unrecognized on their third meeting, the lieutenant gives him the now symbolic offering of a 5-peso piece, the 'price of a Mass', which the priest clutches in his hand as he offers his thanks with the words: 'You're a good man' (138).

With this inversion of moral polarities confirmed, the 'good man' continues his relentless pursuit of the 'bad priest'. At the same time, their roles seem steadily to blend one into the other, as the priest finally embraces his spiritual destiny and begins to desire his martyrdom at the hands of the lieutenant whom he now pursues. Leaving the Eden of the Lehrs, the priest is led by the Judas *mestizo* to a dying American gangster, James Calver, who rejects the offer of confession and resolutely insists that he is 'damned' (185). For the first time in the novel, the priest is in total control of his sacred ministry. He dutifully whispers the words of conditional absolution over Calver (who recalls the unrepentant criminal on the cross next to Jesus at Calvary), just in case his spirit had repented 'for one second before it crossed the border' (186). The lieutenant, tipped off by the *mestizo*, arrives for their fourth encounter and their debate, held over the dead body of the gangster, resembles that between a confident Jesuit proselytiser and an inquisitive proselyte. The priest admits to being a 'bad priest' (189) and sees himself neither as a 'saint' nor even as a 'brave man' (192). But he is insistent that these human failings are irrelevant to the dispensing of his holy ministry:

But it doesn't matter so much my being a coward . . . I can put God into a man's mouth just the same – and I can give him God's pardon. It wouldn't make any difference to that if every priest in the Church was like me. (193)

The lieutenant angrily claims that the priest is angling to end up as a 'martyr' (194) but the priest gently dismisses this idea, joking that he would need to drink much more brandy to be able to attain such a status.

The final encounters of the priest and the lieutenant are defined by the Christian qualities of resolution and compassion demonstrated by both men. The lieutenant offers to fulfil any last request of the priest since he isn't a 'bad fellow' (199). The priest wishes to make a final confession and, true to his promise, the lieutenant tries unsuccessfully to persuade the lapsed and married priest, Father José, to come to the prison. Instead, sipping brandy from a flask given to him by the lieutenant, the priest has to make do with a sincere 'kind of a general confession' (206) and then drifts off into a restless sleep. He experiences another confused religious dream-vision as he sees himself eating hungrily at a café table set up in front of the high altar of a cathedral, while a priest says Mass and the deceased Coral Fellows pours him some wine. Near the altar another priest repeatedly taps out in Morse Code three long taps and one short (equating, unintelligibly, to 'ö'). This message echoes through the whole church when it is imitated by an invisible congregation and Coral explains that it is means 'News'. The priest awakes and finds that his 'huge feeling of hope' dissolves at the sight of the prison yard and the realization that it was the 'morning of his death' (209). Tormented by feelings of despair and regret that with more self-restraint and courage he might have 'been a saint', he poignantly realizes that for a priest and for every man, at the 'end there was only one thing that counted – to be a saint' (209).

The pathetic details of the whisky priest's execution in the prison yard, witnessed by Mr Tench as he tends to the chief of police's teeth, are counterpointed in the following scene with Luis's mother reading aloud from a hagiographical account of Father Juan's martyrdom. The whisky priest cannot walk unaided to face the firing squad while a transcendent Juan faces them with a 'smile of complete adoration and happiness' (217). Instead of the glorious '*Viva Cristo Rey*' of Juan and Pro, the whisky priest utters only a single panic-stricken word that sounds like 'Excuse' (215). The point of similarity in their deaths comes when at each execution the officer mercifully shoots a single bullet into the priest's head to ensure a speedy death. But, just as the priest has previously explained to the lieutenant that the personal moral worth of a priest is irrelevant to his ministering of the sacraments, so this counterpointing of the two executions demonstrates that even if one man dies in tremulous fear and another in heroic joy, both may still be worthy martyrs. Written, it may be argued, as a devout work of anti-hagiography, *The Power and the Glory* proposes that the unreserved gift of one's life for the Divine cause, rather than the way in which it is terminated, offers the only true definition of a Christian martyr.

Later that evening, as Luis looks out of his open bedroom window, the lieutenant walks past and wishes him '*Buenas noches*'. But in silence the boy spits through the window bars so accurately that a 'blob of spittle' (219) lands on the butt of the revolver used earlier to dispatch the whisky priest. During the night Luis hears a knocking on the door and lets in a stranger who tells him: 'I am a priest . . . My name is Father – .' Before he can give his name, Luis 'puts his lips to his hand' (220), thereby ensuring that the unending cycle of missionary work can begin once again in Mexico. Through the flawed but ultimately inspiring character of the whisky priest, followed by this unnamed new arrival and Luis's silent acceptance of his mission, as A. A. DeVitis notes, 'Greene approaches the precincts of myth.'[12]

Wartime and *The Ministry of Fear* (1943)

Soon after delaying his call-up by the emergency reserve, Greene secured a position at the overstaffed Ministry of Information (satirized in his short story 'Men at Work'). He was employed there for six months with Dorothy Glover as his secretary. Together they also served as fire watchers during the London Blitz which began in September 1940 and destroyed the Greene family home at 14 North Side, Clapham Common (described in his 1954 short story 'The Destructors'). Greene's younger sister Elizabeth was already working for the British Intelligence Services and he was accepted for MI6, with confirmation in August 1941 that he would be stationed in West Africa. His voyage in the following December from Liverpool to Freetown, Sierra Leone, was a dangerous one (as recalled in 'Convoy to West Africa'), with the passengers sharing watches with the crew for aircraft and submarine attacks. Greene sometimes warded off anxiety by reciting 'Hail Marys' as they crossed the Irish Sea to Belfast to meet up with the rest of their convoy. He even went ashore briefly to have his confession heard by a young Catholic parish priest whom he had managed to locate in the predominantly Protestant Belfast.[13]

In April 1941 Greene had signed a contract to produce a slim volume on *British Dramatists*, for Collins's 'Britain in Pictures' series, which he completed without any reference books on the voyage out. Typed up on an old French typewriter and published in 1942, its opening words illustrate Greene's now habitual intermingling of religious thought and literary creativity:

> Anyone who goes into a Roman Catholic church during the Holy Week services, can see for himself the origin of our drama: on Palm Sunday the priest knocks on the door of the church and demands to be admitted, the palms are borne along the aisle: on Good Friday the shrill voices of Judas and the High Priest break into the narrative of the Gospel: the progress to Calvary is made more real by human actors.

His hypothesis over how secular drama was initiated in England also proposes a specifically religious perspective as he imagines how the Mass, with its 'dramatic re-enactment of the Last Supper' inspiring the Mystery and Miracle Plays, incorporated Old and New Testament stories, 'often by priests, in the precincts of churches' (7). He then discusses the four great cycles of Miracle Plays and how in Shakespeare's day 'Religion was better left alone for the time' (12). Within only 12,000 words, Greene produced a compact, if highly idiosyncratic, study of the development of English drama. He still found room to sustain his concern with links between religion and artistic creativity, most notably in his discussion of John Dryden, whom he represented as ruled by the 'idea of authority' and who had been obliged to convert to Catholicism when he finally discovered the 'source of his idea' (29). On 3 January 1942 he arrived back in Freetown, seven years after his first visit there, and was flown about ten days later to Lagos for three months' further training.

He returned to Freetown in mid-March 1942, nominally as a member of CID Special Branch but really as an MI6 counter-espionage agent gathering intelligence on industrial diamond smuggling and Vichy airfields in French Guinea. In June he was gratified to learn that *The Power and the Glory* had won the Hawthornden Prize and that Paramount planned to make a film of *A Gun for Sale* (as *This Gun for Hire*). In about April he started another mystery thriller called 'The Worst Passion of All' (pity), which was almost finished by mid-August when he asked his agent to bring it, under its new title *The Ministry of Fear*, to Paramount's attention. The typescript was sent to London in parts between September and November, along with a precautionary surface mail copy, to minimize the risk of loss in the wartime airmail post. To Greene's delight, in September Paramount offered £3,250 for the film rights, even before examining the last two-thirds of the manuscript.

The Ministry of Fear focuses on an outlandish conspiracy of fifth-columnists in England and is told through the experiences of Arthur Rowe, a solitary individual who has been briefly institutionalized in a psychiatric hospital after being acquitted of the mercy-killing of his terminally ill wife on the grounds of temporary insanity. He lives alone on a small private income in rooms in Guilford Street, Bloomsbury (adjoining Mecklenburgh Square where Greene had rented a room for his writing in Dorothy Glover's household), and shelters himself from the outside world by constantly rereading *The Old Curiosity Shop* and *David Copperfield*, childhood favourites untainted by adult connotations. There is a expressionistic quality to this entertainment's foggy, wartime landscapes and its intricate structuring is aptly described by Grahame Smith as: 'a marvel of craftsmanship, a Chinese puzzle of extraordinary ingenuity which finally locks together to disclose meaning rather than mere cleverness'.[14] As in *The Power and the Glory*, its protagonist progresses through three distinct stages of experience, in this case indicated by the titles of the work's three books: 'The Happy Man' (Rowe's idyllic pre-1914 childhood and adolescence), 'The Unhappy Man' (his disillusioned and traumatic adulthood) and 'The Whole Man' (his middle-aged acceptance of the flawed nature of the human condition). Through this progression from innocence to experience, *The Ministry of Fear* fulfils the promise of its title, derived from Wordworth's *The Prelude*: 'It was a Ministry as large as life to which all who loved belonged. If one loved one feared' (258).

The dark sense of conspiracy pervading this entertainment is indebted to both Greene's own espionage work for MI6 and the traumatic experiences of his cousin, Ben Greene, who was briefly imprisoned as a fifth columnist. Ben, the brother of Barbara with whom Greene had travelled through Liberia, was a dedicated Quaker and pacifist. Their mother was German and Barbara also married a German aristocrat, requiring her to spend the entire war in Germany. Ben was an active member of the British People's Party and ran from 'The Wilderness', Berkhamstead, the 'Peace & Progressive Information Service'. He compiled various unpublished tracts on the decadence of contemporary English politics, with such inflammatory titles as 'Party Government and the Downfall of Government' and 'The Party System and the Corruption of Government' (which he continued to revise until the early-1970s). More problematically, Michael Shelden has traced how he visited Germany in 1936 and developed links with the Anglo-German Fellowship. He also gave speeches in praise of Germany after the invasion of Poland and his pamphlet, *The Truth About the War* (1939) was deemed by some as pro-Hitler propaganda.[15]

Unsurprisingly, Ben was soon denounced to the authorities as a fifth columnist, Nazi sympathizer and known critic of British democracy. As W. J. West has demonstrated, the embarrassment for Greene was that his cousin's accuser was none other than his ever-problematic eldest brother, Herbert. Ben was investigated by the security services and at first they decided not to take any further action since a petty family feud seemed to be behind the affair. But MI5 kept Ben under general surveillance and in May 1940 he was detained under the Emergency Powers regulations. He was incarcerated for seven months at Brixton Prison (mentioned in *The Ministry of Fear*) and the straitjacketing of Major Stone in the novel probably reflects Ben's harsh treatment while detained. Barbara Greene supplied the inspiration for Anna Hilfe and her brother, Willi, seems to be based on her German husband.[16] When Arthur Rowe is knocked unconscious by an enemy agent's bomb, he wakes up in a secret psychiatric institution recalling the clinic of Greene's former psychoanalyst, Kenneth Richmond. Although this country nursing-home seems to offer a seductive return to pre-1914 Edwardian England, the entertainment's savage condemnation of the readily exploitable masquerades of psychiatry suggests that Greene was also purging some of his own inner demons in *The Ministry of Fear*.

The plot's religious aspects are generally muted but still remain of central importance to Greene's nostalgic commentary on pre-war English society. Similarly, its vividly realized cameos of the drab austerity of wartime London, interspersed with moments of absolute terror during the Blitz, are powerfully evoked. Although Greene was composing these scenes from the relative safety of Sierra Leone, he could readily imagine the daily anxieties of his family and friends back home in England. All the chapter headings are taken from *The Little Duke*, a favourite novel from Greene's childhood by the Anglo-Catholic writer Charlotte Mary Yonge (1823–1901). The opening scene, set at a traditional English church fête in London reminiscent of the lost world of Rupert Brooke's family vicarage at Grantchester, has the 'inevitable clergyman' supervising a 'rather timid game of chance' (11). It offers a seductively false Eden and evokes Rowe's poignant recollections of his childhood innocence when he used to follow his mother around the stalls. In the fortune-teller's tent he is mistakenly given information about the weight of a cake (containing a hidden microfilm) and duly wins it. As the fête closes, a man dashes out from a taxi into the gypsy tent like a 'mortal sinner in fear of immediate death might dive towards a confessional-box' (18). Under coercion, the vicar and the treasure-hunt lady make half-hearted attempts to persuade Rowe to return the cake but he refuses, thereby setting off a train of nightmarish events in which he becomes that familiar Greeneian figure, the hunted man.

Like Scobie in *The Heart of the Matter*, Rowe is hampered by his excessive sense of pity and indiscriminate compassion for humanity since it disturbed 'his precarious calm' to see people suffering: 'Then he would do anything for them. Anything' (22). This weakness comes into play when he is visited by a dwarfish man called Poole with enormous twisted shoulders caused by infantile paralysis. They share some of the cake won at the fête, which Rowe carefully slices up with his long-treasured multi-blade knife, as the distant sound of an enemy bomber's engines can be heard overhead. Despite his carefully chosen physical differences, Poole seems to express many of the pacifist and pro-Nazi views held by Greene's cousin, Ben (who was six-foot-eight tall), as he laments the sheer 'stupidity of war' (24). Poole deplores the state of the pre-war British government and tells Rowe that true democracy can now only be found in Germany. He also claims that Poland had to be invaded because it was 'one of the most corrupt countries in Europe' (25). Although Rowe is disturbed by Poole's views, he still feels the stirring of his 'dangerous pity' (26), even when Poole finally admits that he has come to reclaim the mysteriously important cake. Suddenly, the house is largely destroyed by a falling bomb. Rowe finds himself in the basement kitchen, looking up at where his room had once been. He is just able to see the cripple lying next to the chair in which he had been sitting as the air-raid wardens arrive to rescue him.

Determined to get to the bottom of this mystery, Rowe visits the decrepit offices of the Orthotex Private Inquiry Bureau run by Mr Rennit. He would have left as soon as he saw their dismal state but for the rousing of his pity, 'more promiscuous than lust' (32). As he ponders the squalid world of infidelities and divorces which seem to make up most of Rennit's cases, Rowe realizes that a godless human society will always be intrinsically ludicrous and dispiriting:

But of course if you believed in God – and the Devil – the thing wasn't quite so comic. Because the Devil – and God too – had always used comic people, futile people, little suburban natures and the maimed and warped to serve his purposes. When God used them you talked emptily of Nobility and when the devil used them of Wickedness, but the material was only dull shabby human mediocrity in either case. (33)

Still furious at Poole's attempts before the bomb intervened to drug his tea with hyocine (which he had used in his wife's mercy-killing), he blurts out to Rennit that he is himself a 'murderer' (35), an indiscretion which also prompts a mental prayer from the Psalms (141.3): 'Set a watch, O Lord, before my mouth and a door around about my lips' (36). Having engaged the agency's services and met his assigned investigator, introduced to him as 'A.2' but soon absent-mindedly called Jones by Rennit, he then attempts to locate the fête's fortune-teller, Mrs Bellairs, who had told him the weight of the cake.

This pursuit takes him to the offices on the Strand of the bizarrely-titled 'Comforts for the Mothers of the Free Nations Fund' (perhaps mocking his cousin Ben's 'Peace & Progressive Information Service') which operates as a cover for fifth-columnist activities. This cameo scene offers an early taster of Greene's skill in concocting farcical parodies of the world of espionage, later brought to full comic fruition in *Our Man in Havana*. Here he meets the attractive but wary Anna and her brother, the charmingly sinister Willi Hilfe, who claims that they are 'technically' (43) Austrians. Their conversations remind Rowe of the lost world of pre-war England, with its fêtes and people who dutifully attended Matins and spent the weekend in the country, now all swept aside by the impending threat of the 'Nazis. The Fascists. The Reds. The Whites' (48). They eventually locate Mrs Bellairs's address for Rowe, and Willi offers to accompany him to her house. He leaves a brief message for his next appointment, a Mr 'Trench' (49), closing the scene with a coded authorial reference since Greene had adopted the pseudonym 'Hilary Trench' for various youthful publications.

The door of Mrs Bellairs's house is opened by an ancient maid whose face seems 'wrinkled and austere like a nun's' (51) and they are invited to join a séance over which Mrs Bellairs is about to preside. Unexpectedly, Anna telephones Rowe there and urges him to leave immediately, warning that they 'will try to get you in the dark' (55). Instead, another guest called Cost is apparently murdered with Rowe's pocket knife in the darkness of the séance and, with Hilfe's assistance (his name is German for 'help'), Rowe escapes through a toilet window. The next chapter, 'Between Sleeping and Waking', places him in a nightmarish world where it becomes increasingly difficult to differentiate between dream and reality and makes extensive use of Greene's long-standing fascination with dream interpretation. In the unnerving darkness of the séance Rowe recalls feeling as though he was trapped in a dream from which he could not escape: 'the feet are leaden-weighted: you cannot stir from before the ominous door which almost imperceptibly moves. It is the same in life' (56).

As Rowe, exhausted and frightened by his flight, takes refuge in an underground air-raid shelter, the author assumes the role of his psychoanalyst:

There are dreams which belong only partly to the unconscious; these are the dreams we remember on waking so vividly that we deliberately continue them, and so fall asleep again and wake and sleep and the dream goes on without interruption, with a thread or logic the pure dream doesn't possess. (63)

Rowe's dreams take him back to the comforting security of his childhood and he imagines himself, although still only a seven-year-old child, confessing to his mother that he has just murdered his wife. She assures him that it is only a 'dream, dear, a nasty dream' (64). As he briefly awakes and hears the terrifying rumble of the air raid above ground, he 'caught the dream and held it' again, since a nightmare seems infinitely preferable to the reality of his current situation. He continues to tell his mother, who died before the horrors of the First World War, about being framed for the murder of Mr Cost at Mrs Bellairs's house and how the Germans are now bombing London. His mother proclaims his world to be a 'madhouse' (65) and Rowe realizes that both his nostalgic dreams of his boyhood self and his present reality are fusing into one seamless nightmare. He is 'filled with horror' over 'what a child becomes' and tries to imagine how his dead mother must feel as she sees his growth from 'innocence to guilt' while remaining 'powerless to stop it' (65).

Although Rowe never expresses any specific religious beliefs, his mind is increasingly permeated, even haunted, by devotional objects and imagery. As he browses through the morning paper following the previous night's raids, he intones to himself the list of casualties and fatalities 'like the closing ritual of a midnight Mass. The sacrifice was complete and the papers pronounced in calm invariable words the '*Ite missa est*' (69). Later, he watches the entrance to Mr Rennit's office from the doorway of a book auctioneer's. At random, he pulls from a shelf an ornamented Roman missal which, oddly, seems entirely in keeping with wartime London, with its 'prayers for deliverance, the angry nations, the unjust, the wicked, the adversary like a roaring lion' (74). He compares his solitary life to biblical anchorites who live in the desert but, as he regretfully notes, 'they had their God to commune with' (76). As the first section of the novel, 'The Unhappy Man', draws to a close, Rowe again fondly recalls his happy childhood with its absolute belief that 'God is good' (89) – just before he is again blown up, this time by a bomb hidden in a suitcase of books.

The second section, 'The Happy Man', traces his gradually emerging consciousness after this explosion in a mysterious clinic where he is now known as Richard Digby. Echoing Richmond's treatment of Greene as an unhappy teenager, some of its inmates are being treated by a Dr Forester with psychoanalysis which, according to the ward-orderly Johns, can sometimes offer 'salvation' (112). Anna Hilfe comes to visit Rowe and, as she stirs his memory by calling him Arthur, they talk of Hitler's coming to power in 1933 and what little he recalls about the ongoing war with Germany. Johns also tells him about Dr Forester's latest pamphlet for the Ministry of Information (for which Greene had worked), titled 'The Psycho-Analysis of Nazidom' (127). While walking in the garden of the clinic, he meets the deranged Major Stone and his pathetic madness induces doubts in Rowe's mind over the true nature of the institution in which they are both incarcerated. He wonders if the sick-bay itself is merely a 'fantasy of disordered minds' and suspects that it has no more 'reality than the conception of Hell presented by sympathetic theologians – a place without inhabitants which existed simply as a warning' (126). As Johns seeks Major Stone, he calls on another orderly to assist him. This 'dwarfish man' with powerful 'twisted shoulders' (127) is the man who tried to steal the cake at the beginning of the novel, although Rowe fails to recognize him. Increasingly disturbed by the flickering re-emergence of his memory, his jailors attempt to persuade Rowe that he is unwell and confine him to his room.

As he seeks to break out of the clinic, Rowe experiences another dream-like return to his childhood but, this time, his fantasies are overtly linked to Greene's psychological problems at Berkhamsted School. He creeps past Dr Forester's study and, discovering a 'green baize door' by the sick-bay, he imagines himself 'back in his own childhood, breaking out of dormitory, daring more than he really wanted to dare, proving himself' (137). In a nearby room he discovers with a 'terrible sense of pity' (141) the straitjacketed Major Stone and feels 'capable of murder for the release of that gentle tormented creature' (141). Rowe eventually makes his escape from the clinic and memories flood back as he is interviewed by the police. He learns that the murder of Mr Cust had been faked and he suddenly recalls that Dr Forester was also present at Mrs Bellair's séance. Rowe is handed over to another section (probably MI5) and their Mr Prentice informs him that a secret roll of microfilm had been hidden by fifth columnists in the cake at the church fête. As they drive past the bombed-out shell of St Clement Dane and the desolation around St Paul's, Rowe thinks that London must look just how Jerusalem once appeared in the 'mind's eye of Christ when he wept' (166). Cost is tracked down and Rowe sees him commit suicide gruesomely with a pair of tailor's shears as Prentice warns him of the dangers of pity: 'a terrible thing . . . Pity is the worst passion of all: we don't outlive it like sex' (172).

The conspiracy of fifth-columnists is finally thwarted, leading to the arrest of Mrs Bellairs and the deaths of Dr Forster and Poole, shot by the idealistic Johns who has grown suspicious of the true nature of the Doctor's loyalties and his clinical approval for the 'Nazi elimination of old people and incurables' (182). The final section, 'The Whole Man', culminates in Rowe's pursuit of Willi Hilfe who commits suicide in a station lavatory with a gun handed to him by Rowe. The latter's mind is haunted by his affection for Anna and the awful thought that he is causing the death of her beloved brother: 'Pity is cruel, Pity destroys.

Love isn't safe when pity's prowling around'. To ensure his country's safety, it seems he must ultimately become a secular martyr:

> his Church had once taught him the value of penance, but penance was a value only to oneself. There was no sacrifice, it seemed to him, that would help him to atone to the dead. The dead were out of reach of the guilty. He wasn't interested in saving his own soul. (218)

Although Rowe finally declares his love to Anna and she reciprocates, such a romantic movie ending seems secondary to Rowe's continuing indifference to the eternal life of his soul. In *The Ministry of Fear* Greene establishes the foundations for Scobie's central dilemma in *The Heart of the Matter* – an excess of pity.

Chapter 5

The Certainty of Doubt: 1944–1954

Adultery, Suicide and *The Heart of the Matter* (1948)

The five-year gap between the publication of *The Ministry of Fear* (1943) and *The Heart of the Matter* was occasioned by Greene's time-consuming wartime intelligence duties and his appointment in 1944 to a senior position as a publisher. His literary life, however, remained intensely demanding. While he was still in Sierra Leone, a theatrical version of *Brighton Rock* was planned, with Vivien acting as his liaison during script-vetting. It opened at Blackpool on 15 February 1943 with Richard Attenborough as Pinkie, Hermione Baddeley as Ida and Dulcie Gray as Rose (the first two reappeared in the 1947 film). Greene arrived back in England on 1 March and attended the first night at the New Theatre, Oxford. He disliked Baddeley's musical-hall inspired interpretation of Ida and he was horrified by the obliteration of the dark spiritual climax of the novel's ending through the excision of the priest's final speech to Rose (also a major problem in the film). He demanded the removal of his name from all publicity and for a while avoided theatrical and film work (including a potentially lucrative offer to draft a film script of Howard Spring's novel, *Fame is the Spur*).

On his return from Africa, he was posted to SIS headquarters at St Albans where he worked closely with the traitor Kim Philby. Much of his knowledge of espionage, later deployed in *Our Man in Havana* (1958), came from this period. Unexpectedly, in June 1944 Greene resigned from MI6 – Philby had been promoted but Greene seems to have wanted to distance himself from him – and moved to the Political Intelligence Department (PID). One of his first tasks there was to edit a cultural anthology called 'Choix' which was to be dropped over occupied France. Continuing this congenial shift from espionage to literary duties, in the following month Greene was granted half-time release from PID so that he could join the publisher Eyre & Spottiswoode, with the specific brief of building up their fiction list. This appointment had been mooted as early as July 1940 and Greene proved a productive publisher. He signed up R. K. Narayan, Wyndham Lewis and Mervyn Peake, established the Century Library of neglected classics and forged a friendship with François Mauriac, resulting in the firm's publication of Gerard Hopkins's acclaimed English translations of his major novels. Greene and Mauriac were well-matched, with each, as Robert Speaight noted, a 'specialist in sin, and the possibility of salvation'. Greene continued to work at Eyre & Spottiswoode until late-autumn 1948 when he resigned to devote more time to his own writings, following the international success of *The Heart of the Matter*.

By the end of the war Greene was firmly established as a writer of national importance whose fame abroad was steadily growing. From June until October 1945 he tried his hand at a weekly book column for the *Evening Standard*; and between 1946 and 1952 Heinemann brought out a uniform edition of his major works. His second collection of short stories, *Nineteen Stories* (1947), included reprints of some of the best from his first collection, *The Basement Room* (1935). In late-summer 1947 he began discussions with Alexander Korda and Carol Reed for a film called *The Fallen Idol*, based upon *The Basement Room* (released September 1948). This powerful psychological drama, told from a child's point of view, led Greene into a productive working relationship with Reed. The typescript of *The Heart of the Matter* was submitted to Heinemann on 27 September 1947 and only two days later Greene was beginning to plan his most renowned collaboration with Reed, *The Third Man*, originally conceived as a man 'risen-from-the-dead' thriller.[1]

While Greene's literary career was thriving during the late-1940s, a personal rather than literary association was to define the intensity of the religious impulse in his writings for the next decade. Apart from the long-term influence of his wife Vivien, from 1946 Greene's adulterous relationship with Catherine Walston exercised the most potent effect over his interests in religious belief and the efficacy of the Catholic faith. Catherine Crompton, the daughter of an Englishman living in America, had been the 18-year-old bride of Harry Walston, a wealthy English landowner who, although from a Jewish family, had been educated as a Protestant at Eton. By 1946 they had been married for 12 years and, despite a strong personal bond with Harry, Catherine freely indulged in other affairs. In an unfolding sexual drama worthy of one of Greene's lesser short stories, she first contacted him as an admiring reader, explaining that his novels had played a major role in her decision to convert to Catholicism. Always adept at gratifying her own wishes, Catherine then telephoned Vivien to ask if her husband would agree to stand as her godfather. Greene could not attend the ceremony himself and, instead, Vivien acted as a godparent when in September 1946 Catherine was received into the Catholic Church. A photograph survives in which a radiant Catherine sits in front of the standing Vivien who gazes quizzically at the future mistress of her husband.

Norman Sherry comments: 'No one touched Greene as deeply as Catherine Walston, even at a religious level. Although Greene had become a convert to win Vivien, he felt a truer Catholic with Catherine.'[2] During the early-1940s he was torn between his love for Vivien and that for Dorothy Glover but, following his contacts with Catherine, his love for them was transmuted into what he regarded as self-destructive pity. The problematic nature of pity had already formed a major element in the dilemma of Arthur Rowe in *The Ministry of Fear*

(1943). With the last third of *The Heart of the Matter* written after his infatuation with Catherine had begun, Greene's treatment of Scobie's marital dilemma focused on the psychological 'sin' of pity and its inevitable consequence, a fascination with the real Catholic sin of suicide as the only available release from personal crisis. Following a climactic argument prompted by the discovery of one of Greene's love letters to Catherine, Vivien dated the spiritual end of her marriage as 20 November 1947 (poignantly, the wedding-day of the future Queen Elizabeth II). Throughout 1948 they were embroiled in acrimonious discussions, often punctuated by Greene's protestations that his suicide would be the best solution, over whether to seek a deed of separation or a judicial separation.[3]

Evelyn Waugh's biographer, Martin Stannard, writes of Greene's crisis of Catholicism during the late-1940s:

> His Church was not a precise organization with absolute rectitude on its side but a tangle of paradox and heretical temptation. In the clashes between authority and the individual in his novels, authority usually corrupts . . . As a writer he felt the need, even with his Faith, to live on the borderline, owing no loyalty which would demand the faithful lie. The novelist, he felt, needed anonymity, like the spy, to observe clearly and to move freely. And he was not only dangerously 'unorthodox' in his work. He was in love with his American, a married woman who still lived with her husband.[4]

If adultery is dubiously endowed with a spiritual significance – a fascinating idea for Greene – then Catherine Walston did indeed reinvigorate his appetite for the exploration of personal scales of sinfulness. Within such a framework, even the Sixth Commandment (against adultery) could be relegated to the level of a debatable suggestion rather than an absolute tenet of belief. During his conversations in 1979 with Marie-Françoise Allain, Greene argued that he found it difficult to accept the idea of adulterous mortal sin since it has to be 'committed in defiance of God. I doubt whether a man making love to a woman ever does so with the intention of defying God.'[5]

Greene's relationship with Catherine revitalized his already ingrained tastes for theological debate. Waugh recalled when invited in September 1948 to the Walston's country house, Thriplow Farm: 'She and Graham had been reading a treatise on prayer together that afternoon. Then she left the room at about 1 and presently telephoned she was in bed. We joined her. Her bedside littered with books of devotion.'[6] To a cynical eye, the image of Catherine strewing her bedroom with a miscellany of male admirers and theological tracts may appear calculatedly self-indulgent. Nevertheless, it usefully exemplifies a tripartite equation of paramount importance to Greene during the next three decades – the intertwining of personal spirituality and sexuality as a catalyst for literary creativity. As Sherry again explains, Catherine's 'influence was paramount during his great creative period. She was the source of his creativity, for

The Heart of the Matter would not have been completed without her and *The End of the Affair* would not have been started'. In his review of the former novel (*Tablet*, 5 June 1948), Waugh quoted Greene's assertion: 'These characters are not my creation but God's. They have an eternal destiny. They are not merely playing a part for the reader's amusement. They are souls whom Christ died to save.'[7] Such a pronouncement seems emphatically wide of the mark since Scobie's moral dilemmas were specifically designed to reflect upon his author's preoccupations with the insidious dangers of pity within a disintegrating Catholic marriage and the allure of suicide to the despairing adulterer. Sherry sees Scobie as 'Greene's emotional and psychological double'; and in *Ways of Escape* Greene admitted that Scobie came from 'nothing but my own unconscious'.[8]

The epigraph to *The Heart of the Matter* quotes the paradoxical perspective of Charles Péguy:

> Le pécheur est au coeur même de chrétiénté . . . Nul n'est aussi compétent que le pécheur en matière de chrétiénté. Nul, si ce n'est le saint.
>
> (The sinner is at the very heart of Christianity. No-one is as expert as the sinner on the subject of Christianity. No-one except a saint.)[9]

While this statement may be readily held against the whisky priest or Pinkie, it is more problematic to gauge the nature of Scobie's sinfulness. At the beginning of the novel his Catholic faith, to which he had converted to please his wife, is obviously wavering, as symbolized by the 'broken rosary' (10) lying in his office drawer. Calling him by his pet name 'Ticki' (used by Vivien for Greene), Louise accuses him of lacking faith. Scobie lamely replies that she has 'enough for both of us, dear' (16). Their marriage had also been strained by the death of their nine-year-old daughter back home in England three years earlier. Scobie's memory is haunted by a poignant photograph kept on Louise's bedside cabinet of a 'little pious . . . face in the white muslin of first communion' (13). Ultimately, he is weary of his dull marriage and unrewarding colonial life. He dreads retirement, hoping that he will die first (33), and he envies those (like Pinkie) who have enjoyed an accelerated route through the trials of a fallen world to either redemption or damnation. If man could be tested in 'fewer years', then he might first sin at seven, ruin himself for 'love or hate' at ten and seek 'redemption' on a 'fifteen-year-old death-bed' (43).

In his relationship with Louise, Scobie has created through his vulnerability to pity a kind of marital purgatory. Greene was intrigued by the Catholic doctrine of Purgatory, the condition of the soul of a deceased person who has not yet been purged or purified from unforgiven venial sins or forgiven mortal sins. In a 1968 interview he noted that he was a 'great believer in Purgatory. Purgatory to me makes sense, while Hell doesn't', and that he could not believe in a Heaven which is 'just passive bliss'.[10] Scobie's personal purgatory is engendered by his diminishing desire for Louise's presence, shifting his feelings from love into a debilitating state when 'pity' and 'responsibility' reach the 'intensity of a passion' (13). Having lost all physical desire for his middle-aged wife, Scobie finds himself trapped by the 'pathos of her unattractiveness' (19). He sadly recalls how 14 years earlier, in grimly elegant ceremony 'among the lace and candles' (49), he made his marriage vows, now pathetically diminished to the self-deluding hope that he might still somehow make her happy. Scobie tries to ignore the inescapable truth of their dying relationship, pretending that in human relationships 'kindness' is worth a 'thousand truths' (48).

In retrospect, Greene was probably too harsh in his assessment of *The Heart of the Matter*. Stylistically, he felt that his wartime distractions had made his writing skills 'rusty with disuse and misuse'. He also admitted that the novel's emotional core rested upon the insubstantial foundations of a personal desire to escape from the responsibilities of his disintegrating marriage. He regretted presenting Louise only through Scobie's eyes since this 'technical fault' allowed little sympathy for her. He even wondered whether Scobie's dilemma could have been better handled as a 'subject for a cruel comedy rather than for tragedy' since he had made Scobie's religious scruples 'too extreme'.[11] Scobie's dilemma leads to an intriguing tension between the debilitating purgatory of his day-to-day world and the refreshing purity of his subconscious mind. Still fascinating by dream-analysis, Greene allows Scobie occasionally to escape from the oppressive heat of Africa into a soothing mental coolness, when in his dreams 'peace' appears as the 'great glowing shoulder of the moon heaving across his window like an iceberg, Arctic and destructive'. Scobie desires not eternal happiness but only peace, the 'most beautiful word in the language'. Even during the Communion liturgy of the Mass he cannot focus upon the transubstantiation but only on the hypnotic power of the word 'peace' as he is driven to tears by the incantatory responses: 'My peace I give you, my peace I leave with you: O Lamb of God, who takest away the sins of the world, grant us thy peace' (50). Scobie's most famous dream combines this haunting pursuit of peace and 'perfect happiness' with a return to an Edenic landscape of a 'wide cool meadow' where even the serpent is benign and his boy Ali walks silently at 'his heels':

> Birds went by far overhead, and once when he sat down the grass was parted by a small green snake which passed on to his hand and up his arm without fear, and before it slid down into the grass again touched his cheek with a cold, friendly, remote tongue. (73)

Tragically for Scobie, these soothing dreams rapidly evaporate in his conscious world as an apparently irreversible immersion in self-deceiving despair takes a firm hold over his mind. Faustus-like, Scobie is seduced by a dangerous pride in his own flawed rationality. He convinces himself that ultimate 'truth' is valueless since it is merely a mathematical or philosophical 'symbol' (48). While acknowledging that despair is the 'unforgivable sin', Scobie flatters himself that only a 'man of goodwill' can truly possess the 'capacity for damnation' since the 'corrupt or evil man' never knows 'absolute failure' (50) and is always able to trump despair with hope. Wearily, he still tries to be a good Catholic – he habitually recites an Our Father, Hail Mary and Act of Contrition as he lies in bed longing for sleep – but the emotional impotence of his life leads to a corresponding escalation of his spiritual malaise. Although he doesn't drink, fornicate or even lie, Scobie is unable to find virtue in mere absence of sin, simply because he no longer regards his life as 'important enough' (103).

A turning point in Scobie's spiritual decline comes when he is sent to Bamba to deal with the suicide of a young colonial officer called Pemberton, an investigation which establishes an insistent motif of innocence versus experience in the novel. Reaching the Mission at Bamba, he meets Father Clay, a youthful Catholic priest from Liverpool (Greene's port of departure for his African travels) who is overwhelmed by Pemberton's death. Clay is an innocent devotee of the 'Little Flower', St Thérèse of Lisieux, and he regards Pemberton's suicide as 'too terrible' in putting him 'outside mercy' (76). Scobie gently reassures him that Pemberton's childlike innocence (also wryly noting that he was non-Catholic) would have protected him from being guilty of such a sin, even though if either of them had done it, 'We'd be damned because we know, but he doesn't know a thing' (78). Later on, Scobie has another disturbing dream in which Louise is sobbing in their bedroom as he drafts a suicide note in the sitting room. Looking around for a suitable rope or weapon he realizes that suicide was 'for ever out of his power' since no cause was sufficient to 'condemn himself for eternity'. He rushes upstairs but a ghostly Father Clay opens his bedroom door with the words: 'The teaching of the Church' (83).

Just as Pemberton provides an innocent contrast to Scobie's experienced colonial officer, so the naïve Father Clay is counter-pointed by the worldly wise Father Rank who has served 22 years in African missionary work (58). Following Pemberton's suicide, the sacraments of Confession and Communion, along with his preoccupation with suicide, preoccupy Scobie's mind. Having fatally compromised himself by accepting a loan from Yusef to finance Louise's trip to South Africa, Scobie and Louise mark their imminent parting by attending Mass and kneel alongside one another at the Communion rail (87). But, as events unfold, this becomes the last time that Scobie is able to seek solace in the sacraments.

The second book opens with Scobie at Pende, awaiting the arrival of exhausted and dying survivors from a shipwreck who have spent 'forty days and nights' in lifeboats. Despite the obvious biblical echoes of Noah's 40 days and nights of rain and flooding (Gen. 6–8) and Jesus fasting in the wilderness for 40 days and nights (Mt. 4.1–2), Scobie still struggles with the 'mystery' of how to reconcile such suffering with the 'love of God' (108). As he watches over a dying six-year-old girl, he earnestly prays: 'Father . . . give her peace. Take away my peace for ever, but give her peace' (112), thereby sowing the seeds of his ultimately fatal tendency to envisage his negation as a worthy sacrifice for the benefit of others. On the next first Saturday of the month Scobie goes as usual to confession. He explains to Father Rank that he feels weary of his religion since it now 'seems to mean nothing to me . . . I am not sure that I even believe'. The priest plays down his scruples but even a light penance of five Our Fathers and five Hail Marys (replacing a decade of the rosary since, symbolically, his beads are broken), brings little relief since there seems 'nothing to relieve' (140).

This crisis in Scobie's Catholic faith coincides with his increasing intimacy, leading to adultery, with Helen Rolt, a young widowed survivor of the shipwreck. Her plainness arouses his pity, that 'terrible promiscuous passion' (147), making her far more seductive to him than a more beautiful and intelligent woman. Once they begin a sexual relationship, Scobie realizes that his pity for her merely echoes his marital pity for Louise and he anticipates how it will eventually replace his lustful passion for her: 'pity always stayed. Nothing ever diminished pity' (163). Helen scoffs at his attempts to preserve his Catholic identity: 'It doesn't stop you sleeping with me – it only stops you marrying me' (164). As he furtively heads for Helen's hut, Scobie resolves to repent and go to confession so that his 'life will be simple again.' But as 'Virtue, the good life, tempted him in the dark like a sin' (171), the clarity of this spiritual insight is fleeting. After a moment's hesitation, he knocks on her door, thereby initiating his final tragedy. As A. A. DeVitis notes: 'Scobie's Catholicism [is] something akin to the Fatality of Greek drama.'[12]

He learns that a passionate love letter pushed under Helen's door the previous night has gone astray, almost certainly intercepted for blackmail purposes. When he returns disconsolately to his own house, he discovers a telegram from Louise, informing him that she is returning home. Nauseous with anxiety and trapped by his pity for both women, Scobie tries to pray but finds that the Our Father 'lay as dead on his tongue as a legal document'. This devotional failure further convinces him that the happiness of others and the peace he so ardently desires can only be achieved through his death. In a perverted supplication he begs: 'O God, give me death before I give them unhappiness.' The remainder of the novel then offers, filtered through the thoughts of its tragically flawed hero, Greene's sustained meditation upon the intellectual and emotional allure of suicide.

Scobie takes some aspirin for his spinning head and wonders if death itself could be drained as 'simply as these aspirins', even though he knows that suicide is the 'unforgivable sin' and the ultimate expression of an 'unrepentant despair'. He seeks to persuade himself that even God had occasionally broken 'his own laws' and rhetorically asks whether God would find it so difficult to 'put out a hand of forgiveness into the suicidal darkness' since he had been able to wake himself in the 'tomb, behind the stone'? Scobie even hubristically speculates that Christ had not been murdered at the crucifixion since it was impossible to murder God: 'Christ had killed himself: he had hung himself on the Cross as surely as Pemberton from the picture-rail' (174). His mental decline seems tinged with Manichaeism here since they vehemently rejected the idea of the physicality of the crucifixion and resurrection and also advocated suicide as a means of escape from the fallen world of the flesh to that of the spirit. At a drinks party, Scobie discusses Pemberton's death with Helen and Dr Sykes and they casually consider other ways of committing suicide. When asked for her expert opinion, Dr Sykes advises that the most undetectable way would be to get oneself diagnosed with angina and then take an overdose of the prescribed medication. Helen is horrified and Scobie says that Catholics are taught that suicide is the 'unforgivable sin'. The result of such action, he explains to Dr Sykes, would be damnation in Hell, which he envisages not as 'flames and torment' but as a 'permanent sense of loss' (179). Hence, Scobie confirms not only the best way to kill himself but also his full understanding as a Catholic that such actions would be a mortal sin.

Louise's return leads Scobie into what he regards as an irreversible travesty of the sacraments of Confession and Communion. She claims that he hasn't been much of a Catholic without her and insists that they should go to communion together, as a reconfirmation of their marital reunion. Scobie discusses with Helen his fear of taking communion while in a state of mortal sin because of his adultery. But he admits, echoing Greene's words to Marie-Françoise Allain, that if he died now he 'wouldn't know how to repent the love' he holds for Helen. Expressing another Greeneian paradox, Scobie even speculates that a 'lack of faith' allows him to see 'more clearly than faith' (194). He eventually escapes communion by taking a swig of medicinal brandy for his faked angina symptoms but Louise's promise that they can take the sacrament together on another day casually sentences 'him to eternal death' (197). As he sits in church and watches Louise receive communion alone, he is tormented by the words of the liturgy: '*Domine non sum dignus*' (Lord I am not worthy).

Eventually, Scobie tries to confess his adultery and, waiting outside the confessional, prays: 'Make me put my own soul first. Give me trust in your mercy to the one I abandon' (204). Recognizing Scobie's acknowledgement of sin but lack of spiritual strength for amendment, Father Rank cannot grant absolution and instead asks him to come back when his mind is clearer. That night Scobie dreams that he is in a boat with a corpse, only to realize that the 'smell of decay' comes from his own body. Louise then shakes him awake to accompany her to Mass. Hopelessly, he thinks: 'I am damned already – I may as well go the whole length of the chain' (206). In a climactic scene, Scobie's mind inverts the solace of the Mass into a living torment. Haunted by the idea that he is 'desecrating' (207) God because of his love for Helen, the progression of the Canon of the Mass towards the Consecration acts as an insistent chorus to Scobie's escalating sense of his unavoidable damnation. As he finally takes the communion host in his mouth from Father Rank, he makes a perverse prayer at the altar or, as he envisages it, the 'foot of the scaffold' (108). He offers up his 'damnation' to God as the taste of the communion host seems like an 'eternal sentence on the tongue' (109).

When Scobie learns that his replacement is not coming, leading to his own promotion, he views himself as now of the 'devil's party' and bitterly expects to proceed 'from damned success to damned success' (212) since the devil always looks after his own. Similarly, he tells the uncomprehending Helen that he is 'damned for all eternity – unless a miracle happens' (216). Driven by despair and pride, he continues to fake angina symptoms and elicits a prescription for Evipan. Planning his suicide in meticulous detail, he guesses that ten times the recommended dosage should be sufficient. He decides, therefore, to store the tablets for nine days and then to take ten on the following night, as well as doctoring his diary to suggest that he was having increasingly frequent bouts of angina. If this is the 'worst crime' for a Catholic, Scobie thinks, then 'it must be a perfect one' (241).

Greene creates an internalized dialogue between the two contrasting sides of Scobie's mind. In the depths of despair, he sits in church and laments how he cannot continue 'insulting' Him: 'I can't face coming up to the altar at Christmas – your birthday feast – and taking your body and blood for the sake of a lie' (241). This disconsolate admission seems to elicit a Divine intervention since another voice speaks to him 'from the cave of his body':

> it was as if the sacrament which had lodged there for his damnation gave tongue. You say you love me, and yet you'll do this to me – rob me of you for ever . . . All you have to do now is ring a bell, go into a box, confess . . . the repentance is already there, straining at your heart.

Even as he ponders these words, Scobie's intellectual pride leads him back into despair and he decides that he will see things through the 'only way I can' (242). This Faustian dialogue between his 'good angel' and 'bad angel' continues until his final moments. About to take the stored tablets he considers himself totally isolated and at the 'freezing-point' of his life. Even then, he still hears one last plea: 'Throw away those tablets. You'll never be able to collect enough again. You'll be saved' (248). Despite this intercession, he swallows the tablets in two mouthfuls, swilled down with whisky.

Scobie makes a final false entry in his diary, leaving it incomplete as though he had experienced a terminal seizure. As he waits for the end, he tries to pray but can no longer remember the Hail Mary and his Act of Contrition stumbles to a halt at the words: 'I am sorry and beg pardon.' Losing consciousness, he falls to the ground and says aloud: 'Dear God, I love' (249), as his holy medal spins under the ice-box. After his death Louise regards Scobie as a 'bad Catholic' and is convinced that he must have been aware of 'damning himself'. In contrast, Father Rank reminds her that no one can fully comprehend 'God's mercy' (254). His concluding thought provides a suitable epitaph for Scobie: 'I think, from what I saw of him, that he really loved God' (255). The ensuing debate over whether Scobie was ultimately saved or damned greatly irritated Greene. He denied that this issue had ever been a key concern of the novel and insisted: 'I have a small belief in the doctrine of eternal punishment (it was Scobie's belief, not mine).'[13]

Nevertheless, it is clear that he went to considerable lengths in the final scenes to ensure that the fate of Scobie's soul, in accordance with Catholic teaching, was not a matter upon which any reader could pass ultimate judgment. Instead, the novel concludes with Father Rank's reminder to Louise that the workings of Divine Mercy are ineffable to human reason.

Faith, Doubt and *The End of the Affair* (1951)

While *The Ministry of Fear* had generated 18,000 sales, over 300,000 copies of *The Heart of the Matter* were sold between 1948 and 1951. This level of success led to the reissue of most of Greene's earlier works, an escalation of his royalties and an international reputation as a writer who explored and challenged the central tenets of Catholicism. However, not all critics were impressed. George Orwell condemned Scobie's self-pitying sacrifice:

> The cult of the sanctified sinner seems to me to be frivolous, and underneath it there probably lies a weakening of belief, for when people really believed in Hell, they were not so fond of striking graceful attitudes on its brink.[14]

Tom Burns, who had commissioned his *The Lawless Roads*, was even more scathing, accusing Greene of using:

> all the apparatus of the Catechism & bad sermons twanging away on an exhausted id & irritated nerves to produce a sham spiritual dilemma: a caricature conventional Catholic couple is very cruelly trotted out to cut capers in the world of apprehensions much more the novelist's than their own. He almost turns things upside-down & hates the sinners while he loves the sin. G.G. is becoming a sort of smart-Alec of Jansenism.[15]

In contrast, Evelyn Waugh offered a balanced critique of the novel, noting how it continued Greene's fascination with the concept of damnation as first explored in *Brighton Rock*. He dissected Scobie's theological misapprehensions and dismissed outright the idea of embracing one's damnation for the love of God either as a 'very loose poetical expression or a mad blasphemy'. Nevertheless, he generously concluded: 'It is a book which only a Catholic could write and only a Catholic could understand. I mean that only a Catholic could understand the nature of the problem.'[16]

In view of Greene's now well-established (if unwelcome) reputation as a Catholic controversialist, from the late-1940s his readers were increasingly alert to his representations of Christian doubt and sin within a distinctively fallen world. In a 1948 short story, 'The Hint of an Explanation', a train passenger listens to the reminiscences of a fellow traveller who recalls how as a child he had been persuaded by an anti-Catholic villager to steal a consecrated communion host. The tale ends with the revelation that the storyteller is now a priest, but its most interesting aspect is its focus on the narrator's agnostic doubts over the existence of an 'omnipotent and omniscient Deity'. When he realizes that he is speaking to a Roman Catholic, he tries to define his own hazily indistinct 'intuition' of God's existence, largely founded upon 'childish experiences and needs', even though he remains intellectually 'revolted at the whole notion of such a God, who can so abandon his creatures to the enormities of Free Will' (32).

This concept of fundamentally decent individuals seeking some sense of moral order in a flawed world is also to the fore in Greene's major project of 1948, the script for Carol Reed's *The Third Man*. Greene had visited Vienna and Prague in February, followed by a brief tryst with Catherine Walston in Rome where he began to draft the film treatment. He returned to Vienna in June with Reed and his film crew and had completed the script by early-August.[17] While Pinkie had been a pathetic and immature child-gangster, infatuated with the concept of damnation, in *The Third Man* Harry Lime is an amorally calculating adult, utterly indifferent to either damnation or salvation. He cynically explains to his friend Holly Martins on the Great Wheel, with a 'boyish, conspiratorial smile', the financial benefits of his diluted penicillin racket. He suggests that the people far below are merely 'dots' and asks him whether he would feel any 'pity' if he could have £20,000 for each dot that stopped moving: 'would you really, old man, tell me to keep my money – or would you calculate how many dots you could afford to spare?' (97).

The action of *The Third Man* is framed by the two funerals of Harry Lime. At the first the coffin really contains the body of Lime's co-racketeer, Joseph Harbin, a hospital orderly who had stolen the penicillin for dilution and been killed for becoming a police informer. This false interment symbolizes how the defeat of evil in a fallen world can be merely illusory, enabling Harry to rise from the dead in a devilish, mock-resurrection. As 'D.' feared in *The Confidential Agent*, in post-war Vienna religious objects have been relegated to the status of museum items. Dr Winkel, Lime's doctor and co-conspirator, is an ardent collector of crucifixes, holy statues and saints' reliquaries, mostly looted from bombed churches. Martins is fascinated by one crucifix in his collection with the 'figure hanging with arms above his head: a face of elongated El Greco agony'. Winkel describes it as 'Jansenist' (perhaps a sarcastic nod to Tom Burns's criticism of *The Heart of the Matter*), with arms above his head because he died 'only for the elect' (49–50).

In another Greeneian moment, two English officers from the Cultural Re-education Section of G.H.Q. (combined into the single character of Crabbit in the film) invite Martins to give a lecture on the 'Crisis of Faith' in the modern novel (57). The only real sense of religious hope in *The Third Man* comes after Lime's 'second death' in the sewers of Vienna and his genuine interment. After the coffin has been lowered into the grave, Martins cryptically comments, 'A man's not dead because you put him underground' (119), to Major Calloway, the head of the British Military Police who is responsible for closing down the penicillin racket. Like the priest's final words to Rose on Pinkie's soul and Father Rank's on Scobie's, this comment suggests that not even a Harry Lime can be regarded as entirely beyond the reach of Divine Mercy.

The film of *The Third Man* was released in August 1949 and published in 1950 as a 30,000 word novelette, along with a reprinting of 'The Basement Room'. From the proceeds of the film, Greene purchased a small villa, 'Rosaio', on the Mediterranean island of Anacapri where drafts of many of his later books were compiled. His study there was plainly furnished with whitewashed walls and was 'apart from a small cross, without ornament – a monastic cell'. During the summer of 1949 he was working with Basil Dean on a dramatization of *The Heart of the Matter* to be staged in New York and Boston, as well as conceptualizing what he then referred to as his '"I" book' (i.e., written as a first-person narration), which later became *The End of the Affair*.[18]

The publication in 1951 of *The Lost Childhood and Other Essays* brought together a selection of Greene's writings on religious and spiritual issues. Of special significance was his essay on 'Henry James: The Religious Aspect', in which he cited James's view of the Catholic Church as the 'most impressive convention in all history' (36), while the Anglican Church, Greene felt, had never taken hold of James's imagination in the same way. He was also attracted to James's preoccupation with supernatural evil and purgatory, as manifested in *The Turn of the Screw*, and he felt that these concerns had drawn him closer towards Catholic teachings. Greene concluded that for James religion mirrored life: 'Experience taught him to believe in supernatural evil, but not in supernatural good' (40). In his essay on 'François Mauriac' Greene famously proposed that after James's death the 'religious sense was lost to the English novel' (76) but in Mauriac he found a writer of Dickensian vividness who created characters whose actions were less significant than the 'force, whether God or Devil, that compels them' (79).

Several lesser figures were also considered in this collection, including the Catholic convert Frederick Rolfe (the self-styled Baron Corvo) whose life of grotesque moral extremes fitted well with Greene's fascination with the polarities of good and evil: 'if he could not have Heaven, he would have Hell' and the 'Inferno' (104). Another flawed Catholic convert, the artist Eric Gill, fascinated Greene primarily because of his inability to fit into the traditional mores of the established Church and his hatred of the priesthood (152). In a pungent essay, 'Don in Mexico', Greene denounced a complacent Cambridge academic who had visited Mexico when he had also been there researching *The Lawless Roads*. Professor John Brande Trend claimed, 'blithely, whimsically, from his Cambridge study' (187), that the state persecutions of Catholicism had been exaggerated. As an ardent admirer of the heroism of the Mexican Jesuit martyrs,

Greene angrily dismissed his views, recalling his first-hand knowledge of how priests had been forbidden to say Mass but had continued to deliver the sacraments to the people 'in secret' (188). In contrast, Greene commended the American historian Francis Parkman, whose *The Jesuits in North America in the Seventeenth Century* (1867) recorded the exemplary courage of missionaries working among the North-American Indians (139–44).

The End of the Affair marks the mid-career culmination of Greene's creative preoccupation with damnation and salvation. In an interview for *Time* magazine, Greene explained how he had written a novel 'about a man who goes to hell (*Brighton Rock*), another 'about a man who goes to heaven (*The Power and the Glory*) and now one about a 'man who goes to purgatory'.[19] The self-created earthly purgatory in which the writer Maurice Bendrix finds himself is defined by two pairs of moral polarities. The first and dominant one binds together love and hate for both humanity and God Himself. David Lodge calculates that the words 'love' and 'hate' in various forms occur in the narrative about 300 and 100 times respectively.[20] Secondly, Bendrix's spiritual doubts, coupled with occasional moments of incipient hope, are often focused upon a Manichaean preoccupation with the sinfulness of earthly women, versus a spasmodic desire to transform them both in life and after death into figures of sanctity (comparable to the *parfaites* of the Cathars).

Sarah Miles, the most psychologically intriguing female character in Greene's fictions, has three devoted lovers. The first, in ascending order of influence, is her loyal but cuckolded husband Henry; the second is the infatuated Bendrix; and the third is God Himself who (at least in Bendrix's eyes) ultimately steals Sarah away from him. From the opening page of the novel, Bendrix envisages these three dominating presences in his life within a triangulated framework of doubt and hate. Prompted by this love affair, Bendrix's distaste for the fallen world is intensified by his sporadic but powerful desire to believe in a perfected heaven. He laments how 'twisted we humans are' even though supposedly a 'God made us' but he struggles to imagine any 'God who is not as simple as a perfect equation, as clear as air'. Honest enough to recognize his own failings (not least as the catalyst for Sarah's adultery), Bendrix's unease at seeing himself reflected too closely in other men prompts him to experience an 'enormous wish to believe in the saints, in heroic virtue' (5). These comments all occur in the first chapter of book one and Greene seems from the outset of the novel focused upon investing Bendrix with the spiritual identity of an earnestly doubting individual who is caused genuine regret by his own failings but is also capable of occasional glimmerings of divinely inspired hope.

Perhaps inspired by one of his favourite poets, John Donne, in *The End of the Affair* Greene draws a persistent equation between human love for a woman and Divine Love. But unlike the neo-platonic ideal, envisaging earthly love as an inspiring route towards an appreciation of heavenly love, Greene paradoxically inverts this scale to suggest that the 'words of human love . . . used by the saints to describe their vision of God' may be exploited to intensify human passions. Hence, the 'terms of prayer, meditation' and 'contemplation' may be applied to the 'intensity of the love we feel for a woman' (36). Similarly, in Bendrix's mind Sarah's progression towards quasi-sainthood grows from his habit of equating his physical passions for her flesh to the intangible world of the eternal spirit. In particular, he is fascinated by her prelapsarian ability to live only for the 'moment' and without any doubts or moral scruples. Even her adulterous affair becomes not just the gratification of reciprocal sexual desire but also an approximation to the sublime 'nothingness' of eternal love: 'Eternity is said not to be an extension of time but an absence of time . . . her abandonment touched that strange mathematical point of endlessness, a point with no width, occupying no space' (39).

A range of other literary and religious influences underpin the narrative of *The End of the Affair*. Greene's atmospheric use of first-person narration was inspired by Dickens's *Great Expectations*; and other stylistic elements were derived from Ford Madox Ford's *The Good Soldier*, T. S. Eliot's 'Ash Wednesday' and Mauriac's *The Knot of Vipers*. Greene's familiarity with Baron von Hügel's study of the fifteenth-century mystic St Catherine of Genoa, venerated for her assistance to plague victims, provided some additional ideas for the novel's dialectic on the interaction of human and divine love as focused on the potential sanctity of Sarah's character.[21] While travelling by sea to America in August 1948 to discuss *The Third Man* with David Selznick, Greene wrote wistfully to Catherine Walston to tell how all he then desired was quiet and peace with her, lying 'on a bed, reading St John of the Cross'.[22]

St John (1542–1591), a Spanish Carmelite friar, priest and mystic called Juan de Yepes, had been a close associate of St Teresa of Avila in her reformation of the 'discalced' (barefoot) Carmelites. His writings were well known to Greene and had also provided inspiration to St Thérèse of Lisieux whose is often referred to in Greene's novels. The bicentennial of his canonization had been celebrated in 1926 (the year following that of St Thérèse of Lisieux), soon after Greene's reception into the Catholic Church. Greene greatly admired St John's eclogue, *Cántico espiritual* ('Spiritual Canticle'), based upon the biblical 'Song of Songs'. It describes how the soul (represented as a bride) passionately seeks Jesus Christ (the bridegroom) after a period of separation. His *Noche oscura del alma* (the Dark Night of the Soul), also an important influence on Greene's imagination at this period, narrates the journey of the tortured soul from its earthly home towards a longed-for spiritual union with God. The night represents the hardships faced by the soul as it painfully seeks to transcend the fallen world. Mark Bosco summarizes the impact of St John's poetry on *The End of the Affair*:

The novel's theological aesthetic pushes most explicitly the spiritual *via negativa* of John of the Cross, a mysticism consisting essentially in a passionate exchange of love with God through a process of purification, trials and temptations, and deliberate detachment from external things. The 'dark night of the soul' entails the experience of utter abandonment by God, the person's spiritual identification with the absence of God felt by Christ at the cruci-fixion; Bendrix's feelings for Sarah encompass an affinity with a kind of spiritual darkness . . . a secular dark night of the soul.[23]

At the heart of Bendrix's dilemma in the novel lies St John's representation of how the individual soul enters a period of trial and purgation through an inevi-table conflict between the spirit and the senses. One of his most memorable images is of the ten steps on the mystical ladder towards Divine Love and this metaphor of the staircase becomes of central importance in *The End of the Affair*. The spiritual climax of the novel occurs when Bendrix and Sarah are lying in bed after making love during a V1 flying bomb attack. He hastens down the staircase to see if they might take shelter in the basement but is knocked uncon-scious half-way down by the bombed-in front door of the house. As he regains consciousness, a relieved Sarah appears and admits that she had been praying, '"To anything that might exist"'. In reply Bendrix teases her: '"There wasn't much to pray for then . . . Except a miracle"' (57). Only later, when he reads through her private diary (purloined for him by a private detective called Parkis) does he realize the full significance of this moment. Her diary entry explains how she had made a promise to God that if Bendrix was allowed to survive the bomb blast then she would 'give him up for ever'. When it seems that her prayer has been (perhaps miraculously) granted, she realizes that the 'agony' (76) for both of them must now start and she even momentarily wishes that he had not survived the blast.

Other imaginary and real staircases appear elsewhere in the novel. In Sarah's diary under 12 February 1946, the final entry read by Bendrix, he learns how she had a dream in which she was 'walking up a long staircase' to meet him at the top. When she could not find him there, she descended sadly 'down the stairs again' as water and mist swirled around her waist (99). Returning to Sarah's bomb-damaged house only 24 hours after her death, since he has been invited to stay by Henry, Bendrix symbolically walks 'up the broken steps into the hall' (119). In his room he finally attains a full understanding of Sarah's spiritual state when he finds her last letter to him, explaining how just before her death she had told a priest of her pledge with God when the V1 bomb hit the house and how she now definitely 'wanted to be a Catholic' (120).

In a return to the gender polarities of Greene's earliest fictions, the female figures in *The End of the Affair* seem to belong either to the fallen world of sexual corruption or to embody for their male admirers saintly and miraculous possibilities. In their local pub, Bendrix and Henry view with distaste the usual lavatory scrawls about the landlord's 'breasty wife' and the bawdy Christmas greeting: 'To all pimps and whores a merry syphilis and a happy gonorrhea' (5). Suspecting that Sarah may have other lovers, Bendrix consults the detective agency of the world-weary Mr Savage, expert in all forms of female betrayals. Later in the novel, filled with Manichaean 'hatred and distrust', Bendrix walks

through the red-light district near Piccadilly and watches the torches of prostitutes flash like 'glow-worms' (45) for prospective clients. He picks up one who
seems younger and more beautiful than Sarah (66) but then abandons her in
a pub when his sexual lust withers away.

Unexpectedly, it is the downtrodden and widowed private detective, Parkis,
who provides Bendrix with the most uplifting appreciation of that familiar
Greeneian archetype, the idealized woman. When Bendrix first meets Parkis,
he suspects him of being an agent in the 'devil's game' of detecting marital
infidelities and always seeking with 'borrowed fanaticism to destroy love' (47)
wherever he can. However, Parkis turns out to be a devoted father who still
mourns the death of his beloved wife. When his son Lance is taken ill with a
life-threatening appendicitis, he tells Bendrix how he prayed to God and to his
wife, 'because if there's anyone in heaven, she's in heaven now', and even to
Mrs Miles, 'if she was there' (148) in Heaven as well. The next morning, Parkis
finds his son is recovering and has no doubts that his wife and Sarah have sought
divine intervention on his behalf. The purity of Parkis's love for his saintly
wife counterpoints the self-destructive bitterness contaminating Bendrix's
memories of Sarah. Prior to this conversation, Bendrix had been interviewed
by a pompous journalist called Waterbury and, almost as a way of spiting Sarah
for leaving him, he begins to seduce Sylvia, Waterbury's young girlfriend. She
innocently accompanies Bendrix to Sarah's cremation and, prompted by his
nascent conscience that such a seduction would be cruel and pointless, he prays
to Sarah: 'Get me out of this, get me out of it, for her sake, not mine' (132). As
though miraculously, Sarah's comic-grotesque mother, Mrs Bertram, suddenly
appears and Bendrix is able to free himself from his planned tryst with Sylvia
by taking her to dinner.

One of the most contentiously 'miraculous' occurrences in *The End of
the Affair* involves Richard Smythe who runs the Rationalist Society of South
London. Sarah consults him when attempting to persuade herself that God is
unnecessary to her life. Smythe is a handsome man whose face is disfigured by
a 'purple crumpled strawberry mark' running from the top of his cheek-bone
down to his chin.[24] After Sarah's funeral Bendrix fortuitously meets him and is
astonished to see that his birthmark has shrunk down to a 'small blue patch no
larger than a half-crown'.[25] Smythe claims to have attended a nursing home and
mumbles something about modern methods and electricity but later rings
Bendrix to explain that this was untrue. Instead, he now claims that his cure
was nothing less than 'a . . .' – but Bendrix puts down the receiver before he can
say 'miracle', that 'foolish newspaper word' occasioned, in Smythe's mind, by
Sarah's intercession (157). Greene later regretted including the scene concerning the 'strawberry mark' and felt that 'every so-called miracle, like the curing
of Parkis's boy, ought to have had a completely natural explanation'.[26] Even
though Greene had suggested in the first edition that such a skin blemish
could be 'hysterical in origin' and removed by a 'mixture of psychiatry and
radium' (234), in later editions he pointedly revised this condition from being

a congenital strawberry mark (only removable by surgery) to urticaria or nettle-rash, a temporary rash caused by allergies.

The latter half of the novel offers a rich miscellany of religious perspectives as it traces the painfully gradual progress of Sarah (and, by implication, Bendrix) from doubt and despair towards the possibility of attaining Sanctifying Grace. The life of St Thérèse of Lisieux was well known to English Catholics from her epistolary and biographical essays published as the *Histoire d'une âme* (*Story of a Soul*). Sarah's private diary occupies a similar but inverted role in *The End of the Affair* as it progressively traces her self-flagellating sense of her own sinfulness, 'I'm a bitch and a fake', and her determined but steadily weakening resistance to repentance, 'believe me, God, I don't believe in you yet, I don't believe in you yet' (81). As Sarah's spiritual struggle is internalized within the secret world of her diary, both Henry and Bendrix begin to respond to the outward trappings of Catholicism. Her husband's mind is literal and unquestioning, neutrally noting that it is a 'materialistic' religion: 'In the Mass they still believe in transubstantiation' (88). In contrast, when Bendrix sees a crucifix in a church he readily imagines the agony of a 'material body on that material cross' (89) and, in defiance of his professed atheism, as he leaves he dips his finger in the holy-water font and makes a cross on his forehead (90). In coincidental confirmation of this action, he then reads in Sarah's diary that she had once bought a cheap and ugly crucifix and kept it secretly in the privacy of her bedroom at the bottom of her jewel-case. But her responses far surpass Bendrix's, since contemplating it leads her into an intense wish for imitative self-mortification: 'Dear God, if only you could come down from your Cross for a while and let me get up there instead. If I could suffer like you, I could heal like you' (96). When Bendrix follows Sarah into a church he spots her sitting in one of the side aisles near a statue of the Virgin Mary (104). As he leaves her for the last time, half-asleep with fatigue and despair, he sees her huddling like a beggar looking for warmth 'at the edge of the candle-light'. Reduced to this pathetic state (she is developing pneumonia), Bendrix is granted a brief moment of spiritual enlightenment as he admits that even he could then readily 'imagine a God blessing her: or a God loving her' (107).

Although Sarah's death is not presented as a calculated act of suicide like Scobie's, her refusal to accept medical attention ultimately leads to her physical self-annihilation since the doctor called by Henry advises that a timely course of penicillin would have saved her (111). Her nurse reports to Henry that she had been asking on her death-bed for a Catholic priest and he readily admits to Bendrix that she may even have 'become a Catholic' (112). These suspicions are confirmed by her final letter to Bendrix in which she admits that she had been praying to God 'all the time that he won't be hard on me' (120) and that she had seen a priest about becoming a Catholic. Her final declaration of faith in her diary presents her love for God as a natural progression from her love for Bendrix: 'I believe there's a God – I believe the whole bag of tricks, there's nothing I don't believe, they could subdivide the

Trinity into a dozen parts and I'd believe . . . 'I've fallen into belief like I fell in love' (121).

An angry debate develops between Bendrix, Henry and her priest, Father Crompton (Catherine Walston's maiden name), over whether Sarah should be buried or cremated. Father Crompton acknowledges that burial is preferred for Catholics even though cremation can have no impact on the final 'resurrection of the body' (128). He also confirms Sarah's genuine intention to become a Catholic and refers, therefore, to her 'baptism of desire' (126), through which she would have received Sanctifying Grace, even though she had not had time to be admitted formally to the Catholic Church through baptism. As the presence of the dead Sarah seems just as strong to Bendrix and Henry as when she was alive, the centrality of the dead to Catholics is emphasized by Father Crompton: 'There are special Masses for our dead . . . We remember our dead' (127). This perspective becomes crucial to the conclusion of the novel since it reminds the reader how the Catholic faith allows prayers to those whom we believe already to be in heaven, asking for their intercession on our behalf. In effect, this is what Parkis has already suggested to Bendrix when he prayed first to God and then to his wife and to Sarah in the hope that his son Lance would survive his sudden illness. Parkis's lasting love for his dead wife provides a clarity of vision denied to the intellectually confused and emotionally weary Bendrix.

Sarah's cremation is as grim an affair as that of Hale in *Brighton Rock* and Anthony Farrant in *England Made Me*. The presiding clergyman, used to conducting funerals for those about whose religious beliefs he knows nothing, preaches in general terms of the 'Great All', which Sarah's mother mishears as the 'Great Auk' (134). Mrs Bertram then stuns Bendrix by telling him that the two-year-old Sarah had been baptized by a French priest. She was, therefore, already a Catholic, although 'she didn't know it' herself. Greene drew the idea for Sarah's infant baptism from the life of Roger Casement, an Ulster Protestant executed for treason in 1916, who became one of the secular pro-Irish martyrs against British rule. When Casement decided just before his death to become a Catholic, the prison chaplain discovered that he had been secretly baptized as a child. This unusual incident, which Greene admitted might for agnostic readers offer the 'notion of magic', serves a specific theological purpose since it completes the complex history of the earthly progress of Sarah's soul.[27] Granted Sanctifying Grace through her childhood baptism, she then loses it through the mortal sin of her adultery. But her baptism of desire ensures that she dies in a state of Grace, She becomes, thereby, one of the (probable) saints in heaven to whom the likes of Parkis, Bendrix and even Henry (who becomes increasingly interested in Catholicism) may pray. Bendrix, however, is still incapable of fully understanding this progression. As he ponders the immediate impact of Mrs Bertram's revelation of Sarah's childhood baptism he angrily comments: 'magic is your cross, your resurrection of the body, your holy Catholic church, your communion of saints.'

The novel's conclusion is dominated by Bendrix's doubting internal dialogue with Sarah's ultimately triumphant lover, God Himself. After her funeral his jealous anger bubbles over and he thinks of God as a ruthlessly usurping rival for her affections. While he admits that 'You won in the end,' he takes a grotesque pride in his sexual union with Sarah: 'When she slept, I was with her, not You. It was I who penetrated her, not You' (137). Now living permanently with Henry and aware that Father Crompton is saying a Mass each month for Sarah, Bendrix notices on the last page of her diary a final prayer for his consolation: 'When I ask You for pain, You give me peace. Give it him too. Give him my peace – he needs it more.' Although Bendrix still strives to keep his waning hate alive, he begins to realize that Sarah's example is one that all humankind can follow simply by 'shutting the eyes and leaping once and for all: if *you* are a saint, it's not so difficult to be a saint. It's something He can demand of any of us, leap'. In a final attempt to dodge the infinite Mercy of God, he takes refuge in Greene's well-worn image of the duality of a Manichaean divinity, conjoining the potential for both good and evil: 'I know Your cunning. It's You who take us up to a high place and offer us the whole universe. You're a devil, God, tempting us to leap . . . I hate You, God, I hate You as though You existed.' Just as suddenly, Bendrix's thoughts are suffused with Sarah's posthumous potency, even though he still feels that it will 'take more than your prayers to turn this hatred of Him into Love' (159). The final words of the novel strike a note of equivocal weariness, suggesting that the progress of Bendrix's own soul is only just beginning: 'O God, You've done enough. You've robbed me of enough, I'm too tired and old to learn to love, leave me alone for ever' (160).

During the early-1950s Greene was frequently travelling abroad in dangerous locations, such as Malaya, French Indo-China and Kenya. Nevertheless, his publications still often focused upon Catholic issues. In 1953 a French collection of his writings, *Essais Catholiques*, was published, including translations of some new lectures delivered in Belgium and previously published works, such as his essay on 'Henry James: the Religious Aspect'. The collection sought to blend his personal perceptions of Christian fortitude and the miraculous with a demonstration of how relevant an awareness of Catholicism had become to contemporary political affairs. In his 'Message Aux Catholiques Français' he recalls how his own beliefs had been strongly influenced in 1938 by observing the ardent devotions during Holy Week of the oppressed Indians at Chiapas in Mexico. More recently, he records witnessing the stigmata of Padre Pio as he celebrated Mass in southern Italy. Ominously, he also declares that now in 'l'époque de Belsen' (9) it seemed that an awareness of Satan is all the more important since the eternal struggle between good and evil has become a defining element in international affairs.[28]

On a lighter note, his 1954 short story 'Special Duties' demonstrates that Greene had no hesitation in occasionally extracting gentle comedy from Catholic traditions. The grandiose William Ferraro views God, like himself, as the managing-director of some 'supreme business'. He is married to an invalid wife who is invariably accompanied (like Catherine Walston) by a Jesuit or Dominican with a 'taste for good wine and whisky'. Mr Ferraro walks through his luxurious private library, 'rather as God walked in the Garden' (23), and admires there his fabulous art collection, collected as a hedge against death duties. He employs the mousy Miss Saunders, with the anonymous face of a 'holy statue', to collect plenary indulgences for him. He seeks, thereby, to manage his smooth entry into heaven as efficiently as the rest of his business concerns.

Miss Saunders's suitability for her post is beyond question since she was the head girl of the 'Convent of Saint Latitudinaria' in Woking, the three-time winner of the school's 'special prize for piety' and possesses an exemplary record as a volunteer 'Child of Mary'. She supplies Mr Ferraro with a monthly triple-column account of the indulgences gained on his behalf and, as a shrewd businessman, he advises her not to spend too much time on the 'lower brackets' (24) of indulgence. These can each offer only a few days off purgatory, although he begrudgingly recognizes that her total of 1,565 days of indulgences in April alone is a gratifying rate of return. He is especially concerned that the dowdy Miss Saunders should always be in a 'State of Grace' (25), since the indulgences would otherwise be invalidated. The comic denouement comes when Mr Ferraro decides to make an unannounced spot-check on her work. He goes to one of her favoured areas, Cannon Wood, but is disturbed to find that her beloved Catholic church of St Praxted (cf. St Praxed Church, Rome, dedicated to a martyred Roman virgin) does not exist. Fearful that the 36,892 days of indulgences accrued during her three years of employment may be questionable, he rushes around to her home in Bayswater. The invalid mother with whom she supposedly lives turns out to be a young man at her bedroom window with his arm around a semi-clad Miss Saunders. Putting his fingers together 'in the shape some people used for prayer', a chastened Mr Ferraro resolves to find himself a new and 'really reliable' (27) indulgence secretary.

In contrast to this jocular tone, one of Greene's most powerful post-war explorations of Catholic scruples was presented in his first theatrical play, *The Living Room* (published at Stockholm, 1952; London, 1953 and New York, 1954). Fittingly, the earliest sketch of the play, recycling fragments from an unpublished novel, had been jotted down on the back end-papers of his copy of *Devotional Poets of the XVII Century* (Nelson Classics). He began drafting it during a visit to Vietnam in November 1951 and it was completed at Kuala Lumpur on 8 January 1952. Its premier was held at Stockholm in October 1952 (where it incurred the wrath of Artur Lundkvist, the chair of the Nobel Prizes committee) and it toured the English provinces before coming to London in a British run lasting from mid-April 1953 until early-January 1954.[29] *The Living Room* was dedicated 'To Catherine with Love' (although Greene also enjoyed in 1951 a brief relationship with Jocelyn Rickards, an Australian artist) and it explored the now familiar Greeneian themes of adulterous passion, Catholic scruples and suicide. A young girl called Rose, whose mother has recently died, enters into an affair with a middle-aged psychologist, Michael Dennis. He has a neurotic, invalid wife and is also the executor of the estate of Rose's mother. His wife recalls Louise in *The Heart of the Matter* and Michael feels trapped in his marital relationship through pity rather than love. Rose comes to live with two aged great-aunts, Teresa and Helen, who are both devout Roman Catholics with a special devotion to St Thérèse of Lisieux. They look after their invalid brother James, who had served as a Catholic priest before being incapacitated in an accident 20 years earlier.

Although cast as a domestic drama, the stage-set of the play is theologically symbolic in that the two aged sisters inhabit only a single room (formerly the day nursery) on the third floor of a rambling old house. All the other rooms have been shut up over the years because someone has died in them. This represents the narrowing of human experience into a claustrophobically restricted sphere and denies the prayerful relationship envisaged by the Catholic Church (and by Parkis and Bendrix in *The End of the Affair*) between the living and the dead. Although James sees himself as a pathetically crippled 'priest who can't say Mass or hear confessions or visit the sick' (21), he acts as a source of spiritual wisdom to the other confused individuals who surround him. He sternly advises the adulterous Michael that he is hurting his wife, himself and the 'God you don't believe in' (28) and gently soothes Teresa's unfounded fears of eternal damnation: 'I don't know anyone who's great enough for Hell except Satan' (40). Father James is a devotee of St John of the Cross and readily sympathizes with his seminal idea of his 'dark night of the soul' in which he experienced a spiritual darkness that left him 'without love' (41) or even the ability to pray.

The escalation of this family's own 'dark night of the soul' is suggested by the gradual shutting down into darkness of the various rooms in the house, leaving the remaining 'living room' as a spiritually crippled microcosm of a fallen world. Tragically, the individual most influenced by this repressive claustrophobia is the previously dynamic Rose who seems to age visibly as the play progresses. Distraught at the irreconcilable problems inherent in her adulterous relationship with Michael, she echoes the despairing language of Bendrix in *The End of the Affair*. She cries out to James: 'Do you think if I left Michael I could really love a God who demanded all that pain before He'd give Himself?' (48). She angrily dismisses James's insistence upon God's Mercy and the intercession of his saints in heaven, insisting: 'I don't believe in your Church and your Holy Mother of God. I don't believe. I don't believe' (57). In total despair, and as an altruistic act (recalling Scobie's), Rose commits suicide in the living room (thereby cancelling its privileged identity as the house's only 'living' space) with the tablets that Michael's wife had previously threatened to use to kill herself. As she dies, Rose's final prayer lapses into the pathos of childish innocence: 'Our Father who art . . . who art . . . Bless Mother, Nanny and Sister Marie-Louise, and please God don't let school start again ever' (58).

The play's religious theme concludes by reiterating Greene's preoccupation with characters unable to conceive of a loving God who will forgive their sins in response to genuine repentance. The audience is invited to wonder whether Rose is damned or saved, despite her mortal sins of adultery and suicide. Through the wisdom of Father James, Greene echoes his familiar motif of the 'appalling' nature of Divine Mercy. The priest quotes from a book of devotions studied long ago as a seminarian: 'The more our senses are revolted, uncertain and in despair, the more surely Faith says: "This is God: all goes well"' (62). After Rose's death Helen remains fearfully fixated on human mortality and tries to prevent Teresa from sleeping in the living room. But the play closes with Teresa's reassertion of her spiritual hope for everlasting life through the efficacious bonds that exist for a Catholic between the living and the dead: 'there'd be no better room for me to fall asleep in for ever than the room in which Rose died' (64).

Chapter 6

The Writer in Search of
New Directions: 1955–1965

Escape and *The Quiet American* (1955)

The 1950s proved a restless decade for Greene when he sought to immerse himself in frequent travelling to distant and dangerous locations. He commented in *Ways of Escape* that the 50s had been a period of great happiness and torment for him: 'manic depression reached its height in that decade'; and Norman Sherry confirms that journeys were 'Greene's means of controlling depression'.[1] Such attempts were generally unsuccessful, as suggested by a passing remark made in a letter of 6 September 1950 to Catherine Walston when he complained of feeling 'useless' and 'homeless': 'Paris, Goa, Malaya, London – there's no point beyond myself in being anywhere.'[2] Inevitably, a sense of not belonging also pervades his fictions from this period. In 1950 his brother Hugh was serving as head of Emergency Information Services in Malaya and Greene received a lucrative commission from *Life* magazine to observe the insurgency there. He recalled that Malaya had provided the 'first of my escapes' between November 1950 and February 1951; and he listed other major overseas experiences, including between 1951 and 1955 four winter trips to Vietnam, reporting the Mau Mau rebellion in Kenya and visits to Stalinist Poland and a leper colony in the Belgian Congo.[3] These arduous assignments were occasionally alleviated by more relaxing breaks, including a holiday in Paris with Catherine (late-February 1951), a cruise on Alexander Korda's yacht in the Aegean (June 1951) and trips (February 1952) to Hollywood to discuss the filming of *The End of the Affair* and New York to receive that year's Award for Fiction from the Gallery of Living Catholic Authors.[4]

The Quiet American was completed in June 1955 and published in the United Kingdom in December 1955 and the USA in March 1956.[5] Its alienated and geographically displaced anti-hero is a world-weary reporter called Thomas Fowler. He takes an existentialist pleasure in his disassociation from the society around him and adopts as his personal 'creed' the mantra: 'let them fight, let them love, let them murder. I would not be involved' (20). Bernard Bergonzi comments that in *The Quiet American* Greene finally 'decided to give God a rest', structuring it around a 'humanistic rather than a religious frame of reference'.[6] Taking an overtly political perspective on the decline of French colonialism and the growth of American imperialism in the Far East, it raises issues relating to human motivation and responsibility within a moral framework defined by the solitariness of scepticism and doubt. Although the novel does not make sustained use of a Roman Catholic background, its author's fascination with religious issues never seems far below the surface of its narrative.

Rather than being an indifferent atheist, Fowler is an individual who insist-ently seeks to reassure himself of the absence of a God from the world of humanity. As his name Thomas suggests (Greene's confirmation name), he resembles the apostle as a rationalist doubter of the intangible. He admits envying those who possess a religious faith while he can only allow himself to believe in loss, impermanence and the ultimate annihilation of earthly life into 'nothing'. He regards death as the 'only absolute value' and both envies and distrusts those who claim a belief in a God: 'I felt that they were keeping their courage up with a fable of the changeless and the permanent. Death was far more certain than God, and with death there would be no longer the daily pos-sibility of love dying' (36). Despite these sentiments, Fowler finds that the alien Vietnamese landscapes are often tinged with Catholic references. At Phat Diem the local bishop has imported a special devotion to Our Lady of Fatima and built a grotto to her at the cathedral which is fronted by a white statue of the Sacred Heart (39). In the face of advancing communists, Fowler notes how Catholics, Buddhists and even pagans fled to the Cathedral precincts for sanctuary (40). After crossing a canal filled with dead bodies, like an 'Irish stew containing too much meat' (43), he sees a small boy wearing a 'holy medal' who had been killed with his mother (45). Shocked by the callous brutality and slaughter all around him, Fowler's thoughts turn once again to wondering why so many people find God essential and whether humanity would be better served by 'not trying to understand' one another: 'Perhaps that's why men have invented God – a being capable of understanding' (52).

Although a professed non-believer, Fowler reveals a fascination with the inter-connectedness of diverse religious beliefs. At Tanyin (Tay Ninh), north-west of Saigon, he ponders with both cynicism and genuine curiosity the beliefs of Caodaism, a syncretistic religion which combines elements from numerous other religions, including Buddhism, Christianity, Confucianism, Hinduism, Islam and Judaism. It still remains the third largest religion in Vietnam after Buddhism and Christianity. Followers of Caodaism believe that the multiplicity of world religions prevents social harmony and peaceful cohabitation by people of differing creeds. God, therefore, initiated a revelation through spiritist means (essentially spiritualism) to Ngo Van Chieu, a Cochinchinese civil servant in the 1920s. Fowler explains to his visitors how Caodaism blends three religions, advocates 'Prophecy by planchette' and venerates Christ, Buddha and the French author Victor Hugo. Caodaists recognize the innate virtues of females and, although their Pope is always a male, women can serve as cardinals in their church. Greene was struck by their use of a planchette (a small moveable platform) placed on an Ouija board since a séance had provided a central scene in *The Ministry of Fear*. As Fowler notes, they place statues of Christ and Buddha alongside one another on their church roofs, in a kind of 'Walt Disney fantasia of the East' (75). Memorably, their church entrances are decorated with 'pale blue and pink plasterwork and a big eye of God over the door' (76); and their adherents venerate an eclectic grouping of three saints: Sun-Yat-Sen (d.1925) who in 1911 had led the Chinese Revolution; Victor Hugo (d.1885); and the Vietnamese poet and prophet, Trang Trinh (d.1587).

Caodaism exerts a strong influence on Fowler's thoughts in the second half of the novel. Their pope's deputy at Tanyin unctuously offers him 'God's blessing' on his work as a reporter and reminds him that 'God loves the truth'. Predictably, the sceptical Fowler enquires: 'Which truth?' and receives the assurance that for Caodaists 'all truths are reconciled and truth is love' (77). In search of shade from the incessant heat, Fowler then takes refuge in the Caodaist cathedral where he sits in the papal chair and idly notes images of Victor Hugo dressed as a French academician and Sun Yat Sen writing on a tablet. This strange visual tableau prompts his deeper thoughts on the puzzling nature of institutionalized religions: 'We make a cage for air with holes . . . and man makes a cage for his religion in much the same way – with doubts left open to the weather and creeds opening on innumerable interpretations' (79). As he ponders the statues of Buddha, Confucius and Christ exposing 'his bleeding heart' on the cathedral roof, he realizes he has 'never desired faith'. Fowler sees himself essentially as a 'reporter' on life rather than as a 'journalist', since a reporter merely seeks to 'expose and record', while a journalist must affirm his own interpretation of a story as truth. He views organized religions in a similar way, regarding believers like journalists, convincing of their personal understanding of the miraculous and seeking to convert others to their beliefs. In contrast, as a reporter Fowler never identifies the 'inexplicable' and seeks only to describe things exactly as he finds them without any sense of 'visions' or 'miracles' (80).

Soon afterwards the car in which Fowler and his young American companion Alden Pyle are travelling runs out of petrol. They take refuge in a watchtower and they casually begin to discuss the human need to conceptualize God (85). Fowler states that he has no personal desire to believe in a God while Pyle quietly insists as a Unitarian that God is central to his world-picture. This reply prompts an irritated expostulation from Fowler over how humanity seems to believe in millions of separate Gods: 'Why, even a Roman Catholic believes in quite a different God when he's scared or happy or hungry.' Pyle responds with a Caodaist logic, as he explains that God is so 'vast' that he must inevitably 'look different to everyone' (86). As the night drags on they continue to discuss a wide variety of topics until Fowler makes the strangely inaccurate assertion that they have talked about virtually everything 'except God', apparently forgetting that God had been the starting-point of their debates. Eventually, they agree to disagree, with Pyle insisting that life would not make sense 'without Him' and Fowler admitting that he cannot make sense of it 'with him' (97)

Ironically, from this point on in the novel the determinedly non-believing Fowler casually but repeatedly tends to invoke the name of God in his conversation, saying, 'I wish to God I had a drink' (98); and thinking, '"Oh God," I thought, "I"m going to sneeze"' (102). This supposedly absent God also begins to exert a shadowy presence in other ways in Fowler's mind. The local inspector of police, a Frenchman called Vigot, is a staunch Catholic and, impressed by his ability to draw out truth from witnesses, Fowler remarks that he would have made an excellent priest since he makes it 'so easy to confess – if there were anything to confess' (160). When the journalist Granger, another self-professed atheist, is distraught to discover that his son back home has been diagnosed with polio he pours out his fears to Fowler as though he was his confessor, 'I was praying . . . maybe if God wanted a life he could take mine' (177), and wishing that he did believe in a God.

Fowler explains to Pyle that he cannot marry his Vietnamese mistress Phuong because his 'High Church' (50) wife back home in England would not agree to a divorce (50). He duly writes to request one but she refuses. Then, at the end of the novel, she finally agrees to his request to begin divorce proceedings in a telegram which concludes, 'God bless you affectionately Helen' (179). Phuong is delighted and Fowler muses upon how everything seems to have gone right since the death of Pyle, who had also offered to marry Phuong. His final thoughts focus upon his spiritual melancholy caused by an absence for him of a personal God and he wishes that 'there existed someone to whom I could say that I was sorry' (180). As Mark Bosco comments on the balance between secular and religious issues in *The Quiet American*: 'The Catholic matrix of Greene's imagination is still unmistakably present even as political struggles and moral commitments to political situations displace the extreme religious dilemma of his characters.'[7]

Other Ways of Escape (1955–1959)

The comic novella *Loser Takes All* was completed during spring 1955 and published later that year, with a film version released in 1956. As Greene's first attempt at a sustained humorous narrative, it confirmed his determination to loosen the shackles of his reputation as a 'Catholic' writer and to experiment with new literary forms. Greene compared this undesired reputation to a 'death mask' which he wanted to 'smash'. In the book's dedication to A. S. Frere of Heinemann he revealed his frustrations with relentlessly Catholic interpretations of his novels. He acknowledged Frere as a reader who, in contrast to his 'Catholic critics', would not confuse the experiences of his fictional creations with those of the author himself.[8] This amusing tale of love and gambling was set in Monte Carlo where Greene had dutifully stayed for the purposes of literary research at the Hôtel de Paris. The generous, if elusive, tycoon Dreuther was modelled upon Alexander Korda, and Greene commented that this was the first and only time he 'drew a principal character from the life'. Dreuther's yacht, the *Seagull*, was based upon Korda's, the *Elsewhere*, on which Greene had enjoyed idyllic Mediterranean trips during the early-1950s. Although set in the secular world of the Riviera and its casinos, and clearly intended as a contrast to the dark psychological and spiritual concerns of *The Quiet American*, *Loser Takes All* is sprinkled with brief references to greed, the Trinity and to those who 'sell systems and those who play roulette with the same dedication that devils and theologians expend on human souls'.[9] Presiding over this comfortably fallen environment is the God-like Dreuther, nicknamed 'Gom' – grand old man, who finally intervenes like an all-powerful divinity to save the happiness (and perhaps the soul) of the middle-aged Bertram (a prototype of Jones in *Dr Fischer of Geneva*) by ensuring the sustained happiness of his marriage to his much younger wife.[10]

In 1957 Greene also drafted in only six weeks a script for Otto Preminger's film version of George Bernard Shaw's 1923 play *Saint Joan*. Joan of Arc had been canonized in 1920 and her spiritual history was of genuine interest to Greene, even though he regarded this scripting assignment as an opportunity to make some quick money. Unfortunately, with the then unknown Jean Seberg cast in the lead role, the film proved a disaster when it was released in 1957. Greene's disappointment was matched by Preminger's and the latter acknowledged:

> I misunderstood something fundamental about Shaw's play. It is not a dramatization of the legend of Joan of Arc which is filled with emotion and religious passion. It is a deep but cool intellectual examination of the role religion plays in the history of man.[11]

At the same period Greene undertook a three-week trip to China where Catholic persecutions were rife, arriving in Peking on 10 April 1957. He bravely involved himself in issues of human rights and before his departure took advice on what to ask to 'serve the Catholic cause'. In 1948 there had been almost 6,000 foreign missionaries in China but by 1957 only 25 were left, with several imprisoned in Shanghai. Greene felt that the religious persecutions which he had witnessed at first-hand in Mexico during the 1930s were now being re-enacted in China. He obtained a copy of a pamphlet, *Religious Freedom in China*, publicizing the dilemma of Father John Tung Tse-tse who was then imprisoned on a charge of counter-revolutionary activity. While in China he asked aggressive questions about the persecution of Catholics and the maltreatment of another noted dissident, Hu Feng. In a combined spiritual and political gesture, he attended Mass on Easter Sunday at the Catholic cathedral in Chungking. The Chinese communist party had adopted a policy titled 'the blossoms in the garden' which in theory allowed freer speech to citizens and visitors. Almost thirty years later Greene wrote for *The Times* (27 May 1985) a withering condemnation of these religious persecutions, titled 'A Weed [i.e., himself] Among the Flowers'.[12]

The plot of Greene's second theatrical play, *The Potting Shed* (1958), was first sketched out in June 1953 when Evelyn Waugh recorded in his diary that Greene had told him of his plans for a drama in which a priest 'sacrifices' his Catholic faith to restore life to a boy who has hanged himself in his family's garden shed.[13] Travels to Kenya, Indo-China, Cuba and Haiti, along with drafting *Loser Takes All*, ensured that the completion of the play was slow. It finally went into rehearsal for its world premier at New York in January 1957 (with the London premier at the Globe Theatre in February 1958). As a young boy, James Callifer had hanged himself when disturbed by the loss of his religious faith due to the rationalist and atheistic arguments of his father, a friend of H. G. Wells and Bertrand Russell (90). His uncle, Father William Callifer, is a Catholic priest and he discovers the apparently lifeless boy in the potting shed. His fervent prayer, 'Take away my faith, but let him live' (125), is answered and the boy revives. However, Father William then lives a tormented life for the next thirty years as an alcoholic priest who practises his ministry without true belief. James's father also loses his 'faith' in secular rationalism due to this seeming miracle.[14]

The first act opens in the Callifer family's home, 'Wild Grove', once set in an idyllic rural landscape but now surrounded by encroaching industrialization. As the stage directions explain, The Grove has become a 'grave' (77) and H. C. Callifer is dying in the best bedroom. As his wife recalls how he always hated 'those sentimental myths, virgin births, crucified Gods' (82), their son James arrives with his pet dog which is left outside in the potting shed. Echoing Greene's unhappy experiences as a trainee editor, James is a newspaper man working in Nottingham and his dog recalls Greene's pet there, Paddy. Kenneth Tynan was comically wide of the mark when he claimed that the barking of this off-stage dog symbolically represented God.[15] Nevertheless, following James's boyhood loss of faith, the dog now represents his only genuine emotional contact with the rest of the world. James's estranged wife Sara bitterly laments that their failed marriage rest upon 'Nothing': 'In the night you'd wake loving Nothing. You went looking for Nothing everywhere . . . I was jealous of Nothing as though it was a woman; and now you sleep with Nothing every night' (87). Questioning another once-trusted belief system, Greene also gives short shrift to an ineffective psychoanalyst, Dr Kreuzer, whose theories are clearly based upon those of Greene's Jungian therapist, Kenneth Richmond.

The miracle of James's apparently Lazarus-like resurrection (a biblical motif used in his 1929 short story, 'The Second Death') has perversely infected his uncle, Father William, with an unshakeable inner lassitude. He explains to his shrewish housekeeper, Miss Connolly, how his brother believed in 'nothing' and now for thirty years he had also believed in nothing, even though he was 'condemned' (120) to being a priest for life. Driven to the depths of despair, Father William consoles himself with drinking cheap altar wine and secretes in his study a whisky bottle behind a volume of the *Catholic Encyclopaedia*. The priest's scruples dominate the second act of the play as he encapsulates for James the torment of extreme spiritual doubt. He prays each night to 'nothing' and still resolutely practises his faith even though he does not 'believe one jot of it' (123). Poignantly echoing St John of the Cross, Father William falls into the trap of attempting to rationalize the workings of Divine Mercy: 'if God existed, why should he take away his faith from me? I've served him well. I go on serving him. The saints have dark nights, but not for thirty years' (124–5). More optimistically, towards the end of the play James's discovery of what really happened to him in the potting shed rekindles his belief in the possibilities of religious faith and there are even signs that Father William may regain his vocation.

Greene wrote two different third acts. For the New York staging James explains his glimmerings of regained faith to his wife Sara, thereby emphasizing the resurrection of their marriage. For the London version, James instead explains his new sense of enlightenment to his mother, who for thirty years has loyally attempted to sustain her husband's failing 'faith' in his own rationalist beliefs. In private, Evelyn Waugh regarded the play as 'great nonsense theologically' but Greene took its spiritual musings seriously. He made clear that Father William's dilemma, describing it as a 'contract made in the dark', was really the central one in the play. In a *Life* magazine article (1 April 1957), provocatively titled 'Mr Greene Promises No More Miracles', he explained that when the boy lives, the priest thinks that his offer has been accepted by God: 'But faith is "a gift from God, not a merit, and therefore was not his to give away", as is proved when he recovers his faith.'[16] Overall, the play dismisses the impotence of sceptical rationalism and reaffirms the tripartite dialectic between intellectual doubt, psychoanalysis and Catholicism which lies at the heart of Greene's writings. Mischievously, the finale of the drama focuses not on James Callifer or his uncle Father William but instead on the young girl Anne, the daughter of James's brother, John. She happily dreams of going down to the now purged potting shed and finding there a lion fast asleep who (in the final words of the play) gently 'licked my hand' (138). This perhaps refers to C. S. Lewis's God-like Aslan in *The Lion, the Witch and the Wardrobe* (1952) or, more likely, to the 1952 film *Androcles and the Lion*, based upon George Bernard Shaw's 1912 play (since Greene had recently worked on Preminger's *Saint Joan*).

The fact that this theologically complex play was followed by Greene's brilliant comic novel, *Our Man in Havana* (1958), confirms his determination to diversify his literary output during the 1950s. Widely acclaimed as a satiric thriller, this entertainment drew upon his wartime SIS experiences, especially in Wormold's creation of a bizarre selection of fictitious agents. Greene based this device on the activities of the Lisbon-based Czech double-agent Paul Fidrmuc (Ostro) and Juan Pujol García (Garbo). In Greene's hands, the morally decadent world of pre-revolutionary Cuba is transmuted into a playground for human folly. *Our Man in Havana* offers 'a thriller in which the thriller form is no longer being taken seriously', violence and danger are 'clothed in an atmosphere of irony and black comedy'.[17] An important precursor to the comic perspectives of this novel is also found in an outline film-sketch from the late-1940s. 'Nobody to Blame' (first published in 1985 with *The Tenth Man*), recounted the escapades of Richard Tripp, a hapless Singer Sewing Machines salesman set in a Baltic city like Tallin. As Greene recalls in *The Tenth Man*, the British Board of Film Censors rejected this film outline because they would not certificate a film 'making fun of the Secret Service' (17).

It has been assumed that by realizing the full potential of his satiric talents in mocking the world of espionage, Greene temporarily sidelined his pre-occupations as a novelist with Catholicism and personal doubt. A. A. DeVitis concludes: 'Anyone looking for deep philosophical and religious meaning in *Our Man in Havana* will be disappointed, for Greene does nothing more in the entertainment than entertain.' Similarly, Mark Bosco explains how in this novel: 'Greene's use of Catholicism becomes more a satirized, stereotypical cultural signifier than a religious lens through which to focus on reality.' Never-theless, *Our Man in Havana* still contains in Wormold's precocious daughter, Milly, one of Greene's most memorable comic Catholic characters.[18]

Wormold himself also offers a complex male character-type, occupying in Greene's fiction a pivotal position between comedy and tragedy. He shares not only the world-weariness of Fowler in *The Quiet American* and Querry in *A Burnt Out Case* (1961) but also the touching innocence of the eponymous hero of *Monsignor Quixote* (1982). Like a less fraught Scobie, Wormold's overpowering sense of duty has left him trapped in an inhospitable foreign location by the memory of his marriage vows to a Catholic wife who has deserted him. Although an agnostic and suspecting that his wife has long since abandoned her Catholic principles, Wormold dutifully shoulders the responsibility of bringing up his beloved but often overpowering daughter Milly as a good Catholic. This intense father-daughter relationship lies at the heart of the comic energy of the first half of the novel.

The 17-year-old Milly attends the local American convent school and effort-lessly assumes the comic dual persona of a pious child-saint and a ruthlessly materialistic young woman. Wormold fondly imagines that the ostentatiously virtuous side of Milly is habitually accompanied by an invisible duenna (an elderly female chaperone), as was the custom among rich Catholic Cuban families. In church Milly always sits 'with the rigidity of a nun' and follows the Mass in a gilt-edged missal, with a morocco binding matching her hair colour. Her imaginary duenna also ensured: 'she ate fish on Friday, fasted on Ember Days and attended Mass not only on Sundays and the special feasts of the church, but also on her saint's day. Milly was her home-name: her given name was Seraphina' (11–12). It seems memorably inappropriate that the beautiful Milly, who even chooses her prayer book to match the colour of her hair, should be devoted to this particular saint. St Seraphina, widely venerated in Cuba, was a poor but once attractive Italian peasant girl who, unlike Milly, was noted for her self-denial and for performing menial chores for her widowed mother. Mysteriously, she had been struck down by an affliction which rendered her deformed, ugly and paralysed, although she bore these sufferings without complaint and interpreted them as a calling to imitate the sufferings of Christ. Milly effortlessly blends her devotion to this maimed saint with more materialistic concerns, such as when she spends her entire monthly allowance from her father on earrings and a 'small statue of St Seraphina' (14). Milly's vanity as a burgeoning young woman is counterpointed by Wormold's fond memories of her precocious piety when she used to pray loudly at the age of four, 'Hail Mary, quite contrary' (12), and her childish insistence on keeping in her bedroom a candle permanently lit in front of a statue of Our Lady of Guadalupe.

Periodically, a devilish side of Milly surfaces and at such moments her imaginary duenna wisely makes herself scarce. Wormold is first introduced to his daughter's dark alter-ego when he is summoned to her convent school and informed that she had set fire to a small boy called Thomas Earl Parkman, simply because he pulled her hair. She defends her behaviour by explaining that the boy was a Protestant and if any persecution was needed, 'Catholics could always beat Protestants at that game.' Her father's attempts to elicit a proper explanation are deftly countered by Milly:

'Why did you set fire to Earl?'
'I was tempted by the devil,' she said.
'Milly, please be sensible.'
'Saints have been tempted by the devil.'
'You are not a saint.'
'Exactly. That's why I fell.'

Similarly, she flatly denies that she has ever smoked cigarettes and only when repeatedly pressed by her anxious father does she admit that she exclusively smokes cheroots (13–14). The unworldly Wormold is also bewildered by his daughter's keen interest in her treasured set of 'artistic' postcards of the classical nude, including the naked version of Goya's 'Draped Maja' (13). When it is proposed that her eighteenth-birthday party will be held in a nightclub she shocks her father by wondering if he has booked the Shanghai Club, notorious in pre-Castro Cuba for its live sex-shows (15). After leaving school she contemplates becoming a governess to the children of Señor Pérez who has had four wives since she claims a 'special vocation to sinners' (16) – especially handsome male ones.

Milly deviously persuades her father to give her a horse. She has already secretly agreed to purchase a chestnut filly from the sinister Chief of Police, Captain Segura. The animal is aptly called 'Seraphina' and appears in the stud-book as out of 'Santa Teresa by Ferdinand of Castile' (17). When Wormold momentarily hesitates, even God and Our Lady run the risk of incurring Milly's disapprobation for not responding appropriately to her devotions. She is furious that her two novenas have not worked, even though she was in a 'state of grace' when she said them. Angrily, she proclaims: 'I'll never believe in a novena again. Never, never . . . I've done two extra Masses as well.' Fearful that his daughter might now even reject the 'existence of God', Wormold senses that she is craftily placing on his shoulders her 'disappointment in the old familiar magic'. Helplessly, he gives in to her demands and Milly instantaneously reinstates her belief in the efficacy of novenas. She then wonders which saint's assistance should be invoked to ensure that the sale proceeds smoothly and her father advises that St Jude, the patron saint of 'lost causes' (19) is the most appropriate choice.

Milly's self-interested calculations provide Greene with a rich fund of comedy at the expense of those who ostentatiously parade their superficial pieties. She prays that her absent mother will become a 'good Catholic again' (30) and patronizingly assures her hapless father that he may be saved alongside other good 'pagans', such as Socrates and the Zulu King Cetewayo. She even claims that she has been hearing voices in the 'watches of the night', advising her to be frugal. To counter her father's scepticism, she insists that she is ripe for such divine visitations since she is now older than 'St Thérèse' when she entered a convent. However, she is not intending to enter a convent herself since Captain Segura – known as the 'Red Vulture' from his torturing of prisoners and, therefore, a memorably inappropriate spiritual adviser – has suggested that she is not the 'right material for a convent' (42). Milly has a good claim to be regarded as Greene's finest female comic creation until the appearance of his Aunt Augusta in *Travels With My Aunt* (1969).

Greene had begun *Our Man in Havana* in October 1956 and completed the final draft in June 1958. This was a period of great personal trauma, encompassing his break-up with both Catherine Walston and a Swedish widow, Anita Björk, with whom he had formed another passionate attachment. He had also accepted in June 1957 a directorship of The Bodley Head publishers, a congenial but time-consuming post which he retained until 1968, leading him into such literary ventures as securing the memoirs of Charlie Chaplin and the popular singer Gracie Fields. The simultaneous publication in the United Kingdom and the USA of *Our Man in Havana* in October 1958 coincided with the finalizing of discussions for Columbia's rights to the film (1960), produced and directed by Carol Reed. Greene travelled to Havana in October for the commencement of filming and made six visits to Cuba between 1957 and 1966.

Despite the incessant demands of these commitments, by mid-1958 Greene was keen to follow on the success of *The Potting Shed* with another drama for the public stage.[19] *The Complaisant Lover* tells the story of a 38-year-old antiquarian bookseller, Clive Root, who has an affair with Mary, the wife of an older dentist called Victor Rhodes. Echoing Greene's relationship with Catherine and Harry Walston, the twist in the play lies in the response of the cuckolded Victor when he learns of his wife's liaison. He allows it to continue but only on his specific terms, thereby ensnaring the lover Clive into a position of total dependency. The script was completed by early-March 1959 and, after performances in Manchester and Liverpool, the play moved to the Globe Theatre in London on 18 June where it ran for almost a year until 8 June 1960. Produced by Sir John Gielgud and with a stellar cast of Ralph Richardson (Victor), Paul

Scofield (Clive) and Phyllis Calvert (Mary), the play was a box office success and demonstrated Greene's growing confidence as a comic writer, this time in a dramatic form. In an interview for the *New York Times* (29 October 1961), Greene explained that he wished to incorporate into his play 'awful emotional situations and practical jokes . . . exploding all over the stage at the same time'.[20] Although the play received a disappointingly muted reception from its American audiences, it reaffirms Greene's ambitious determination during the 1950s to test himself as a writer in a wide range of genres.

The Complaisant Lover offers no specific references to religious matters, although it focuses strongly upon the spiritual emptiness that motivates the adulterous behaviour of Clive and Mary, despite the obvious devotion of her loyal husband, Victor. This play's staging, however, was framed by the repeated publication of a substantial short story with a strongly theological bent, 'A Visit to Morin', first in the *London Magazine* in 1957, then as a separate booklet in 1960 and also with three other stories in *A Sense of Reality* (1963). It is narrated by Dunlop, an English wine-merchant, who as a schoolboy had been intrigued by the work of the Catholic French writer Pierre Morin. His once famous novels with Mauriac-like titles, such as *Le Diable au Ciel* and *Le Bien Pensant*, explored the logic of religious extremities, thereby alienating 'orthodox Catholics' in his homeland but delighting 'liberal Catholics abroad' (216). Although a non-believer, Dunlop decides when in France to attend Christmas Midnight Mass where he fortuitously meets Morin and is invited back to his house.

Dunlop learns that Morin is trapped in a paradox worthy of one of his own novels, in that he has lost his 'belief' in rational arguments for justifying the existence of God, although he retains a hopeful 'faith' in the ultimate truth of the Church. Morin seeks to interpret his loss of belief as evidence of the presence of a stern Old Testament God whom, he assumes, is punishing him by letting his belief wither away. Morin's dilemma demonstrates how vestiges of faith may survive the demise of even the most rigorous of intellectual doubts. Scrupulously, Morin has denied himself the sacraments of confession and communion for the past 20 years because he knows that he is unable to repent sincerely for his extramarital relationships. He explains to Dunlop that he has excommunicated himself 'voluntarily' and given up confession since he was too much in love with a woman to pretend that he would ever leave her: 'You know the condition of absolution? A firm purpose of amendment. I had no such purpose. Five years ago my mistress died and my sex died with her.' Despite thus escaping the compromising allure of female sexuality, Morin remains fearful of resuming his Catholic observances in case he finds that they do not resurrect his belief. 'The alienated man remains alienated,' Roger Sharrock notes, 'because in his alienation lies the only guarantee that Christianity may be true'.[21] In a disturbing mixture of crumbling intellectual pride and escalating spiritual fear, Morin defines the irresolvable stasis of his dilemma since he regards his 'lack of belief' as conclusive proof that the 'Church is right and the faith is true'. Paradoxically, he denies any belief in 'God and His Son and His angels and His saints' but still regards the teachings of the Church as 'true'.

Provided he avoids the sacraments he feels that his 'lack of belief is an argument for the Church'. But if he was to resume his observances and they 'failed' him, then he really would be a 'man without faith' (227).

It becomes impossible to ignore the numerous self-reflective elements inserted by Greene into this narrative. The author seems to be tempting the reader into viewing Morin's spiritual dilemma as an image of his own, not least in his depiction of Dunlop's school-teacher, Mr Strangeways, who had a 'principle of leaving the author's views out of account' (218) and, thereby, always missed the obvious. In an interview with David Lodge, published in 1991, Greene echoed Morin's hopeful doubting as he explained how he distinguished between 'Belief' which he had lost and 'Faith' which he still had, although it seemed to him more like a 'wistful kind of Hope, that the whole Christian myth might improbably turn out to be true after all'.[22] Like Morin, Greene frequently made the gesture of spiritual abstinence by not taking Communion and he shared with his fictional creation a sense of the watchfully oppressive presence of the Catholic clergy who feared the apostasy of so public a figure. Morin recalls how priests 'swarmed like flies' around him and his women, treating him as an 'exhibit for their faith' and proof that 'even an intelligent man could believe'. At first the Dominicans, who enjoyed the 'literary atmosphere and good wine', pursued him. But, later, when his novels dried up and they began to smell 'something – gamey – in my religion', the Jesuits took over the pursuit since they 'never despair of what they call a man's soul' (225). The list of semi-autobiographical references could be extended, but it is clear that Greene threaded through 'A Visit to Morin' various anxieties from his own spiritual history and angry spurts of resentment at the Catholic Church and the expectations of those readers who viewed him as a 'Catholic' writer.[23]

If the fearful doubts of 'A Visit to Morin' represent Greene's fictionalized 'dark night of the soul', then the sojourn of a nihilistic architect in a Belgian Congo leper colony in *A Burnt Out Case* (1961) offers through its focus upon the practicalities of missionary work a temporary release from such cerebral anxieties. Its protagonist Querry, a once renowned architect specializing in ecclesiastical buildings, is psychologically burnt-out and tormented by a root-less sense of belonging nowhere. Like Morin, Querry had stopped attending Mass some twenty years earlier (17) but, unlike Morin who still possesses vestiges of hopeful faith, Querry is numbly resigned to his loss of hope: 'I suffer from nothing. I no longer know what suffering is' (8). Neither sexual passion nor professional acclaim can any longer feed his waning sense of self-worth: 'I have no interest in anything anymore . . . I don't want to sleep with a woman nor design a building' (37). Once again, Greene's own anxieties seem to be pressing down upon the vitality of his fiction and Cedric Watts defines this now familiar authorial challenge:

It is the characterisation of Querry which is problematic. What makes him hard to credit is that repeatedly he seems to be a vehicle for thinly disguised autobiography. Greene the author seems to be infiltrating the characterisation of Querry, creating an oddly ambivalent and even embarrassing effect.[24]

Nor does the psychological development of the other characters in the novel seem of any real significance, as Greene satisfies himself with character-types and caricatures. The leprosarium's atheist medical officer Doctor Colin, its sensible Father Superior and two of its diligent priests, Father John and Father Philippe, are sympathetically sketched but seem attractive primarily because they are too busy dealing with the practicalities of daily life at the mission to be distracted by spiritual scruples. The one problematic member of the mission, Father Thomas, is an insecure individual who might have come more to life as one of the problematic priests of Greene's stage dramas. There is also a theatrical quality to two of his more grotesque characters. André Rycker is a Belgian colonialist who manages a local margarine factory. As a former seminarian and pompous Catholic he assures Querry that he has only married his younger wife because, as St Paul instructed, it is better to marry than to burn with lust. Even more loathsome is the itinerant English journalist Montague Parkinson, an obese fraud who regards the distinction between fact and fiction in journalism as a trivial irrelevance.

The relationship between Querry and his native helper Deo Gratias proves a conspicuously more successful element in the novel. Deo Gratias is a burnt-out leprosy case whose disease has run its course, leaving him severely disfigured but no longer contagious or in pain. While Doctor Colin and the missionary priests teach Querry important lessons about human compassion, it is the lepers who teach him most about the intense but transient nature of human suffering and despair. Deo Gratias and Querry come to parallel one another, as the former's physical mutilations and numbness correspond to the latter's spiritual condition. Through the support of Deo Gratias and the leprosarium workers, Querry gradually seeks a route back into social integration and practical usefulness. He becomes absorbed into the daily work of the mission and begins to plan the construction of new hospital buildings. Querry even experiences moments of grim humour at the leprosarium. Viewing the acute discomfort of an old man with elephantiasis and a hugely enlarged scrotum, Doctor Colin drily enquires: 'Could a famous ecclesiastical architect design a chair for swollen balls?' (71), since such a mundane task would be of far more value to the mission than another chapel. Querry is also fascinated by Deo Gratias's haunting memories of a better place. A. A. DeVitis explains:

Querry's search for usefulness is symbolized by Pendélé, a place of contentment that Deo Gratias remembers from childhood. Pendélé, neither the Christian heaven nor a pagan sanctuary, becomes for Querry a reason for living – usefulness, innocence perhaps, an escape from success and the demands of the ego. Paradoxically, it is Querry's reawakening interest in human suffering, the rebirth perhaps of compassion, that keeps him from finding Pendélé and ultimately brings about his death.[25]

Querry innocently passes time in the company of Rycker's frustrated young wife Marie and, in a thinly disguised act of authorial confession, he tells her the story of a famous jeweller with great wealth and many lovers who was also devoutly loyal to his godlike King. Eventually, however, he grew weary of producing major artistic works and instead preoccupied himself with ornately trivial ones. Strangely, his 'reputation of being a very good man' (145) was sustained by his adoring public, even though his belief in both his artistic skill as a jeweller and his King, as well as his sexual desires, steadily waned and died. In the end, he could no longer rationally believe in the potency of his King and the fable ends by returning to Morin's struggle between belief and faith. Once again, doubt becomes the only way men can convince themselves of God's existence: 'there were moments when he wondered if his unbelief were not after all a final and conclusive proof of the King's existence. This total vacancy might be his punishment for the rules he had wilfully broken' (150).

If Greene's self-doubting trajectory as a novelist during the late-1950s does lie behind Querry's tale of the jeweller, then its allegory may have been intended as an ironic double take at the expense of those readers who still loved to hunt out deep 'Catholic' meanings in his writings. Querry advises Marie Rycker, when she asks whether he was really the boy in the allegory, that she should not seek 'close parallels' since it is usually assumed that a 'novelist [*sic*] chooses from his general experience of life, not from special facts' (143). The most teasingly obscure moment of authorial self-reflection perhaps comes when the intrusive Rycker tries to find out which prayers mean most to Querry. His reply is evasive, claiming that he rarely prays, except in moments of danger or from 'habit', and even then only for a 'brown teddy bear' (32). This puzzling reference may recall Greene's short story, 'The Bear Fell Free', in which a teddy bear becomes a totemic survivor of a plane crash. Closer to this period, from the 1950s onwards the globe-trotting Greene habitually carried around with him a brown bear called Ted as his good luck charm. A photograph has survived taken in Cuba of, as Greene called him, 'Our Ted in Havana'.[26] In moments of personal duress, one may need the comfort of God Himself or a favourite teddy bear – or, preferably, both.

Similarly, Rycker's intrusive curiosity over Querry's religious habits suggests that Greene is treating him as one of those tiresome 'fans' who accosted him with such self-introductions as: 'Ever since I heard you were here I've looked forward to a conversation with an intellectual Catholic' (30). Rycker is a failed Jesuit seminarian whose spiritual pomposity leads him to assure Querry that 'God rules the weather' and he ridiculously proclaims: 'In the seminary I formed the habit of thinking more than most men' (31). It seems possible, then, that the most vulnerable figure in *A Burnt Out Case* is the ultra-orthodox Catholic reader, teased by a novelist who no longer has any patience for his own wearisome reputation as a great Catholic writer. Of relevance here is 'Congo Journal', the first item in Greene's *In Search of a Character: Two African Journals* (1961), which included some of his research notes for *A Burnt Out Case*. In his entry for 4 February 1959 at Yonda, Greene records how he had been pursued by an earnest schoolmaster who tried to exert a kind of 'spiritual blackmail' over him. He notes how he replied that he was 'not competent in matters of faith' and that the schoolmaster would be better served by finding himself a priest. This incident also prompted a weary footnote:

> I would claim not to be a writer of Catholic novels, but a writer who in four or five books took characters with Catholic ideas for his material. None the less for years . . . I found myself hunted by people who wanted help with spiritual problems that I was incapable of giving. Not a few of these were priests themselves. (24)

In Querry's fable of the jeweller, the boy's career as a fabricator of exquisitely carved precious stones has become for him a second best option since he has 'always wanted to carve statues, as large and as important as the Sphinx' (144). This passing reference hints at the personal significance for Greene of his play *Carving a Statue*, an unsuccessful experiment in dramatized theological debate, first staged in London on 17 September 1964 at the Haymarket Theatre. This expressionistic and obscurely allegorical drama is set in the studio of a fanatical artist based, according to Greene, upon Benjamin Haydon, who devoted himself to grandiose biblical paintings and eventually committed suicide. The sculptor in Greene's play (played by Ralph Richardson) is pre-occupied with his gigantic representation of God, so vast that only its lower limbs and torso are visible on stage. At this period the Lord Chamberlain decreed that no representation of the Christian God could be allowed on the public stage in England. Hence, Greene used his stage-set to adhere, with a conscious sense of the ridiculous, to this legislation. This largely incomplete giant statue is a work-in-progress and unlikely ever to be finished. When in the second act its head is finally lowered down to the stage by pulleys, it turns out to be only roughly prepared stone. The central theological question posed by the play is whether 'God is created in the sculptor's (or man's) image or the sculptor is created in God's image'.[27]

The play's action revolves around a characteristic Greeneian query. How can an artist define God if not through his own sinfulness, which is all that fallen man can truly know? The statue is the culmination of the career of an obsessively deranged artist whose neglected son (played by Dennis Waterman) watches his father with increasing incomprehension. The Father is lost within his private world of irreconcilable theological paradox: 'He isn't only power. He isn't only wickedness . . . Did He love? Didn't He love? What's love? There's the tricky question.' As he rightly concludes, but without realizing the truth of his own Manichaean observation: 'how do you carve a contradiction? He has to be wicked and He has to be loving at the same time' (220). In his preface to the published text, 'Epitaph for a Play', Greene explains that he had found *Carving a Statue* especially fatiguing to write and bring to production and he expresses gratitude to those critics whose panning reviews ensured that it only enjoyed a short run. Nevertheless, his 'Epitaph' offers a robust defence against an accusation of 'over-lading the play with symbols', and instead suggests that his diverse use of 'association of ideas' had been mistaken for the symbolic. While this argument is at least feasible, Greene's claim that there was 'nothing theological' in *Carving a Statue* seems deliberately misleading, not least because he admits in the same 'Epitaph' that theology was the 'only form of philosophy' (211–12) which he still enjoyed reading.

The play repeatedly contrasts, A. A. DeVitis explains, 'the concept of a loving God with that of an unheeding or detached deity who has forgotten that creation for which he is responsible'.[28] The naming of the main characters – the Father, the Son, the First Girl, the Second Girl and the Statue of the Father – has a distinctly biblical ring and the Father is preoccupied with God's creative vision. His statue's eyes are especially problematic since they seem to look either askew or indifferently down upon the world and His creations. The Father echoes this unfocused indifference in his treatment of his son and his first girlfriend. As he is talking to them he lowers the head of God down onto the stage and cries out: 'Now I can see Him properly again with his head in the clouds. Tomorrow I'll get back to work on that left eye. Like it was when He looked at the world and loved what He'd made.' But, as the First Girl confesses that his son had 'wanted to make love', the Father ignores her plea for personal guidance and instead remains fixated upon the dilemma of God Himself: 'They double-crossed Him while He rested on the seventh day. No wonder He took a turn against the world' (242). Soon afterwards, the Father sexually assaults the First Girl. The Son's second girlfriend, who is deaf and dumb, is then killed in a road accident while trying to escape from the lascivious Dr Parker who has raped her (and may have been implicated in the earlier death of the Son's mother).

Throughout the play the Father remains impotently self-deluding in his blindness to the corrupting presences all around his vulnerable and sexually awakening son. His spiritual hubris allows him to assume that God is really just a great artist like himself, and he triumphantly proclaims as the second act closes: 'I don't have to worry about love. God doesn't love. He communicates, that's all. He's an artist. He doesn't love.' To his Son's question, 'Did He hate his son?', the Father can only reply that he neither loved nor hated him but, instead, 'used him as a subject. That's what the Son was for' (246). The play ends without hope as the Father climbs up the statue once again with a self-deluding cry: 'All I needed was a new idea' (262). When an artist has left only an adherence to his own failing creativity, Greene's play tells us, no hope remains for his personal salvation. He may also, through the sin of indifference, destroy those innocents around him who should have been able to rely upon his wisdom and love.

Chapter 7

The Disguise of Tragicomedy: 1966–1973

Hellish Comedy and *The Comedians* (1966)

Conor Cruise O'Brien remarked that Greene had been 'looking for Hell all his life and . . . found it at last in Haiti'.[1] Written slowly (often in Antibes in the south of France) during 1964 and 1965, *The Comedians* is a satiric politico-thriller set during the blood-thirsty regime of Doctor 'Papa Doc' Duvalier. On a sea-passage to Haiti an opportunistic but world-weary Englishman called Brown, who has inherited a hotel there from his raffish mother, meets a cheerful soldier-of-fortune, 'Major' Jones. Both of their characters echo elements of Anthony Farrant in *England Made Me* and Greene's unreliable eldest brother, Herbert. Also aboard Brown's ship are an elderly, genteel American couple called the Smiths. He is a former politician who stood against Truman in the 1948 presidential elections on a vegetarian ticket and, with his vociferous wife, is travelling to Haiti to set up a vegetarian centre. On the island they meet Dr Magiot, a Marxist idealist who opposes Duvalier's vicious oppression of the people. He stands for a co-operative alliance of Catholics and communists against tyranny – a conjunction which came to matter greatly to Greene during the rise of liberation theology in Latin America. Other characters encountered there include Brown's dying mother Yvette, a decorated hero of the French Resistance, who has transformed herself via one of her numerous male liaisons into the Comtesse de Lascot-Villiers After her death her inconsolable and much younger black lover, Marcel, poignantly hangs himself in her bedroom. In one of the numerous dark ironies around which the novel is structured, Brown shares his discovery of his mother's distinguished service in the Resist-ance with his mistress, Martha Pineda, the daughter of a Nazi war-criminal and wife of a South American diplomat. Several other minor characters sporadically burst into life, recalling the vitality of Minty in *England Made Me*, most notably a tiny, sharp-witted *métis* journalist called Petit Pierre, a black Catholic-Voodooist called Joseph and Martha's fascinatingly unbearable son, Angel.

Greene had been in Haiti in 1963 and published an article, 'The Nightmare Republic', in the *Sunday Telegraph* (29 September), describing the daily lives of the natives who were descended from the liberated slaves of Hispaniola. He compares the 'unconscious' nightmare world of the Haitians, in which the

'Ego and the Id seem joined in unholy matrimony' to that of 'Hieronimus Bosch'. Voodoo's Baron Samedi, with his sunglasses, cigar and top hat and tails 'haunts the cemeteries' and, according to some, resides in the 'Presidential Palace, and his other name is Dr Duvalier' (221).[2] The devil-like figure of Baron Samedi occupies a place of special interest in the novel. Noted for his vibrant delight in debauchery and obscenity, the Baron escorts the dead from the graveyard to the underworld but can also, if he so wishes, offer resurrection to those close to death. It lies within his powers either to grant everlasting life to the dead or to ensure that their bodies rot in the grave. Sometimes, if he is displeased, he may allow living burials or the resurrection of mindless zombies. Clad in his characteristic garb of a top hat, a black tuxedo and dark glasses, Baron Samedi is assisted by a legion of servile, devilish spirits. Greene's conflation of his identity with that of Duvalier and Samedi's agents with the Tonton Macoute is comically astute since a 'reign of terror' often has an 'atmosphere of farce' (222). Samedi also offered to Greene yet another example of the duality of a Manichaean God who, as it pleases him, dispenses either damnation or resurrection to his fearful human servants.

The ingrained cultural blending of Catholicism and Voodoo rites in early-1960s Haiti was actively promoted by Duvalier and it provides a striking background to *The Comedians*. 'Papa Doc' had been excommunicated in 1961 for his persecution of the Catholic hierarchy, but in the same year he ordered a *Te Deum* to be sung in the cathedral at Port-au-Prince on Inauguration Day and required the Papal Nuncio to attend, threatening otherwise to close down the Catholic schools on the island.[3] The Tonton Macoute, wearing their distinctive soft hats and dark glasses, brought sub-machine guns to this Mass and even searched the altar, with armed marksmen taking up positions in the choir (224). Greene also described in his *Sunday Telegraph* article attending a black mass in which Catholic and Voodoo elements were liberally mixed together. Incessant drumbeats, saints' banners and Latin prayers were heralded the arrival of a priest swinging a censer:

> But the censer was a live cock, and after the priest had incensed the congregation, he put the head in his mouth and crunched through the neck. Then, using the neck like a tube of red-brown paint, he made his mystic designs upon the earth-floor. (221)

This bizarre scene of a Voodoo priest, his sacrificial cock and the banner of St Lucy was transposed into the novel and viewed through Brown's eyes with horrified fascination (179–80). Born in Monaco in 1906, Brown had been educated at the Jesuit College of the Visitation and believed in the 'Christian God' (24). Due to his early passion for theological study he was half-expected to develop a vocation for the priesthood. At school he took the presence of God and the fate of fallen humanity seriously and envisaged Him 'incarnated in every tragedy. He belonged to the *lacrimae rerum*'. But the experiences of adult life have taught Brown that the 'confused comedy of our lives' is better viewed as a divine farce enacted upon His creations by a sometimes benign and sometimes vengeful God. As Brown grew older, only his sense of humour allowed him to believe in God and that life inevitably became a 'comedy, not the tragedy for which I had been prepared' (24–5). The Voodoo Baron Samedi is noted for his outrageous practical jokes and for Brown a Christian (or even Manichaean) God is best envisaged as the 'authoritative practical joker' who consistently drives his human toys towards the 'extreme point of comedy' (25). At the casino Brown and the cashier discuss the necessity of evil and, just before seducing Madame Pineda for the first time, he assures the cashier that he must be a 'Manichean like myself' (78).

Defining the exact nature of Brown's lapsed (but still lurking) Catholicism becomes central to his characterization in the novel. A. A. DeVitis explains:

> Brown has been brought up a Catholic but he is unlike the Catholics Greene has previously portrayed. The passionate pity of Scobie has given way to a tragicomic irony, which is also the chief mood of the novel . . . it is instead a cloak of indifference, a means whereby the stupidities and the atrocities of the world can be warded off, and perhaps explained. Yet Brown's rejected Catholicism remains for him a standard of measurement, in Haiti a valid one, for Catholicism liberally sprinkled with Voodooism is the religion of the majority.[4]

The agnostic Brown continues, literally, to be haunted by his boyhood Catholicism since his dreams are preoccupied with religious imagery. At the moment of his mother's death, Brown dreams that he is walking in the moonlight alongside a lake 'dressed like an altar-boy' (70). Similarly, Brown experiences later in the novel another Catholic 'dream-vision', this time tempered by the subversive comedy of a subconscious recollection of the obese Angel's addiction to sweet biscuits. He falls asleep and dreams of kneeling at the communion-rail of his Monte Carlo college. The priest carefully places a 'bourbon biscuit' in the mouth of each boy but omits Brown and, as the communicants come and go, he obstinately remains kneeling: 'Again the priest distributed the biscuits and left me out. I stood up then and walked sullenly away down the aisle which had become an immense aviary where parrots stood in ranks chained to their crosses' (207).

The point of these surreal, religious dreams is that they offer no significant insight into Brown's spiritual dilemma. Rather, they reinforce an insistent feeling in the novel that the iconography and ceremonies of institutional religion have been reduced to the status of incidental props in the lethal comedy of 1960s Haitian society. In retrospect, even Brown's earlier contacts with Catholicism seem tinged with either farcical elements or a sense of nihilism. His unreliable mother regularly failed to pay his fees at his Jesuit College but, on her death-bed, dutifully leaves her rosary and missal (66) to the fathers of the

Visitation. Brown's expulsion from the college had been occasioned by his well-intentioned indiscretion in dropping a roulette token instead of five francs (57) into the collection-bag at Mass. Lying in bed one day with his married mistress, Brown reasserts his nihilist spiritual state as a lonely and disappointed adult: 'I am nothing.' But Martha presciently emphasizes the need for those raised in a specific religion, even if now doubting, to categorize themselves as either a 'Protestant nothing' or a 'Catholic nothing'. Her words make Brown realize that ultimately everyone does need to believe in a non-tangible something, even if it is no more than a resolute commitment to a lack of belief. He imagines 'coloured balls flying' through the air with a different 'colour for every faith – or even every lack of faith', as well as 'existentialist' and 'logical-positivist' balls (226).

At the end of *The Comedians* Joseph and a small band of valiant rebels against Duvalier's tyranny have been killed. Earlier Joseph had been described as a 'good Catholic as well as a good Voodooist' (48), and his demise becomes a culminating event in the closure of the novel. Brown meets the bedraggled remnants of the rebels' forces as they are carrying the dead Joseph on a stretcher towards their refuge, appropriately situated in a lunatic asylum near Santo Domingo. Momentarily lost for words, Brown blurts out that Joseph always made excellent 'rum punches' (284). Understandably, his surviving comrades disapprove of such a flippant comment in the face of death. But, obliquely, it is entirely appropriate since Baron Samedi is notoriously fond of rum and Joseph's Voodoo credentials are thereby reaffirmed by Brown over his dead body. A Catholic Mass is also said for the deceased rebels at the local Franciscan church by a young Haitian refugee priest who preaches a powerful sermon, drawing on St Thomas the (doubting) Apostle. His message upholds the heroic value of Christian engagement with the forces of evil and insists that the Church is both in and sharing the 'suffering' of the world:

> though Christ condemned the disciple who struck off the ear of the high priest's servant, our hearts go out in sympathy to all who are moved to violence by the suffering of others. The Church condemns violence, but it condemns indifference more harshly. Violence can be the expression of love, indifference, never. One is an imperfection of charity, the other the perfection of egoism. (288)

The seeds of Greene's personal engagement with liberation theology in Latin America during the 1960s and 1970s (reminiscent of his admiration for Catholic missionary work in Mexico during the 1930s and in China during the 1950s) are much in evidence in this sermon. They are again confirmed by a Voodoo-like 'letter from the dead' (290) which soon after Joseph's funeral Brown finds lying on his pillow from the deceased Dr Magiot. In this mysterious missive, Magiot explains from beyond the grave the links between their respective codes of belief (or non-belief). He envisages Communism as more than merely Marxism, just as Catholicism is more than the 'Roman Curia. There is a *mystique* as well as a *politique*'. Like Brown, Magiot was born a Catholic, but he sees them both as 'humanists'. Although Catholics and Communists have been guilty of 'great crimes', he argues that they have at least not 'stood aside, like an established society' in the face of suffering: 'I would rather have blood on my hands than water like Pilate.' By this stage in the novel, Brown has moved to the neighbouring Dominican Republic and finds work as an assistant undertaker in Mr Fernandez's funeral business. Clad in his black funeral suit and hat, Brown is transformed into a parody of Baron Samedi and seems, both literally and symbolically, more associated with the world of the dead than the living, since his hotel is defunct, 'Major' Jones is dead and Martha is about to leave with her husband for his new posting at Lima. Brown's final thoughts are unremittingly dark and he expresses a total absence of hope for the future. He regards himself as entirely incapable of both 'love' and 'guilt': 'There were no heights and no abysses in my world – I saw myself on a great plain, walking and walking on the interminable flats. Once I might have taken a different direction, but it was too late now' (290–1). Unlike Querry who begins to reconnect with the lepers around him, or Morin whose spiritual doubts paradoxically serve to confirm his hope for the existence of God, Brown finds in Haiti only a world of brutal nothingness. *The Comedians* concludes with the tragicomic implication that Hell is to be found not only in 'other people' (to echo Sartre's famous words) but also in the isolated and despairing psychological landscapes of the inner self.

The Comedians prompted an outraged response from Duvalier's 'Department of Foreign Affairs'. It published a pamphlet, *Graham Greene démasqué*, memorably describing him as: 'A liar, a crétin, a stool-pigeon . . . unbalanced, sadistic, perverted . . . a perfect ignoramus . . . the shame of proud and noble England . . . a spy . . . a drug addict . . . a torturer.'[5] A contract for a film of *The Comedians*, directed by Peter Glenville (the director of *The Living Room*) and starring Richard Burton (Brown), Elizabeth Taylor (Martha), Peter Ustinov (Pineda), Alec Guinness (Major Jones) and Lilian Gish (Mrs Smith) had been signed with MGM before the publication of the novel. Given the response of the Haitian government, the film was shot in Dahomey (Benin).[6] The composition of the screenplay – the last Greene undertook for one of his books – proved a demanding exercise since it disallowed his preferred 'escape' from the world of his fictional characters once a novel had been completed. He also greatly disliked having to accommodate the multiple-perspectives narratives required in films when as a novelist he always preferred telling a 'story from a single point of view'.[7]

New Ventures (1967–1972)

Returning with relief to single-perspective narratives, Greene's next major publication, '*May We Borrow Your Husband?' and Other Comedies of Sexual Life*, appeared in March 1967. It comprised twelve sardonic short stories in the style of Maupassant and focused upon the comedy of sexual manners. They were written, Greene commented, in a 'single mood of sad hilarity' while he was settling into a two-roomed apartment overlooking the small port of Antibes.[8] These tales blend farcical and tragic elements, as in the first (providing the title of the collection), tracing the seduction of a young man on his honeymoon by two predatory homosexuals. Although none of the stories is specifically concerned with religious issues, the often unsatisfactory nature of traditional Christian marriage provides a persistent theme. In the first story, the worldly wise narrator is drafting a life of the notoriously unfaithful husband and Restoration rake, the Earl of Rochester, while watching the collapse of the newly-weds' marital relationship. In 'Chagrin in Three Parts' the narrator is again a voyeuristic writer, this time labouring over a fictional courtship as he watches the first tentative steps of a lesbian relationship between an older widow and a younger woman with an unfaithful husband. 'Mortmain' recounts how a former mistress tries to keep a hold over her now happily married lover; and 'Cheap in August' tells of a 39-year-old wife having a passing affair in an off-season hotel with a lonely old man. 'The Invisible Japanese Gentlemen' focuses on a pair of soon-to-be married but mismatched lovers; and the collection closes with the sad tale of 'Two Gentle People', a middle-aged woman and man who fleetingly meet on a park bench before returning home to their unsatisfactory spouses, respectively, a homosexual husband and a neurotic wife. The only idealized relationship in the collection, in 'A Shocking Accident', blooms from pure farce. A young man, whose father had been killed by a pig falling onto him from a Neapolitan tenement block, finds his ideal marital partner when she not only shows sympathy for his embarrassing paternal dilemma but is also concerned for the pig's welfare.

In March 1966 Greene was invested by Queen Elizabeth II as a Companion of Honour (having refused a knighthood a decade earlier), and he was appointed as a Chevalier of the Légion d'honneur in January 1967. This award confirmed his permanent departure from England in favour of residence in France and later Switzerland. The draconian levels of taxation then current in England, along with the complexities of his personal relationships, prompted this move abroad, although his relocation to Antibes was complicated by the arrest of his tax-avoidance advisor, Tom Roe, who was later imprisoned for major fraud and counterfeit-currency offences. Greene's personal losses were considerable and they provided an unexpected catalyst for a surge in his literary productivity to recoup some of his losses.[9]

Greene's fantastic black-comedy, *Travels With My Aunt*, was published in November 1969 and, Norman Sherry explains, its long first section comprises, essentially, a 'series of short stories . . . akin to scraps stitched together, a quilt of picaresque adventures'. Its episodic structure also incorporates fragmentary storylines originally intended for the *'May We Borrow Your Husband?'* collection.

Only in the shorter second section does this anecdotal accumulation gel into a more coherent novel form.[10] Offering, Cedric Watts notes, a 'saturnalia of self-referentiality', it is rich in literary in-jokes for avid readers of Greene's earlier works, with sections of the first part of the novel set in Brighton and the outlandish character of Aunt Augusta based upon Dottoressa Moor, an eccentric friend from Capri whose memoirs, *An Impossible Woman* (1975), were edited (and partly ghosted) by Greene. The second section exploited his recent travel experiences in Argentina and Paraguay. In *Ways of Escape*, Greene commented: 'If *A Burnt-Out Case* in 1961 represented the depressive side of a manic-depressive writer, *Travels With My Aunt* eight years later surely represented the manic at its height – or depth'.[11]

Henry Pulling, a lonely bachelor resigned to a retirement growing dahlias in the suburbs, is a former bank manager who recalls the middle-aged ennui of the accountant in *Loser Takes All*. There is little direct discussion of Catholic matters in *Travels With My Aunt* and Pulling claims to be only an indifferent Protestant. Mark Bosco observes of this novel: 'Greene's use of Catholicism becomes more a satirized, stereotypical cultural signifier than a religious lens through which to focus on reality.'[12] When Pulling's Aunt Augusta (really his long-lost mother) mysteriously appears, she ironically comments that they only ever seem to meet at 'religious ceremonies', the last time being Henry's baptism. Her sister, a 'very saintly woman' (8), had adopted him as an infant and passed him off as her own child, even though, at least in Augusta's eyes, her Protestant virtues were of a stiflingly censorious kind. Recalling her sister's disapproval of her rackety lifestyle, Augusta comments tartly that she may well have been a saint: 'but a very severe saint. She was certainly not angelic' (52). Despite his surrogate mother's best intentions, Henry's adult views of the English Church echo Greene's youthful disillusionment with his family's comfortable Protestantism at Berkhamsted. Attending Midnight Mass at his local church, Henry relegates his religious appreciation of the Nativity of Christ to mere aesthetic pleasure in a 'beautiful legend' and its delightful 'commemoration service' (167).

In contrast, Augusta proclaims herself to be an enthusiastic (if only sporadically devotional) Catholic convert. But as her personal history is pieced together from a flurry of madcap anecdotes, her Catholic practices seem even more farcical than those of Milly in *Our Man In Havana*. She describes how in her youth she considered various religions but 'hadn't finally plumped for Catholicism, though I was on the brink' (16). The turning point in Augusta's personal journey towards what she considers as spiritual enlightenment began when she met one of her former conmen-lovers, the Rev. Curran, who set up in Brighton a dogs' church. He claimed that his title stood for 'Revered' rather than 'Reverend' (40), so as to avoid civil prosecution for masquerading as a clergyman. Still harbouring fond memories of this charming charlatan, Augusta recalls that once she knew Curran she became 'interested in religion' (38) and

she credits him for stimulating her preposterous biblical studies. Despite close
scrutiny, she found little 'favourable to dogs in the Old Testament':

> It was the Christians who began to carve dogs in stone in the cathedrals,
> and even while they were still doubtful about women's souls they were
> beginning to think that maybe a dog had one, though they couldn't get
> the Pope to pronounce one way or the other, not even the Archbishop of
> Canterbury. (41)

A later lover, Mr Visconti, is described as Catholic, 'even though a non-
practising one' (104), and had insisted on Augusta being formally received
into the Church. During the Second World War he had escaped the advance of
the Allied Forces by disguising himself as a Catholic monsignor but, mistaken
for a real priest, had been obliged to hear confessions, including that of the
adulterous wife of a German general (116). She then abandoned her husband
to provide Visconti with a seat in her fleeing car since he brought with him the
protection of our 'Holy Mother Church' (117). Previously, Pulling's knowledge
of other religions had been limited to mistyped letters from Miss Keene, a
spinster friend living in South Africa, who sends him a dismissive description of
her local 'Dutch Deformed' (135) church. In contrast, Augusta passionately
describes herself as a 'half-believing Catholic' and reverentially notes the feast
of the 'Little Flower', St Thérèse of Lisieux who is a persistently present figure
in Greene's fictions. Bamboozled by Augusta's crazy stories of the Rev. Curran
and Visconti, Henry asks if she is a real Roman Catholic and receives a
Greeneian reply: 'Yes, my dear, only I just don't believe in all the things they
believe in' (147).

It would be pointless to attempt any deep reading of Greene's playfulness
over religion in *Travels With My Aunt*, but its second section offers hints of an
author beginning to refocus upon a 'more intense exploration of writing about
religious faith and political commitment'.[13] Visconti's Catholic aphorisms –
'Scepticism is inbred in a Catholic' (235) – increasingly impinge upon Henry's
sensibilities as he is drawn into the complex world of South American politics
and Catholicism. His picaresque adventures conclude with him resident in
Paraguay and soon to marry the 16-year-old daughter of the local Chief of
Customs. He happily whiles away the pleasant evenings sharing with his future
wife favourite lines from Browning's poetry, especially (as the last words of the
novel), 'God's in his heaven – / All's right with the world!' (262).

Despite this closing tone of optimism, there are signs in *Travels With My Aunt*
of more serious preoccupations emerging from its rambling narratives. Augusta
and Wordsworth, her black lover from Sierra Leone, are heavily involved in
currency smuggling. The entire plot relates to the work of a master forger, a
motif which echoes Greene's problems with his renegade tax-advisor, Tom Roe.
The novel also satirizes the imperialist tendencies of the CIA via the hippy girl,
Tooley, whom Henry meets on a train to Istanbul. Her father works for the

agency in Paraguay and has contacts with the extreme right-wing dictator, General Stroessner, whose regime was notorious for sheltering Nazi war criminals. Greene had visited Israel in autumn 1967 during the aftermath of the Six-Day War and in an article for the *Daily Telegraph Magazine*, 'The Worm Inside the Lotus Blossom' (3 January 1969), he referred to Jewish agents hunting down 'war criminals in the German colonies around Encarnación'(263).[14] The article also outlined the bloody history of Paraguay's dictators, including Marshal Solano Lopez (whose war with Argentina reduced the male population of his country to only 30,000) and the cruel intellectual Dr Francia (known as El Supremo). For Greene, Paraguay's current censorship regulations are readily summarized: 'One mustn't attack the President – or the United States' (258).

In this article Greene forges an explicit link between the social impact of Catholic missionary work and communism. He describes how in Paraguay dictators of various kinds, 'civilian, military, ecclesiastical, the cruel and the kind' have always existed. In contrast, he recalls that during the seventeenth century the Indians received welcome protection from their Spanish oppressors from the 'benevolent Communist rule of the Jesuit missions' (259). He attributes the survival of the native language, Guaraní, to the benign influence of the Jesuits. Noting the ruins of the 'magnificent red baroque churches, the size of cathedrals' (259), he recalls how the exploitative Spanish imperialists finally drove the Jesuits out of Paraguay. Another wave of missionary churches was initiated by the Franciscans but by the late-1960s it was once again the Jesuits who were providing the only viable humanitarian challenge to Stroessner's regime. In Asunción the Jesuits had instituted what is known as 'Open Mass', an egalitarian church service in which the priest's offices were combined with native Guariní devotional music and sermons from politically active lay members of the congregation. It seems to Greene that only the 'new movement' in the Church, and the 'Jesuits in particular', seem occasionally now to 'threaten the surface of the still pool'. He also draws attention to a martyred priest, Camilo Torres who had been shot with the guerrillas in Colombia, recalling the self-sacrificing heroism of Father Pro in Mexico and rendering him the 'Catholic equivalent of Che Guevara' (264). This determined linking of Catholic missionary work and the humane face of communism takes the reader, W. J. West concludes, into a 'uniquely Greene territory the world of the underground struggle against the state by Catholics who might be priests or who might not even believe in God but fight on the right side'.[15]

A strong sense of historically politicized Catholicism also surfaces in Greene's acceptance speech, 'The Virtue of Disloyalty', delivered when he received the Shakespeare Prize at the University of Hamburg on 6 June 1969.[16] He polemically attacks Shakespeare as the 'supreme poet of conservatism' (266) and 'this bourgeois poet' (267). Although the son of a non-conforming Roman Catholic, Greene finds it puzzling that Shakespeare's only reference to the desecrations of the Reformation is in a single lyrical line in the sonnets (slightly misquoted): 'Bare ruined choirs where once [late] the sweet birds sang' (sonnet 73). The paradoxical relationship of disloyalty and virtue had also recently preoccupied Greene when he drafted a sympathetic introduction to the traitor Kim Philby's memoir, *My Silent War* (1968). Contrasting the brutal state persecution of the poet Southwell, 'disembowelled for so-called treason' (268), with Shakespeare's idealized jingoism in John of Gaunt's, 'This blessed plot, this earth, this realm, this England', Greene remarks how these lines were published in 1597, only two years after Southwell's execution after 'three years of torture'. He suggests that if Shakespeare had ever expressed some comparable level of 'disloyalty', then we might have 'loved him better as a man' (268).

For Greene, this contrast between Southwell and Shakespeare encapsulates his conception of the writer's political and religious roles. Since repressive states always tend to 'poison the psychological wells' and 'to restrict human sympathy', he argues that the storyteller's role must involve acting as the 'devil's advocate', in order to 'elicit sympathy and a measure of understanding for those who lie outside the boundaries of State approval'? Hence, Greene feels strongly that a writer's vocation inevitably leads him to be a 'Protestant in a Catholic society, a Catholic in a Protestant one, to see the virtues of the Capitalist in a Communist society, of the Communist in a Capitalist state' (268–9). He then draws for his Hamburg audience a striking contemporary connection with the persecutions of Elizabethan England as he describes how a German theologian had viewed the conflicts of the Second World War as the ultimate moral challenge for German Christians. The evils of Nazism had made them choose between the 'defeat of their nation in order that Christian civilization may survive' or the 'victory of their nation and thereby destroying our civilization' (270). Greene's speech concludes with an adroit parallel between the martyred Southwell and the German pastor, Dietrich Bonhoeffer, who had chosen to be hanged rather than comply with the immorality of Nazi totalitarianism.

As he approached his mid-sixties, original composition became more arduous for Greene, and it is perhaps inevitable that several of his later books merely offered collections of earlier materials (such as in 1972 his *Collected Stories* and *The Pleasure-Dome*, reprinting a selection of his film reviews from 1935–1940). In 1969 The Bodley Head published his *Collected Essays*, including various pieces with religious concerns, such as 'Henry James: The Religious Aspect', 'François Mauriac' and 'G. K. Chesterton'. It also drew together three disparate but revealing pieces of journalism under the title 'Three Priests'. The first item reprinted Greene's passionate review (1959) of Waugh's biography of Ronald Knox, in which he judiciously balances the productive but privileged cosmopolitan life enjoyed by Knox with priests whom he had met on the 'borders of a battlefield in Vietnam, in the region of the Mau Mau or in the dying white world of the Congo' (283). The second item, 'The Paradox of a Pope' (1951), considers the historical role of the Papacy and the life of Eugenio Pacelli (1876–1958) who served as a Papal Nuncio in Germany (1917–1929) and became Pope Pius XIII in March 1939. This essay offers a sympathetic assessment of Pacelli's papacy, despite his much criticized adoption of diplomatic neutrality in the face of Nazi persecution of Christians and Jews and, significantly for Greene, his severe measures (enacted in 1946) against Catholics who collaborated with Communists. The third item, 'Eighty Years on the Barrack Square', reprinted Greene's generous review (1965) of the diary of Pope John XXIII, *Journal of a Soul*, a volume blending long litanies of 'retreats, spiritual exercises, meditations' (298) with more touching stories of his modesty, his excessive love of 'mirth' (299) and examples of his genuine warmth as a man of the people occupying an extraordinary spiritual role.

Greene explained that he was encouraged to compile his volume of autobiographical reminiscences, *A Sort of Life* (1971), by a Catholic psychiatrist whom he had consulted when suffering from recurrent bouts of depression.[17] Drafted as a form of literary self-psychoanalysis, these 'scraps of the past' (9) record his memories of Anglican Christmas celebrations at Berkhamsted and the purgatorial torments of his schooldays. *A Sort of Life* intersperses a chronological progression through his early life with thoughts and incidents from later periods, detailing his amused responses to official Vatican censorship of *The Power and the Glory* (58) and his enduring delight in Browning ('Better sin the whole sin, sure that God observes; / Then go live his life out!') whose poetry can transcend, Greene suggests, even the lyricism of the Beatitudes (84). He also recounts his instruction in the Catholic faith at Nottingham before his reception into the Church in 1926 and his choice of Thomas as confirmation name, 'after St Thomas the doubter and not Thomas Aquinas' (121).

Political Theology and *The Honorary Consul* (1973)

In his 'Chile: The Dangerous Edge' (*Observer Magazine*, 2 January 1972), Greene offered his tempered support to the Marxist-Socialist President, Doctor Salvador Allende, along with an attack on USA and CIA involvement in South America. He was also impressed by the markedly politicized role of the Catholic Church in Chile. Allende headed a 'Popular Unity' coalition of Socialists, Communists and Christian Democrats and Greene recorded with wry amusement the National Day celebrations (18 September) at the cathedral where the archbishop presided over a remarkably eclectic *Te Deum*. The Catholic worshippers were joined by the Marxist President and representatives of various communist states, including China, with prayers offered in rapid succession by a 'Methodist, a Protestant, a Baptist and a Jewish Rabbi'. A Catholic priest then preached on the urgent need for the congregation to 'expel the Cain' within them all (278). Genuinely impressed by the broadly ecumenical nature of Chilean socialism and liberation theology, Greene's essay concludes that the Marxist-Communist ideal in that country might just 'have a sporting chance' (283). Such optimism was proved sadly unfounded by the military coup of

September 1973 – at first supported by the Christian Democratic leadership –
leading to a four-man junta led by General Augusto Pinochet who abolished
civil liberties, banned union activities and dissolved the National Congress.

The action of *The Honorary Consul* (1973) is set in a small port on the River
Paraná on the Argentinian side of the Paraguayan border and its plot condemns
US support for General Stroessner's right-wing dictatorship. A motley group of
guerrillas led by León Rivas, a married Catholic priest, plan to kidnap a visiting
US Ambassador who is in Paraguay to view its 'Jesuit ruins' (12). They hope to
force the release of some Paraguayan political prisoners but succeed only in
catching Charley Fortnum, the alcoholic British Honorary Consul. Doctor
Eduardo Plarr, the son of a Latin American mother and an English father who
had been imprisoned for his opposition to Stroessner's regime, is unwillingly
drawn into this chaotic plot when the guerrillas bring him to tend Fortnum
after he is taken hostage. The intimacy of these characters is further complicated by Plarr's secret affair with Fortnum's much younger wife, an ex-prostitute
called Clara. The character of Plarr is derived from Greene's earlier jaded
expatriate Brown in *The Comedians*. Both men have English fathers and foreign
mothers and are lapsed Catholics who were educated by the Jesuits, and both
are conducting desultory affairs with the wives of low-level diplomats.

The sense that *The Honorary Consul* extends Greene's thoughts in *The
Comedians* on the ingrained social functions of Catholic traditions within
repressive Third World environments is supported by the wealth of carefully
worked incidental references to religious iconography scattered throughout
this novel. When, for example, the town's English teacher, Doctor Humphries,
is thought to possess the 'evil eye' (14) by an Italian waiter at the local Italian
Club, he makes passing reference to the Madonna of Pompeii. Greene's choice
of this Catholic cult honouring the Madonna (Our Lady Queen of the Rosary)
is entirely appropriate since it had been founded in the nineteenth century
by Bartolo Longo, a reformed Italian Satanist who at his baptism had adopted
as his second name 'Maria' as a sign of repentance. Although all the male characters are either problematic or lapsed in their religious faith, female devotion
is depicted as universal within South American society. Plarr's aging mother at
Buenos Aires relishes the company of indulgent Jesuit priests; and his virginally
unobtainable medical secretary, Ana, always wears a 'small gold cross round
her neck', regularly attends confession and carries a prized 'missal bound in
white vellum' with her to Sunday Mass (95). At the unusually decorous local
brothel, each girl has a 'little shrine with a lighted candle' (48) to her favourite
saint in the cubicle used to service clients. Predictably, the hard-working prostitute Teresa is devoted to her 'statuette of Saint Teresa of Avila' (62) – on whose
feast day Greene had married Vivien in 1927.

Such minor and often implicitly comic details provide a recurrent sense of
local religious traditions surviving despite a callously repressive regime. They
are complemented by Greene's more sustained meditation on the theme 'of
political commitment and the political duty of a Christian in an unjust society'.[18]

Greene had conducted extensive first-hand researches for *The Honorary Consul* and travelled to Paraguay in late-summer 1968, with a second visit there in March 1970. The drafting of the resulting novel (Greene's personal favourite) sporadically occupied much of his time from 1970 until its publication in the United Kingdom and USA in September 1973.[19] As his creative focus increasingly centres upon the doomed political activism of Father León Rivas and his relationship with Plarr, the narrative of the latter half of the novel is frequently interrupted by lengthy theological debates. While these digressions are perhaps a structural flaw in the literary cohesion of the novel, they nevertheless offer an informative window onto the development of the author's radical religious views at this period.

When Plarr first sees Rivas again by the light of a candle in a hut on the *barrio* he is reminded of a 'shy seminarist' (23). He recalls how as an earnest theology student Rivas used to explain the Trinity to him in a way that was more 'complicated than the catechism' (25) and like a 'sort of higher mathematics' (98). Even when he fries eggs in the hut, Rivas's fingers recall those of a priest when he 'breaks the Host over the chalice' (104). But through the injustices of the political system in Paraguay, Rivas is now alienated from the traditional securities of his Catholic faith. Emphasizing that a priest is no more than a witness at a marriage, Rivas explains to Plarr how he and his wife Marta had merely 'made our vows to each other' (96) and that he had decided to marry when he lost his faith since a 'man must have something to guard'. Along with the injustices of Stroessner's brutal regime, it is clear that the radical changes engendered within the Catholic Church by the Second Vatican Council (1962–1965, instituted by Pope John XXIII and completed by Pope Paul VI), have also exerted a marked effect on Father Rivas's waning commitment to his ministry. He proudly recalls to Plarr that he had been ordained when John XXIII was Pope and that he cannot 'wait for another John' (98) since his marriage directly contravenes Paul VI's stance on the retention of priestly celibacy (*Sacerdotalis Caelibatus*, 1967). In contrast, the Council's renewed emphasis upon missionary vocations and its recasting of the Church as comprising the 'pilgrim' people of God (Paul VI was known as the 'pilgrim pope') seem more in accordance with Rivas's strong Christian-Socialist compassion for his fellow citizens and the poor.

When the kidnapped Fortnum half-seriously asks Rivas to hear his confession, the ex-priest scolds him for joking about sacramental 'things like that' (109). Then, in a reversal of their roles, he replies to Fortnum's query over why he chose to marry as if he was 'kneeling in the confessional box himself'. This question pinpoints Rivas's spiritual dilemma and forces him to admit that it was not just loneliness but also anger with 'my Mother the Church' (110) which prompted him into marriage. At this point Greene justifies these digressions by emphasizing Fortnum's natural cunning, as he realizes that theological debate will engage the sympathies of his captor. His innocuously phrased question: 'What's wrong with the Gospels, Father?' produces a torrent of humanitarian anger from Rivas who feels that they no longer make 'sense . . . anyway not in Paraguay' (111). He denounces the luxurious lifestyle of the archbishop when the poor suffer from malnutrition and wonders what use a Communion Host can be to a starving child who desperately needs a nourishing *chipá*. Even Communion wine seems an unobtainable luxury in Paraguay and Rivas concludes: 'Why could we not use water in the sacrament? He used it at Cana'. Only the missionary fortitude of the Jesuits meets with his unqualified approval. He also recalls with admiration Father Camilo Torres, 'shot with the guerrillas in Colombia' (112), whose heroism was commemorated in Greene's 1969 article, 'The Worm Inside the Lotus Blossom'.

Greene uses the historical example of Father Torres, hailed as a martyr after his death in February 1966, to validate his portrayal of Rivas's revolutionary Christianity. Torres was from a wealthy Colombian family and he challenged the traditional hierarchies of his Church and State by calling for the creation of a revolutionary mass movement to seize power, if necessary using violence, as a means of establishing an egalitarian socialist society. Even though Pope Paul VI had explicitly denounced violence in his *Populorum Progressio* (Progress of the People, March 1967) as a means of supporting the faithful poor, Torres provided Greene with tangible proof that the concept of a revolutionary socialist (and Marxist) Christian was a viable model for repressed Third World countries. A famous image of Jesus carrying a rifle across his shoulder, reprinted in the *New York Times* (12 August 1970), encapsulated this alluring concept of militant Christianity and recalled Torres's most famous axiom: 'the duty of every Catholic is to be a revolutionary'.[20]

Although Rivas consciously separates himself from the institutional Church he is by no means a spiritual outcast from his priestly ministry and his wife Marta longs to see him once again, 'all dressed up at the altar . . . turning to bless us' (189). As the state forces close in on their hideaway, Rivas is persuaded by his fellow guerrillas to say Mass without an altar or vestments. Recalling the whisky priest's hurried Mass in *The Power and the Glory*, Rivas hastens through the Gospel (which, pointedly for post-Vatican II, he reads in Latin rather than vernacular Spanish), the Canon of the Mass and the Consecration. But just before he reaches the '*Domine, non sum dignus*' (241), the voice of Colonel Perez, the leader of the state militia hunting them down, blares through a loudspeaker, making final demands for them to release their hostage and surrender.

Earlier, Rivas angrily retorts to Plarr's accusation that he had 'left the Church' by asking how he could ever 'leave the Church' since it is the 'world', this '*barrio*' and this 'room: There is only one way any of us can leave the Church and that is to die' (196). From Rivas's perspective, his Mother Church has abandoned him and the poor of this blighted country. Instead of relying upon the justice of an omnipotent God who, like Sherlock Holmes, used to pursue and punish the 'wicked man' as he 'discovered all', Parguay now only has the 'law and order' of General Stroessner with his reliance upon 'Electric shocks on the genitals' (204). Rivas expresses a passionate desire for faith in a higher power but, in despair, he regards his Church as impotent and alienated from the people. This frustration is symbolized by the dried beans which he casually tosses in his hands 'like the beads of a broken rosary' (212), recalling the symbolic potency of Scobie's broken rosary in *The Heart of the Matter*. Even the figure of Christ Himself has become problematic in Rivas's mind as he can focus only on His incarnate identity, even if some people believe that he was 'God as well'. The Romans killed him not because he was God but because he was an ordinary man, a 'carpenter from Nazareth'. Such an individual, Rivas thinks, could not imagine the 'kind of world we would be living in now'. Contemporary religious and secular philosophies seem to have betrayed the common people and Rivas bitterly concludes that he is now no more interested in the Catholic Church than in Marxism: 'The Bible is as unreadable to me as *Das Kapital*' (216).

As these earnest theological discussions continue between Rivas and Plarr, it becomes clear that the former has taken refuge in an extreme evolutionary concept of both the Divinity and the human condition. These eclectically derived theories proposed that it was possible to trace the ongoing struggle within a still-evolving universe between the bright and dark sides of God Himself. Echoing a Manichaean suspicion that in Paraguay the dark side of God is temporarily in control of the secular and theological orders, Rivas's logic derives from the controversial Jesuit theologian and palaeontologist, Pierre Teilhard de Chardin (1881–1955). Seeking to combine Christianity and science, he had proposed that humankind is gradually evolving through its apparently endless trials and tribulations towards a final spiritual unity. Another strong influence over Rivas's thoughts is Thomas Hardy who supplies the title-page epigraph for *The Honorary Consul*: 'All things merge into one another – good into evil, generosity into justice, religion into politics.' Rivas echoes the heresy of 'evolutionary meliorism', traceable in Hardy's *The Dynasts* and his poem 'God's Education', that God is animated by both a benevolent and malevolent impulse and that He can only finally evolve into full benevolence through the active interaction of His human creations with their Creator.[21]

Pitying rather than blaming God (217), Rivas explains to Plarr how the concept of Free Will has been used as the 'excuse for everything. It was God's alibi'. While it seems simple to blame all evil on either Satan or humankind, Rivas admits that his central dilemma as a seminarian and priest had been that he could never fully believe in Satan since it was 'much easier to believe that God was evil'. His co-conspirator, Aquino, reiterates this idea, cynically insisting that God is indeed evil: 'God is capitalism. Lay up your treasures in heaven – they will bring you a hundred per cent interest for eternity' (223). This support from like-minded brethren prompts Rivas into an impassioned evolutionary-revolutionary sermon; sampled here in extract:

> I believe in the evil of God . . . but I believe in His goodness too . . . He made us in His Image . . . and so our evil is His evil too. How could I love God if

He were not like me? . . . I can feel his fear and his gratitude and even his treachery . . . The God I believe in must be responsible for all the evil as well as for all the saints. He has to be a God made in our image with a night-side as well as a day-side . . . I believe the time will come when the night-side will wither away . . . and we shall see only the simple daylight of the good God . . . It is a long struggle and a long suffering, evolution, and I believe God is suffering the same evolution that we are, but perhaps with more pain . . . I believe in the Cross and the Redemption. The Redemption of God as well as of Man . . . Because the evolution of God depends on our evolution. Every evil act of ours strengthens His night-side, and every good one helps His day-side. We belong to Him and He belongs to us. But now at least we can be sure where evolution will end one day – it will end in goodness like Christ's. It is a terrible process all the same and the God I believe in suffers as we suffer while He struggles against Himself – against His evil side . . . God when He is evil demands evil things. He can create monsters like Hitler; He destroys children and cities. But one day with our help He will be able to tear His evil mask off forever. (223–6)

An evolutionary-revolutionary metaphysic offers to Rivas a rational route towards reconciling the past and present sufferings of the world with a desire for a more perfect world of social and Divine interaction.

The tragic climax of the novel finally draws together Plarr and Rivas in a reverential parody of a shared Christian ministry. With their hideaway surrounded by Colonel Perez's forces, Plarr decides to surrender and walks outside with his hands raised. He is treacherously shot in the back of his right leg and loses consciousness for a few moments. When he comes round, he realizes that Rivas, who had been shot in the stomach, is lying close behind him. Their final words to each other echo the sacramental formula of contrition and absolution. Plarr hears Rivas utter in a whispered voice a word which sounds like 'Father' and a heartfelt apology: 'I am sorry . . . I beg pardon.' With their roles reversed – 'Nothing in their situation seemed to make any sense whatsoever' – Rivas becomes the penitent with Plarr assuming the priest's role. Intending to recall their Jesuit schooldays, Plarr grants him the words of absolution, '*Ego te absolvo*' (250), but is too short of breath to laugh. As they lie silently together, three paratroopers advance with their rifles at the ready to finish them off in a final act of state brutality. As Mark Bosco explains, for both Rivas and Plarr:

their words intimate a sharing in the mediation of God's grace, a perhaps ironic portrayal of the 'priesthood of the people,' which was a central theme of the documents of Vatican II. God's grace is thus surprisingly manifested on both the vertical plane of a cultic priesthood and the horizontal plane of a 'priestly people' who are showing care for and forgiveness for each other.[22]

The concluding chapter of *The Honorary Consul* opens in the cemetery at Plarr's funeral. As a final twist, the eulogy spoken over the coffin presents Doctor Plarr as a priest-like missionary who worked unremittingly in the '*barrio* of the poor without recompense – from a sense of love and justice'. It is then falsely claimed that Plarr had been assassinated 'without mercy by a fanatic priest' (253), thereby sacrificing his life to save that of Charley Fortnum. The State, it seems, is once again triumphing over the liberation theology of Rivas and his associates by simply rewriting its own history. The poor are still as poor as they ever were and the powerful remain unchallenged. Only the final words of the novel, describing Fortnum's genuine love and forgiveness towards his wife Clara, offer a positive conjunction with the spiritual bonding of Plarr and Rivas in their final moments. Once again, Mark Bosco provides a succinct summation of this concluding perspective:

> The end of the novel emphasises two places in which the religious and the political imagination intersect: hope and love. Human hope can ground political belief only when it is experienced in a personal commitment to others, and human love has a stake not only in creating communities of commitment but also in the evolutionary union of humanity with God. Indeed, love is the transcendent signifier in the novel that keeps human action focused on correct practice.[23]

Chapter 8

The Self-Reflective Writer: 1974–1991

Almost the Last Phase (1974–1980)

The last years of Greene's career as a published writer have something of a miscellaneous feel. Yet his preoccupation with Catholicism and the tragicomic nature of the human condition remains vigorous. His writings also become increasingly self-referential, as he cultivates a sense of nostalgia for his own past and literary reputation, thereby sustaining his stance as a sceptical rationalist fascinated by the workings of devotional faith, hope and doubt. The publication of *Lord Rochester's Monkey* (1974), a biography of the Restoration poet and rake John Wilmot (1647–1680), Earl of Rochester, readily illustrates these facets of his literary activities during the early-1970s. Greene had first compiled this study during the early-1930s, but it was rejected by Heinemann, fearful that it would be regarded as pornography. The typescript lay neglected for some forty years until Greene's international fame (and the rise of Rochester's reputation within academia) ensured a ready market. Greene began finalizing the revised typescript soon after proofing *The Honorary Consul* in January 1973. His first reassessment of the original 1930s draft during the late-1960s at Antibes forms the writing project of the author-narrator in 'May We Borrow Your Husband?'; and the darkly comic ethos of this short-story collection is also in keeping with the epigraph to *Lord Rochester's Monkey*:

> Most human affairs are carried on at the same nonsensical rate, which makes me (who am now grown superstitious) think it a fault to laugh at the monkey we have here, when I compare his condition with mankind. (Rochester to Henry Savile)

Rochester was a Hobbesian sceptic, persistent adulterer and prolific writer – the appeal of his life-story to Greene is obvious. He detailed how Rochester had converted to Catholicism (more for political than spiritual reasons) but then, as advancing syphilis consumed his body, he underwent a renewal of faith and a deathbed reconversion to the English Church (215). Greene's Preface explains how, as his 'spirit' constantly fought with his 'flesh' and blended 'love' and 'lust' with 'hate' and 'death', his 'unbelief was quite as religious as the Dean of

St Paul's faith' (10). Echoing his literary fascination with unsatisfactory fathers, Greene's biography emphasizes how Rochester's father had also been a decadent sensualist. A sermon preached by his mother's chaplain at his father's funeral acerbically comments: 'so confirmed was he in sin, that he oftentimes almost died a martyr for it' (16). He also quotes how the dramatist George Etherege had polarized Rochester's moral behaviour in the character of Dorimant in *The Man of Mode*: 'I know he is a Devil, but he has something of the Angel yet undefac'd in him' (17). Greene concludes his biography by quoting Robert Parsons's eloquent sermon preached at Rochester's funeral in August 1680 for 'so great a man and so great a sinner' (220).

Greene's next literary venture was his dramatic comedy, *The Return of A. J. Raffles* (1975), loosely based on E. W. Hornung's *The Amateur Cracksman* and focusing on the gentlemanly housebreaker and his friend 'Bunny' (who is also his lover). Substantial roles are given to Lord Alfred Douglas (Oscar Wilde's 'Bosie'), his father the Marquess of Queensberry, and the Prince of Wales, disguised as 'Mr Portland' for an assignation with his mistress Alice (the renowned Mrs Keppel). Apart from the occasional line, for example, when the Prince compares his insubstantial public role to a 'plaster image in a Roman church' (299), religious concerns play no part in this fast-moving comedy of manners. Produced in a six-week run by the Royal Shakespeare Company at the Aldwych in London, the play instead seeks to exploit the recent relaxation of theatre censorship by showing homosexual relationships (among Bosie's set and between Raffles and Bunny) and female nudity (as Alice sheds her voluminous Edwardian garments before bathing). Ultimately, its dramatist seems to be taking a temporary respite from his customary theological and moral concerns, in favour of exploring further the comic impulse that so enlivens his writings from *Our Man in Havana* onwards.

The Return of A. J. Raffles prompted two other late excursions into dramatic comedy: the one-act play *Yes and No* and a longer comedy, *For Whom the Bell Chimes*, both performed in March 1980 at The Haymarket Studio Theatre, Leicester, and published in 1983 in a limited edition. *Yes and No*, about the staging of a play by Frederick Privett, is a slight two-hander between an actor and his director, poking gentle fun at Sir Ralph Richardson and Sir John Gielgud. Privett is an enthusiastic follower of Harold Pinter but supposedly with his own distinctive style, as the director explains: 'His pauses are quite different from Pinter's. They are Privett pauses' (360). *For Whom the Bell Chimes*, incorporating the corpse of a murdered woman and a transsexual police officer, reveals Greene's admiration for Joe Orton's black farces. This latter play was in rehearsal when Greene was drafting the conclusion to his autobiographical *Ways of Escape* (1980). He explained in this memoir his sheer delight in 'testing the spoken word' in dramatic compositions and in 'working with a group' thereby 'escaping solitude'.[1]

The Human Factor was completed in April 1977 and published in the United Kingdom and USA in March 1978. The defection in 1963 of Kim Philby,

Greene's former boss at the SIS (Secret Intelligence Service), to the Soviet Union proved a catalyst for this sombre depiction of the British security system. Greene had penned a sympathetic introduction to Philby's *My Silent War* (1968), in which he compared Philby to the Catholic martyr-conspirators during Elizabeth I's reign. These thoughts prompted preliminary drafts for *The Human Factor*, which includes passing references to Philby, Burgess and Maclean (75). But unlike the comic sketching of the bungling British security services in *Our Man in Havana*, in this novel the murderously amoral SIS is depicted as cynically collaborating with the repressive apartheid regime in South Africa.

As with several of Greene's later works, there is a pervasive self-reflective quality to *The Human Factor*. Echoing the first names of the lovers in *The End of the Affair*, Maurice Castle is a long-serving MI6 operative who has married a black wife, Sarah, and is devoted to her son, Sam. They live quietly in Berkhamstead, Greene's childhood home, and the characters of Castle's mother and Mrs Hargreaves, the American wife of a high-ranking figure in the Secret Service, are based, respectively, on Greene's mother and Catherine Walston. The novel returns to Greene's perennial fascination with personal betrayal since Castle has been passing low-grade secret information to the Russians, in return for their assistance in extricating Sarah and her son from persecution and probable death in South Africa. Castle is depicted by Greene as another example of the paradoxical 'virtue of disloyalty' since, after a long and unblemished service to the SIS, he has become a traitor to his country only through personal loyalty and love.[2]

Although not an overtly religious man, Castle's mind seems haunted by the traditional devotional practices of English provincial life. He is plagued by fears that his treachery will soon be detected, as the biblical words, 'Those that are in Judaea must take refuge in the mountains' (13), flit through his mind. These lines (Mt. 24.16) relate to the prophesied destruction of Jerusalem and the end of Jewish society and civilization, thereby hinting at an apocalyptic future for a morally bankrupt English society. When Castle walks down Berkhamsted High Street one Sunday morning, on impulse he goes into the local parish church just as a service is concluding. The middle-class congregation heartily sing, 'There is a green hill far away', and he feels himself drawn towards 'sharing their incredible belief'. Sam is then recovering from the measles and Castle thinks that he might as well 'mutter a prayer of thanks' to his childhood God that Sarah's son was now recuperating (51).

For a character who professes no firm religious convictions, Castle's imagination often seems richly Christian in its associations. One night, as he lies in bed with Sarah recalling their lives in South Africa, they discuss his former contact Carson who had arranged Sarah's escape to England via Lourenço Marques (Maputo), formerly the capital of Portuguese East Africa. News has recently reached Castle that Carson had died in prison from pneumonia, although it seems more likely that he has been eliminated by BOSS, the South African Secret Service. Castle recalls how Carson had been a committed

Communist and man of the people who had 'survived Stalin like Roman Catholics survived the Borgias' (100). These memories prompt an illuminating confessional moment from Castle, with his wife Sarah cast as his confessor. He explains that he was never especially religious, and 'left God behind in the school chapel'. But sometimes missionary priests whom he met in Africa rekindled his desire to believe and, if he had stayed there, he might eventually have 'swallowed the Resurrection, the Virgin birth, Lazarus, the whole works', rather than ending up as a mere 'half believer' (101). Castle's thoughts periodically return to the attractions of the confessional as he compares Boris, his Russian control, to a Catholic priest who listens to confessions 'without emotion' (111). Boris is much younger than Castle, prompting him also to muse that old men often catalogue their sins to younger priests in the confessional (112).

During the war Castle's first wife, Mary, had been blown up in Oxford Street by a buzz bomb while he was working in Lisbon (105), recalling the accidental killing of 'D.'s wife by fascists in *The Confidential Agent*. For both characters, unexpected bereavement leads to a sense of alienation from human society and a questioning of all political and religious codes. 'D.' and Castle share a belief that their worlds are in a state of terminal decline, as Castle casually recalls a phrase from one of his schoolboy hymns: 'Change and decay in all around I see' (119). His existential angst is compounded by the sudden death of Arthur Davis, another SIS operative with whom he shares an office. Davis had wrongly fallen under suspicion of being the source of documents leaked by Castle and his sudden demise is caused by a dose of aflatoxin, a traceless poison specifically identified for this novel by Greene's medical brother, Raymond. This clinically efficient 'in-house' assassination is enacted (rather too hastily) by another British Intelligence Officer, Dr Emmanuel Percival, in whom political expediency has superseded personal morality and the Hippocratic Oath. Understandably disconcerted by these events, Castle wonders if his sense of alienation from others is caused by an inability to love power, success or beauty or perhaps because he always tries to seek a proper balance in his personal affairs, 'just as Christ had, that legendary figure whom he would have like to believe in' (141). At Davis's funeral held at St George's in Hanover Square the uninspiring delivery of the presiding vicar depresses further the despondent tone of the novel by reducing the sublime mysteries of life and death to the mundane logic of a mathematical theorem. As he reaches the familiar words, 'O Death, where is thy sting?', the vicar sounds like a 'bad actor' delivering Hamlet's soliloquy. His droning academic conclusion, 'The sting of death is sin, and the strength of sin is the law,' sounds like a 'proposition of Euclid', so much so that the amoral Dr Percival automatically intones not 'Amen' but 'QED' (155).

As desolation and despair encroach ever more deeply into Castle's mind (or soul, since he harbours such a powerful longing to believe in the legendary figure of Christ), he turns once again to the concept of confession and its alluring promise of purgation and forgiveness. Mark Bosco sees Castle as the 'displaced religious person who searches for surrogate priests who can assist him with kindness through the crises of his life'.[3] Seeking out his Russian contact Boris in a safe house at Watford, he glances through the window of a suburban dining room where he sees a family saying grace before their meal. Although he recalls the custom from his childhood, he had assumed that it had gradually died out but then wonders if the family might be 'Roman Catholics' since 'customs seemed to survive much longer with them' (176). This train of thought tempts him into the local Catholic church and, on the spur of the moment, he decides to make his confession, rationalizing it as a form of secret service interrogation or summary trial, '*in camera*' (177). Sadly, Castle's expectations of a sympathetic ear and spiritual solace are confounded by a short-tempered priest, as isolated and lonely as himself, who rattles his rosary like a 'chain of worry-beads'. Admitting that he is not a Catholic, Castle is brusquely advised that he should go to priest in his own Church. When he confesses that he hasn't 'got a Church', the priest loses patience and tells him that he really needs a doctor, before slamming closed the shutter of the confessional (178)

It eventually becomes necessary for Castle to be spirited away from the West by the Soviet Security Services to Moscow, and it falls to Dr Percival to inform Sarah of his safe arrival there. Her grateful expostulation: 'Thank God', elicits a wry reply from Davis's phlegmatic assassin who is not 'sure about God' but confirms that she can at least thank the 'K.G.B. (One mustn't be dogmatic – they may be on the same side, of course.)' (238). Castle ekes out a lonely existence in Moscow and discovers that even his treachery has been worthless since his low-grade documents have been leaked back to London as a means of establishing the trustworthiness of a Russian triple agent. The only hope sustaining him is that he will eventually be reunited with Sarah and Sam. Apart perhaps from Charley and Clara at the close of *The Honorary Consul*, Greene offers in Castle and Sarah's relationship his first sustained depiction of mutually supportive married love. In this sense, he seems to be responding to contemporary Catholic teachings. Mark Bosco explains:

> This representation of married love differs sharply from Greene's earlier Catholic cycle . . . post-Vatican II theological discourse [challenged] the body-soul dualisms and the Jansenistic dread of anything sexual in favour of a more holistic, incarnational understanding of married love as a reflection of the divine image in human relationships . . . Greene's late novels offer glimpses of married love as the new *Imago Dei*, the only divine-human factor that visibly makes a claim over all the isms and abstractions of contemporary life. In a world where God seems absent, married love becomes God's trace . . . the text's tenuous transcendent signifier.[4]

But Castle experiences a final blow when it becomes apparent that Sarah will not be allowed to join him. The betrayer is cruelly betrayed, as he senses an 'exile inside his exile' and longs even more for Sarah (243). As Sarah, his loving wife and quasi-priestly confessor, pleads with him to continue 'hoping', their telephone connection is cut off and in the sombre last words of the novel her line to 'Moscow was dead' (259).

Castle's tragic isolation can now be alleviated only by the reader's hope that Sarah and Sam will somehow be able to join him in Moscow, since through his 'virtuous disloyalty' Castle has crossed an irreversible border. Greene thereby places the burden of hope not upon his central characters, who are merely helpless pawns in the chess-game of secret intelligence, but instead upon his readers who must try to come to terms with the post-Christian political tensions between the Western allies and the communist Soviet Union. Bosco's perspectives are again instructive, as he explains how the 'search for a stable "factor" – the human factor of the title – is uneasily negotiated in a universe denied and deprived of Greene's usual recourse to explicit Catholic images and beliefs'. Instead, the moral wasteland of the espionage genre allows Greene to formulate a complex political allegory of his long-standing religious concerns. Although lightly sketched in the novel, the clinically efficient South African BOSS agent, Muller, whose face is unmarked by the 'torments of any belief, human or religious' (90), typifies the starkly dehumanizing effects of the cold war. Only the love for Sarah and Sam unwaveringly held by Castle, a half-believer in both religious and political terms but an unconditional lover of humanity, offers a beacon of hope in this starkly secular modern world.

The publication in 1980 of Greene's *Doctor Fischer of Geneva or The Bomb Party* was greeted with both intrigued interest and bewilderment. Decades later, there is still no general agreement over its subject-matter, literary aims or even genre. Set within the clinical austerity of the super-wealthy of Switzerland, this cautionary tale on the corrupting nature of power and greed blends a rich variety of narrative forms, including thriller, parable, fable, allegory and love story, to challenge the reader – and perhaps simply to amuse its author – with a complex framework of possible ways of reading the narrative of this 'black entertainment'. A lonely, middle-aged widower called Alfred Jones, whose wife and baby died in childbirth, earns a mundane living as a translator of foreign correspondence for an international chocolate manufacturer at Vevey. Jones's familial and physical incompleteness – he lost both parents and one of his hands in December 1940 during the London Blitz – matches a resignation to his emotional and spiritual emptiness. He has a chance encounter in a café with Anna-Luise, a beautiful girl some thirty years younger than himself, who is the estranged daughter of the eponymous Doctor Fischer, a cruelly malicious manufacturing tycoon. His enormous fortune is based upon Dentophil Bouquet toothpaste which fights the decay caused by eating to many Swiss chocolates.

Fischer's supposed friends, known as the 'Toads' from Anne-Luise's mishearing of the English word 'toadies', regularly tolerate gross personal humiliations at dinner parties arranged by Fischer, in the hope of lavish gifts usually presented at the end of their culinary ordeal. These appalling social events read like 'a motif from the grimmer kinds of folklore' or a reverse-Volpone plot in which the 'rich manipulator pretends to be dying so as to extract gifts from

the toadies, each of them hoping to be his heir'.[5] The guests usually include
an international lawyer called Kips, crippled with osteoarthritis; a smooth tax
consultant, Monsieur Belmont (perhaps recalling Tom Roe); the Divisionnaire,
a high-ranking Swiss army officer who has never seen active military conflict;
Richard Deane, a fading, alcoholic film star and Mrs Montgomery, a gushing
American woman with blue hair. Incredibly, Jones is drawn into their circle
when Anna-Luise falls in love with him and they marry. Although they forgo the
presence of either a priest or Anna-Luise's father at their union, their mutual
sense of marital completeness is encapsulated in her loving exclamation: 'You're
my lover and my father, my child and my mother, you're the whole family – the
only family I want' (17). Her words echo Mark's Gospel when Jesus says of his
newly chosen apostles: 'Who is my mother, or my brethren? . . . whoseoever
shall do the will of God, the same is my brother, and my sister, and mother'
(3.33–35). Anna-Luise and Jones are thereby pointedly associated with the
sufferings of Jesus and His unconditional love for humanity. Their devotion to
one another also recalls that of Castle and Sarah in *The Human Factor*. Once
again, the aged Greene represents a loving marriage as the only viable bulwark
against a cruelly indifferent and destructive world.

If Greene's depiction of the tender relationship between Jones and Anna-
Luise represents the transcendental dimension of married love, then Doctor
Fischer's contempt for the infinite greed and self-abasement of his 'Toads'
encapsulates the fallen nature of the human condition. The fable-like structure
of the novella casts Fischer not only as a perverted parody of Christ at the Last
Supper as he presides over his series of dismal banquets but also as a Satanic
inversion of the omnipotence of God the Father through the malevolent
potency endowed upon him by his wealth. At the end of the novella, Jones
recalls how he used to compare Fischer 'with Jehovah and Satan' (141). His
conversations with Anna-Luise firmly establish the Manichaean aspects of her
father's brooding dominance over this self-enclosed society which so readily
blends an outward sense of austerity with inward greed. Once again, Mark's
Gospel seems to have been in Greene's mind since it describes how the scribes
from Jerusalem thought that Jesus, the Son of God, was satanically possessed:
'He hath Beelzebub, and by the prince of devils casteth he out devils' (3.22).
Jones grows to hate Fischer not only for his satanic pride, cruelty and 'contempt
of all the world' but also for his denial of love: 'He loved no one' (10). Anna-
Luise confirms this interpretation in her pithy summation of her father: 'He's
hell' (18). Yet they both regretfully acknowledge his god-like status in Vevey
society. Jones comments that when his wife talks of her father she makes him
seem like 'Our Father in Heaven – his will be done on earth as it is in Heaven'
(24). When she thanks God that her husband has not been invited to one of
her father's dinner-parties, Jones pointedly ripostes: '"Thank Doctor Fischer . . .
or is it the same thing?"' (29).

Jones eventually receives an invitation to a dinner-party and Anna-Luise is
horrified that he plans to accept in case Dr Fischer will take him 'into a high

place' and show him 'all the kingdoms of the world?' Jones light-heartedly confirms the God-Devil duality of her father's identity, insisting that he is 'not Christ', nor is Fischer 'Satan' since they had previously agreed that he was more like 'God Almighty', even though to the 'damned God Almighty looks very like Satan'. Anna-Luise can only wearily reply that he should then 'go and be damned' (33). Like Milton's Satan, Doctor Fischer is tormented by his 'infernal pride' (39) and hatred of free will, as his daughter notes how he hates 'freedom as much as he despises people' (47). He radiates contempt for humanity, and it seems that he even would have despised Christ, except for the fact that the New Testament had proved 'in time to be such a howling commercial success' (41). Anna-Luise concludes that her father definitely has a soul but that it 'may be a damned one' (83). At the dinner attended by Jones, Fischer fancifully suggests that his greed may be compared to God's, and Jones is understandably intrigued by this comment. Fischer's response is characteristically Manichaean as he insists that he really does not believe in God any more than he does in the devil. But (like Greene) he has always found 'theology an amusing intellectual game' and, he argues, to believers God is 'greedy for our love'. Cynically, Fischer suspects that his devilish god is really only 'greedy for our humiliation, and *that* greed how could he ever exhaust? It's bottomless' (61–2).

On Christmas Eve Jones and Anna-Luise, although non-Catholics, attend midnight Mass in the old abbey at Saint Maurice since they consider Christmas to be the 'universal feast of childhood' (80). Their anticipated enjoyment is rudely shattered by the presence of several of Fischer's 'Toads' who seem to reduce this climactic devotional event to the triviality of a 'cocktail party' (81). Despite this disappointment, images from this Midnight Mass (a central event in the novella's progress towards a tragic conclusion) remain fixed in Jones's imagination. When at his last dinner-party Fischer brandishes a Christmas cracker he seems to hold it like the priest at Midnight Mass 'had raised the Host . . . "This is my body"' (109). Similarly, when Jones is boiling a solitary egg in his flat for his supper he spontaneously repeats a line spoken by the priest at Midnight Mass at St Maurice: '"As often as you do these things you shall do them in memory of me"' (143).

Doctor Fischer's final 'Bomb Party' is held at night on his mansion's snow-covered lawn, lit by bonfires and tree-lights. This chilling landscape creates the impression of a nightmarish Garden of Eden in which vital greenness is transformed by Fischer's malignancy into a lifeless frozen landscape (recalling the White Witch's icy impact on Aslan's lush terrains in C. S. Lewis's *The Lion, the Witch and the Wardrobe*). The guests are invited to pull a cracker from a bran-tub, knowing that each of the six crackers contains a cheque drawn against Crédit Suisse for 2 million francs, except for one which contains a probably lethal explosive charge. Although Mr Kips declines to play, the other guests are too greedy to abstain and Jones, desolate after the death of Anna-Luise in a skiing accident, sees this game of Russian roulette with crackers as a convenient means of committing suicide. As he clutches his cracker he feels Anna-Luise's 'closeness' and his love for her triggers a fleeting moment of religious hope: 'She could only continue to exist somewhere if God existed.' But, as Jones pulls his cracker without the desired explosion, a sense of despair overwhelms him. He imagines Anna-Luise withdrawing her hand from his and walking back towards the lake to 'die a second time' (132). On impulse, Jones reaches into the bran tub again and draws out Mr Kips's cracker. He is again disappointed when it fails to explode and Fischer mockingly derides him as 'greedy for death' (133).

When Jones decides to keep one of the cheques for 2 million francs from his crackers, Fischer's devilish interest in him is renewed. He hopes that he might still create in Jones a man as greedy for material gain as the other guests: 'I shall have created you. Just as much as God created Adam' (134). This transparent allegory of Satan's temptations takes another twist when Jones grabs the Divisionnaire's still-unpulled cracker in exchange for his cheque for 2 million francs. As he strides down to the lake to pull it, Fischer's angry exclamation exposes the crumbling Manichaean duality of his power over his guests: 'damn you. Tell me, what in Christ's name do you mean?' But Jones's hopes for death are yet again confounded when this last cracker also fails to explode and he realizes that Fischer has 'stolen' (135) his own longed-for demise by not putting an explosive charge in any of the crackers.

Unexpectedly, Jones meets at the lake a Mr Steiner, who had once enjoyed a platonic friendship with Anna-Luise's mother, Anna, through their shared love of Mozart. Like Satan, Fischer is unable to appreciate such heavenly harmonies, and Anna-Luise had explained how music seemed to taunt him with his 'failure to understand it' (39). Enraged with envy and wealthy enough to act in Vevey like 'God Almighty', Fischer had ensured that Steiner was driven from his job as Mr Kips's secretary and his wife had withered away and died in the face of his marital envy. Having heard about Anna-Luise's death, Steiner's fury at Fischer's revives, and he has come to his mansion to 'spit in God Almighty's face' (137). But when Fischer arrives at the lake, Steiner's hatred melts into pity and Fischer realizes that he has failed to corrupt Jones through material temptations. He walks away from them into the darkness and shoots himself through the head. Jones is left wondering how Fischer's lifeless corpse, now as insignificant as a 'dead dog', had once been compared to 'Jehovah and Satan' (141).

The novella concludes with Jones again alone and without purpose in life, pathetically treasuring a few tangible memories of Anna-Luise, including two snap-shots and a hand-written note, venerated 'like the relics of bone they keep in Roman Catholic churches' (143). Although he senses at the Bomb Party a 'sufficiency of despair', Jones feels a total failure in his attempts to become a martyr to love by pulling three of the crackers. He finally loses all hope of ever seeing Anna-Luise again and regrets that if only he had 'believed in a God' he could have dreamt of a '*jour le plus long*' for both of them: 'It was as though my small half-belief had somehow shrivelled with the sight of Doctor Fischer's body. Evil was as dead as a dog and why should goodness have more immortality than evil?'. Jones can now only appreciate the threat of evil rather than the love and forgiveness of absolute goodness. As his despair deepens, even death itself seems ultimately to 'lose its point' (142). Jones's final tragedy is cast not as a loss of religious faith but rather as the waning of his appreciation of human mortality since he can no longer hope to follow Anna-Luise if it is only 'into nothingness' (142), Jones concludes that without an understanding of death, which has become an 'irrelevance' (143) to him, life becomes meaningless.

The Last Phase (1981–1991)

Following on from the account of his early years in *A Sort of Life* (1971), Greene published in 1980 another autobiographical volume, *Ways of Escape*, drawing upon various newspaper and journal articles and the introductions for The Bodley Head edition of his works, detailing the contexts within which his books had been 'conceived and written' (9). Compiled 50 years after Greene's first published novel *The Man Within* (1929), there is a sense in *Ways of Escape* of an author offering his own assessment of the most important elements of his prolific writing career. Predictably, religious issues frequently figure in a variety of moving and comic contexts. Recalling his correspondence with Herbert Read during his terminal illness, he is struck by a reference to Lourdes from this 'most Christian of unbelievers' (43–4). From his Hollywood days he recounts David Selznick's madcap plans for a film of a life of St Mary Magdalene (67); and Sam Zimbalist's unease over the script for a remake of Ben Hur because he felt that the Crucifixion led to an anticlimax in the action (68). *Ways of Escape* also analyses the impact on Greene's writings and private life of his unsought reputation, in that 'detestable term', as a 'Catholic writer'. Categorizing himself as 'not a Catholic writer but a writer who happens to be a Catholic' (74), he recalls how as a young convert he had not been 'emotionally moved' but merely 'intellectually convinced'. He never intended to bring together his professional life and his religious views and sought to preserve them entirely separately. But political and international affairs in Mexico and Spain, described as 'clumsy life again at her stupid work', had ensured otherwise. He began to scrutinize more closely the effects of 'faith on action' since Catholicism was no longer merely 'symbolic' but much closer now to 'death in the afternoon': 'It was in Mexico too that I discovered some emotional belief, among the empty and ruined churches from which the priests had been excluded, at the secret Masses of Las Casas celebrated without the Sanctus bell' (75–6).

Ways of Escape offers a miscellany of other brief but telling religious observations. It describes the spiritual solace of confession for Catholics during the London Blitz (112); Greene's scepticism over the doctrine of 'eternal punishment' (121); the natural proximity to Catholicism of the native spirituality of the African Kikuyu tribe; how rebels during the Mau Mau rebellion often converted to Catholicism in the condemned cell, 'when hope was over' (202)

and the deeply ingrained Catholicism of Polish society (223). On a personal level, Greene laments how in the years between *The Heart of the Matter* and *The End of the Affair* he found himself 'used and exhausted by the victims of religion'. Although he knew that he lacked any 'apostolic mission', an unending stream of pleas for spiritual guidance left him feeling like a 'man without medical knowledge in a village struck with plague' (253–4). Surprisingly, his only positive words relate to 'Catholic and Marxist critics' who often seem more 'perceptive' and less 'subjective' in their criticisms:

> I wrote to the Communist paper that as a Catholic I considered myself able to treat loss of faith just as freely as discovery of faith, and I trusted that if I were a Communist writer in his country I would be able to take as a character a lapsed Communist. (254)

Despite such long-standing concerns over his literary identity among Catholic readers, *Monsignor Quixote* (1982) offers a sustained meditation – by turns comic, tragic and celebratory – upon the interaction of institutional and personal Catholicism within the confines of a state where secular and religious authorities uneasily co-exist.[6] The 1978 Christmas issue of the Catholic journal the *Tablet* included Greene's short story, 'How Father Quixote Became a Monsignor', later revised as the opening chapter of *Monsignor Quixote*. Set in post-Franco Spain, the novel traces the picaresque adventures of the unworldly Father Quixote of El Toboso who, in a playful blurring of fiction and reality, is supposedly a descendant of his namesake in Cervantes' *Don Quixote*. Greene's humble parish priest is unexpectedly elevated to the rank of monsignor through the influence of a visiting curial bishop from Rome, whom he impresses by fixing his broken-down car (a mechanical 'miracle' achieved by filling the empty petrol tank). His pompous local bishop is unimpressed by this unmerited promotion, and he forces Quixote temporarily to leave his parish. Quixote sets out for a leisurely summer peregrination in the company of the communist ex-mayor of the town, Enrique Zancas, whom he nicknames 'Sancho'. They travel around the Spanish countryside in Quixote's battered old Seat 600, fondly known as 'Rocinante', after Don Quixote's beloved horse. The scenic descriptions of the novel, along with the endless theological discussions between Quixote and Sancho, are based upon Greene's travels in Spain with his close friend, Father Leopoldo Durán, a Catholic priest and former lecturer in English literature at the University of Madrid.

Exploiting the traditional comic device of the 'innocent abroad', *Monsignor Quixote* is rich in tiltings at theological windmills and its dialogues explore numerous issues of ecclesiastical authority and Catholic religious practices. Its well-meaning hero is led into potentially threatening situations, including farcical moments in a brothel, a pornographic film and a public toilet where he is obliged to hear confession. Happily, Quixote is always protected from harm by his genuine innocence and trust in the essential decency of humanity. The novel is light-hearted in tone, and its deftly executed set pieces ally it with the comic impulse of *Our Man in Havana* and *Travels With My Aunt*. But from a theological perspective *Monsignor Quixote* marks a distinct and culminating shift in Greene's exploration of literary representations of personal spirituality.

From the 1970s onwards, Greene became preoccupied with the aging process. He wrote to Catherine Walston in December 1975: 'Death as one gets old seems more & more a friend.'[7] *Monsignor Quixote* offers, in this respect, a meditation upon his own impending mortality and marks a theological shift in Greene's writings from rational scepticism towards a more hopeful perspective on the possibility of redemption. The novel gnaws away at the supposed potency of human rationality in favour of a resigned half-acceptance of the mysteries of Divine compassion. It also confirms how in the literary works of his final decade, Greene increasingly tends to cast a nostalgic eye over the spiritual preoccupations, religious iconography and half-beliefs of his earlier writings.

After a series of ludicrous escapades during his first period of travels, Quixote's local bishop has him kidnapped and brought back to his parish. With the help of Sancho he manages to escape and they head off in Rocinante to Galicia. As in Cervantes's original, this second phase of the novel adopts a much darker tone. The picaresque excursions of the first section are transformed in the second into a testing form of pilgrimage. As he bids farewell to his loyal housekeeper, Teresa, Quixote answers prophetically her enquiry as to his plans, by saying that he hopes, 'God willing', to have a 'long rest in a quiet place' (188). When, from habit, he raises his hand to 'make the sign of the cross in blessing', he finds that he cannot complete it. A distinctly Greeneian thought flits through his mind as he wonders why whenever he mentions belief he senses the 'shadow of disbelief haunting' (189) him. It becomes clear as his travels continue that disbelief, doubt and half-belief are all unavoidable attributes of human rationality. When Sancho explains that he had first been drawn to Quixote because he seemed to be 'without doubts', his friend reminds him that priests are often no different in this respect from their parishioners in being 'riddled by doubts':

I am sure of nothing, not even of the existence of God, but doubt is not treachery as you Communists seem to think. Doubt is human. Oh, I want to believe that it is all true – and that want is the only certain thing I feel. (197)

The habitual way of counteracting doubt for Quixote is rooted in his observance of daily private devotions and the familiar words of the Catholic Tridentine liturgy. The power of prayer and his ministry as a priest become of the utmost importance to him when he finally reads a letter from his local bishop, stuffed into his pocket and then forgotten when he was fleeing his 'house arrest'. This heartless missive issues a *Suspensión a Divinis*, a formal suspension of his duties which forbids him from saying Mass, either in public or private, or from hearing confessions unless in an 'extreme emergency'.

Quixote, however, is determined to continuing saying Mass in his room since, as he explains to Sancho, he remains a priest: 'but a priest only to myself' (200).

While in Galicia, Quixote and Sancho stock up on supplies at a vineyard. The owner tells them how his grandson, a priest, has been driven from his parish because he refuses to charge his poorest parishioners a thousand pesetas for Responses for the Dead. A pervasive sense of veniality within the Spanish Church is confirmed when they then hear about a local festival in honour of Our Lady, at which the priest auctions the honour of carrying her statue in the procession to the four highest bidders. When they arrive there, Quixote finds that the priest has become even greedier by auctioning this year not four but six places. This ancient Catholic ceremony is so debased that the crowd is now expected to plaster the statue with large-denomination banknotes. Quixote is horrified and thinks: 'Was it for this she saw her son die in agony? To collect money? To make a priest rich?' (219). Determined to prevent this sacrilege, he tears some notes from the statue but is accidentally hit on the head by the swinging processional censer. In the ensuing chaos, the statue comes crashing down and he is denounced by an angry Mexican statue-carrier as a 'Thief! Blasphemer! Imposter!' (222). Dazed and with a bleeding head-wound, Quixote is dragged away and driven by Sancho towards the sanctuary of the Trappist monastery at Osera.

This farcical fracas marks the end of the novel's hitherto predominant mode of narrative realism. The final chapter of its second part, 'How Monsignor Quixote Rejoined His Ancestor', is divided into four sub-sections and alternates picaresque comedy with more dreamlike and elegiac interludes. In the first section the Osera monastery is described in expressionistic terms. Its ancient and battered statues assume an 'appearance of life, as sad memories do, when the dark has fallen'. Almost as though the monastery is a half-way staging point between earth and heaven, Greene compares it to an 'abandoned island' on which some new colonialists are trying to 'make a home in the ruins of a past civilization' (225). The second section briefly revives the comic mode as one of the Trappists, Father Leopoldo, cooks an unappetizing meal for the monastery's only guest, a Professor Pilbeam, whose virtually untouched plates are brought back to the kitchen by an unnamed lay brother.

Through this unlikely trinity of characters, the novel's rich sense of comedy again briefly flickers into life. The lay brother by-passes his vow of silence by the cunning eloquence of his winking, and Father Leopoldo turns out to be a frustrated Descartian rationalist and debater who finds himself stranded in a monastery dedicated to silence. Pilbeam, a professor of Hispanic Studies at Notre Dame University, is regarded as the greatest living expert on the Jesuit saint Ignatius Loyola. But he is really a dour pedant who deems Cervantes' imaginative richness too 'fanciful' and remains a Catholic only because he couldn't be bothered to 'change the label' of his birth. He cares nothing for his saint's spirituality and instead hopes to find hitherto undiscovered documents about Ignatius's life – 'Facts are what I like' (229). As Father Leopoldo and Pilbeam idly discuss the difficulties (especially for Catholics) of distinguishing between fact and fiction, they hear sounds of gunshots and a crash outside the monastery. The Guardia Civil, pursuing Quixote and Sancho after their debacle over the procession of Our Lady, have shot out Rocinante's tyres, causing the car to crash into the wall of the church. Sancho is left bloodied and the semi-conscious Quixote is carried into the monastery on a mattress. As he is taken through the church and up the nave towards the guest room, he hopefully asks if he might say a Mass but, instead, he is given a strong sedative.

In the third section Quixote awakes in the early hours and is still delirious, muttering muddled quotations from Cervantes and promising Sancho, 'Come with me, and you will find the kingdom' (238). Rising from his sickbed with the triumphant incantation, 'Bugger the bishop', Quixote takes some staggering steps and solemnly pronounces: 'By this hopping . . . you can recognize love' (239). Politely seeking directions to the moon-lit church from a painted wooden statue, he is followed by his apostolic trinity of Sancho, Father Leopoldo and Pilbeam. He steps up to the altar and initiates an 'oddly truncated' version of the Tridentine Latin Mass (240). Much of his native speech lapses into Babel-like confusion ('Lamb of God, but the goats, the goats', 241), although key phrases from the Tridentine liturgy remain crystal-clear ('*Hoc est enim corpus meum*', '*Hic est enim calix sanguinis mei*' and Pinkie's '*Agnus Dei qui tollis peccata mundi*'). Through this reverential parody of the Tridentine Mass, Quixote finally achieves a long-desired 'truth on his deathbed' (16). As he gives an imaginary communion host to his trusty compañero, Sancho, Quixote collapses into his arms and dies in a final, triumphant confirmation of his priestly ministry.

The fourth section of this chapter concludes with Sancho and Father Leopoldo discussing whether Monsignor Quixote had really celebrated Mass. Pilbeam predictably insists on the fact that there was no consecration, no Host and no wine, while Father Leopoldo observes that Quixote 'obviously believed in the presence of the bread and wine. Which of us was right?' (245). The communist Mayor is moved enough to admit that when he was young he had once 'partly believed in a God, and a little of that superstition still remains' (246). As he leaves the monastery, Sancho wonders how hate, even for someone like Franco, tends to fade with death while his love for Father Quixote may ultimately transcend mortality. All that lasts of their friendship is 'love' and the final words of the novel simply reiterate the culminating question of all religious belief-systems: 'to what end?' (248).

Roger Sharrock suggests that the Italian curial bishop who sets in motion Quixote's adventures may be interpreted as the disguised presence of the author himself.[8] Certainly, this bishop physically resembles Greene and shares his partiality to Spanish wines, cognac and cheeses. It may have simply amused the author to cast himself in such a disguise as the visitor to his fictional El Toboso (there is also a real El Toboso village in Spain) who initiates the novel's plot. As Father Leopoldo comments when discussing Quixote's last hours with Pilbeam: 'Fact and fiction again . . . one can't distinguish with any certainty' (244). In Cervantes's *Don Quixote*, the Don's (perhaps imaginary) beloved is known as Dulcinea del Toboso; and it is ironically noted of the monsignor's plain housekeeper, Teresa, that no one in El Toboso had ever even thought of nicknaming her 'Dulcinea' (7). Similarly, when the curial bishop admits to being an admirer of Cervantes, Quixote humbly notes that his local bishop dismisses his immortal creation as a mere 'fiction'. However, the curial bishop concludes wisely: 'Perhaps we are all fictions, father, in the mind of God' (16).

Some of Greene's favourite religious authors, including St Francis de Sales, St Augustine and St John of the Cross, are loved by Quixote (236). Similarly, ideas drawn in the novel from progressive post-Vatican II theologians and responses to Pope Paul VI's *Humanae Vitae* (1968) on sex and birth control by Edward Schillebeeckx and Hans Küng echo Greene's current reading. On a more sustained level, references in *Monsignor Quixote* to three figures of especial importance to Greene – St Teresa of Avila, St Thérèse of Lisieux and the Spanish philosopher and writer Miguel de Unamuno (1864–1936) – are worth exploring further since their cumulative impact on the spiritual preoccupations of the novel is considerable.

When a replacement, Father Herrera, is sent to El Toboso by the local bishop to take over Quixote's parish, they discuss their preferred theological reading. As a recent seminarian, Father Herrera regards *Moral Theology* by the German theologian, Father Heribert Jone, as an easy-reference handbook for busy parish priests. In contrast Quixote finds greater spiritual depth in the imaginative potency of 'St John of the Cross, St Teresa, St Francis de Sales. And the Gospels' (32). Later in the novel (87), Sancho cunningly confuses two Guardia officers by claiming that he and Quixote are on the way to Avila to say prayers for Franco before the ring finger of St Teresa, preserved there in a convent (and visited by Greene in July 1976). Franco was a pious Roman Catholic and had kept the saint's hand as a holy relic by his bedside until his death in 1975.[9]

Sancho eventually decides to avoid Avila, suspecting that the Guardia Civil will be looking out for them there. He muses to Quixote that even if he could suspend his 'profound disbelief', he would still find it difficult to believe that God had ever wanted these two officers to be born: 'not to speak of Hitler and the Generalissimo – or even if you like Stalin. If only their poor parents had been permitted to use a contraceptive' (91). Predictably, these thoughts prompt discussions about whether sperm have souls (92) and contemporary Catholic attitudes towards birth control. Quixote soon wearies of such endless arguments, and they happily set off again on their travels. When Sancho asks if he has ever fallen in love with a woman, Quixote's mind turns from St Teresa of Avila to another saint of that name. Although he has never been tempted into a personal relationship with a woman, he fosters a special devotion to a 'girl called Martin' (96), the family name of St Thérèse of Lisieux, whose letters were a great consolation to him during his struggles with his local bishop. That evening they arrive at the city of Segovia and find an *albergue* near the Church of St Martin. Its name again reminds him of this saint who had been a favourite of Greene's wife and is frequently referred to in his fictions. Quixote prefers to think of her as 'Señorita Martin' (97) rather than as St Thérèse or

'The Little Flower', fancying that this ploy might help him to catch her ear amidst thousands of other prayers addressed to her.

As a young man, Quixote had once dreamt of studying at the great University of Salamanca (15). He is delighted to learn as they leave Segovia that Sancho wishes to pay a visit to Salamanca, even though he remains unaware of the true purpose of their 'pilgrimage' (101) there. Quixote wishes to see the lecture room in which St John of the Cross listened to the teachings of Fray Luis de León and, again blending fact with fiction, he amuses himself by imagining that Fray Luis might have met Don Quixote. Sancho then admits that he had once studied at Salamanca and attended the lectures of Miguel de Unamuno y Jugo, who was Professor of Greek at the university and became its rector in 1901. Like Greene, Unamuno explores in his writings the tensions between reason and Christian faith. His most famous work, *The Tragic Sense of Life* (included on the *Index Librorum Prohibitorum* until Vatican II) viewed the finality of human mortality as a tragedy that cannot be comprehended or justified by reason alone. Greene also admired Unamuno for his heroic self-sacrifice in readily involving himself in political activism and controversy. He first lost his post as rector of the University of Salamanca in 1914 for political reasons, and again in 1924 when he was exiled to Fuerteventura in the Canary Islands for criticizing the military dictatorship of General Primo de Rivera. He lived as a political exile in France until Rivera's death in 1930. Returning to Salamanca he was reappointed as rector in 1931 but was again denounced in 1936 and removed from his post for his opposition to Franco's Falangists. He was placed under house arrest and died on 31 December of that year in Salamanca, soon after the outbreak of the Spanish Civil War.

Greene takes his readers to the house in Salamanca (recalling his own visit with Father Durán), where Unamuno had died and to his grave in the cemetery on the edge of the city. Unlike Franco's grandiose mausoleum in the 'Valley of the Fallen', which Quixote had previously inspected with some distaste (78–9), Unamuno's final resting place turns out to be a simple box, denoted only by the number 340 in a long white wall of burial caskets. In *Ways of Escape* Greene recalls reading Unamuno's *The Life of Don Quixote and Sancho* (1905) in which Saint Ignatius of Loyola is compared to Cervantes's heroic knight. He also notes how Unamuno regarded Don Quixote as endowed with almost Christ-like qualities, echoing Father Leopoldo's comment at the end of the novel: 'one of our great modern philosophers compared Saint Ignatius to Don Quixote. They had a lot in common' (229).[10]

Greene and Unamuno also had much in common since both questioned the irreconcilable tension between reason and belief and regarded doubt as essential to the pursuit of faith. Like Greene, Unamuno viewed suffering as central to the human condition and argued in *The Tragic Sense of Life*:

> Suffering tells us we exist; suffering tells us those who love exist; suffering tells us the world we live in exists, and suffering tells us that God exists and suffers; and this is the suffering of anguish, the anguish to survive and be eternal.

It is anguish which reveals God to us and makes us place our love in Him. To believe in God means to love Him, and to love Him is to sense His suffering and have compassion for Him.[11]

Viewed within this context, Quixote's travels may be read as a tragicomic pilgrimage towards death and the celebration of a hopeful trust in Divine love. Such sentiments may or may not have matched Greene's personal thoughts as he drafted *Monsignor Quixote*, but throughout his adult life he had taken refuge, like his fictional creation Morin, in the soothing security of intellectual uncertainty. Even before his conversion to Catholicism, he had written in May 1925 to his future wife Vivien: 'When I'm just going to die . . . I daresay that I shall turn a trifle religious, as a kind of insurance, in case there is something in it . . . You see I haven't the courage of my non-faith.'[12] These words, although penned five decades earlier, seem relevant to the conclusion of *Monsignor Quixote* when a humble parish priest, transformed into an unwilling monsignor, enacts a devout parody of the sacrament of communion, before taking the invisible host on his tongue and raising the invisible chalice to drink some of the invisible wine (242). As Father Leopoldo observes, Quixote clearly believed in the living presence of the 'bread and wine' but, for those observing this final sacramental drama – Sancho, Father Leopoldo, Pilbeam and the readers of the novel – it is impossible 'logically' (245) to disprove or prove such matters.

It is perhaps surprising to discover that this comic but theologically profound novel was written under highly stressful circumstances. Greene had first met Yvonne Cloetta in 1959 and, living near his flat in Antibes, she became his closest companion for the last 25 years of his life. He grew fond of her eldest daughter, Martine, but from 1978 until 1984 was drawn into a series of acrimonious disputes with her husband, Daniel Guy, from whom she was seeking a divorce and custody of their daughter, Alexandra. Guy had been imprisoned and Greene became convinced that he was heavily involved in the Nice mafia. Concerned that Guy was trying to manipulate the courts over Martine's divorce, Greene wrote impassioned letters of denunciation to the authorities and the English press. His defence of Martine culminated in a bilingual pamphlet, *J'Accuse* (echoing Emile Zola's intervention in the Dreyfus case), claiming that the thuggish Guy was seeking favour from corrupt officials. Lawsuits inevitably followed, and Guy was awarded damages against Greene and his publisher. Greene received anonymous death threats and Father Durán comments:

I knew two Grahams: one belonged to the period before 1979 and the battle with the mafia; the other, to the period afterwards. The struggle against the wretched mafia affected his nerves and his sleep more than ever . . . one had to bear in mind the colossal mental and psychological pressure on the man during those ghastly years. He was very tired and he would get upset much more easily.[13]

Nor, despite advancing infirmities, was this the limit to Greene's involvements between 1975 and 1985 in the 'dangerous edge of things'. Although comfortably based at Antibes, Greene remained an indefatigable traveller and an outspoken commentator on international affairs. In addition to trips to Belize, Costa Rica and Cuba, and twice acting as an intermediary in political kidnappings in El Salvador, he became embroiled in Panamanian politics through his friendship with its dictator, General Omar Torrijos Herrera. He even agreed to be a member of the official Panamanian delegation to Washington in 1977, when a treaty was ratified between President Carter and Torrijos, in the presence of such controversial figures as General Pinochet of Chile, General Stroessner of Paraguay and General Videla of Argentina (104). Greene's personal admiration for Torrijos, who was killed in a suspicious plane crash in August 1981, is recorded in his volume of autobiographical journalism, *Getting to Know the General* (1984), which bravely voices the unsubstantiated rumour that the CIA had planted a bomb on his aircraft.[14] He was also sympathetic to the cause of the Sandinista guerrillas in Nicaragua, not only visiting the country but later splitting the Spanish royalties of *Monsignor Quixote* between the Sandinistas and the monastery at Osera which features in the novel.[15]

When recalling his experiences in Panama, Greene adopts a self-reflective tone as regards his interests as a writer. The second chapter of *Getting to Know the General* addresses the question as to why Spanish and Latin American affairs had so long preoccupied him. He describes how he first used a Spanish setting for his early, unpublished novel, 'The Episode', dealing with Carlist refugees and their exiled Spanish general (also called Torrijos). Like *Monsignor Quixote*, his third published (but later suppressed) novel, *Rumour at Nightfall* (1931), was set in Spain; and the landscapes of Mexico, Cuba, Haiti, Paraguay and Argentina were all familiar to his loyal readership. The attraction of these torrid worlds, Greene explains, lay in their ready access to the ultimate duality for any writer – the timeless and culminating clash in their political oppositions between 'life and death' (11).

Religious concerns offer at first a sporadic, but then much more sustained, element in *Getting to Know the General*. Apart from an earnest native who wishes to talk with the 'Católico' Greene about 'Religión' (52), the role of the Catholic Church in socialist Panama plays no part in the first part (dealing with his 1976 visit) of the book. But in the second part (his 1977 trip) Greene's characteristic fascination with religious paradox springs into life through the presence of his memorable guide, Professor José de Jesús Martínez (known as Chuchu), a sergeant in General Torrijos's security guard and also a poet, a linguist and a former professor of Marxist philosophy and mathematics. Chuchu's habitual blending of intellectual rationalism with the tastes of a melancholy hedonist strongly appealed to the like-minded Greene. In darkly comic vein, the personal theology of the often childlike Chuchu recalls the adolescent Pinkie in his habitual cry: 'I believe in the Devil. I don't believe in God.' Similarly, his bizarre attempt to prove the Devil exists by 'pushing at a swing door in the wrong direction' (75) connects him with the engaging religious charlatans of *Travels With My Aunt*.

The inert complacency of the established Catholic Church is condemned in *Getting to Know the General* through Greene's scathing comments on Archbishop McGrath of Panama. When he visits the small village of Coclesito, he is impressed to find that General Torrijos has built himself a small house there but, in stark contrast, the local church is sadly decaying and no priest has visited it during the previous year. Inevitably, he thinks disapprovingly of Archbishop McGrath and acknowledges that in the Panama of the 1980s the natives looked not to the Church but to the General for practical help (96–7). When he is obliged to listen to one of the archbishop's personal prayers, especially written for the signing of the US-Panama treaty, his mind is filled only with thoughts of 'chickens in the aisle of the ruined church' which he never visited. Greene concludes that the derelict church at Coclesito was in the 'same country' but not the 'same world as the Archbishop' (103).

In contrast to Archbishop McGrath, Greene is greatly impressed when on his 1978 trip to Panama he visits George Cadle Price (b.1919), the Prime Minister of Belize, a man who, General Torrijos advises him, wished to become a 'priest, not a prime minister' (120). As a person, Greene finds Price a 'shy, reserved man with the touch of uneasy humility one often finds in priests'. Their discussions cover theology and literature and he is delighted to find they share an interest in the Jesuit philosopher Teilhard de Chardin and the Swiss Catholic theologian Hans Küng (125). Price becomes in *Getting to Know the General* Greene's projection of an ideal model for a dedicated and incorruptible Catholic socialist leader in South America. As a young man Price's political and pastoral principles had been formulated by the 1891 encyclical of Pope Leo XIII, *Rerum Novarum*, on the 'Rights and Duties of Capital and Labour', with its dominant concern for the working classes. Price thinks of Belize, Greene suggests, as though it is his 'parish' and, as a former seminarian who was unable to become a priest because of the needs of his family when his father died, Price still lives as a 'priest might live' (126), rising each day at 5.30 a.m for Mass and Communion before resuming his official duties. Price served as Prime Minister of Belize from 1981 to 1984 (and again from 1989 to 1993) and was named in 1982 as a Privy Councillor to the United Kingdom. After almost five decades of interest in Latin American affairs, Greene finally found in George Price a living expression of his dream for a unified Catholic and socialist guardianship of the rights of all citizens, both rich and poor.

Spain was once intended to be the setting for Greene's *The Tenth Man* (1985), an ingenious novella about a double imposture which Greene had begun in December 1937 and completed in 1945. It had then, supposedly, been forgotten in Metro-Goldwyn-Meyer's archives until it was discovered almost forty years later by a researcher. However, Michael Shelden argues, this was something of a publishing escapade (happily promoted by Greene) since he had already been in correspondence in 1967 about the possible publication of this novella.[16] The Spanish Civil War location was modernized to occupied Second World War France, where ten prisoners face the atrocity of decimation. The richest, a lawyer called Jean-Louis Chavel, draws the longest match and swaps his entire fortune with another prisoner, a young man called Michel 'Janvier' Mangeot, in return for his own life.

Some years later, after being freed and without possessions, Chavel anonymously visits the other man's family who now possess all of his fortune. Having assumed the name Jean-Louis Charlot, he meets Janvier's twin sister, Thérèse, who is consumed by hatred for what Chavel did to her brother. She bitterly assumes that as a clever lawyer he will still be able to cheat his way into heaven when he dies with the 'sacrament in his mouth, forgiving all his enemies. He won't die before he can cheat the Devil' (85). Through her brother's death Thérèse has lost her Catholic faith and, as he falls in love with her, Chavel/ Charlot wonders if by removing her hatred he could give her once again the 'possibility of salvation' (98). The plot is further complicated when a down-at-heel actor, collaborator and murderer called Monsieur Carosse turns up at the house. Carosse has overheard another of the prisoners talking about Chavel's deathly deal with Janvier and decides to try his luck by coming to his native village and claiming to be the returning Chavel. Carosse gradually assumes a devilish identity as he inveigles his way into Thérèse's sympathies, liberally acting out a Mauriac-like role of a sanctimonious sinner with his repeated mantras of 'God bless you' and 'God may forgive you' (141).

Carosse persuades Thérèse that Chavel's account of the prison contract with Janvier is false and that his fabricated one is the true version. Delighted by his own malevolent wit, he orders Chavel to leave. He explains that his assumption of Chavel's identity had proved a masterstroke because the post-war French government had only two days earlier decreed that property exchanges made during the German occupation are to be regarded as illegal if one party now rejects them. Hence, Carosse can claim Chavel's entire estate by simply denouncing the contract made with Janvier in the prison cell. The real Chavel finally sees Carosse in his true identity as the Devil himself, on the 'axis of the globe offering him all the kingdoms of the world' (143). Earlier, the local parish priest had come with the 'sacrament in his bag' (130) to give the last rites to the dying Madame Mangeot. Chavel then realizes that both God and the Devil had been simultaneously present in the house: 'God came into the house in an attaché case, and when God came the Enemy was always present. He was God's shadow: he was the bitter proof of God' (143). Carosse's laughter at his own deviousness sounds to Chavel as though he is in the 'company of the Devil' (144). The denouement of the story becomes an overt struggle between the forces of good and evil as Chavel feels divinely inspired to protect Thérèse from this wicked scheme: 'even the gifts of the Enemy were gifts also of God. The Enemy was unable to offer any gift without God simultaneously offering the great chance of rejection' (144–5). Carosse finally shoots Chavel who dies with the solace of knowing that he has finally purged Thérèse of her hatred. Through this self-sacrifice he also perhaps atones for his original sin towards her brother Janvier and ensures that the good side of God finally triumphs over His own dark side.

Greene's last substantial work published during his lifetime, *The Captain and the Enemy* (1988), recalls elements from his first published novel, *The Man Within*, in a strikingly self-referential way. This tale, partly set in the Panama of General Torrijos, recounts how its schoolboy protagonist falls into the company of an older man, known only as the Captain, a slippery trickster who recalls Greene's numerous fictional charlatans. The Captain eventually dies in an unsuccessful attempt, betrayed by the CIA, to bomb President Somoza of Nicaragua. These political thriller elements clearly grew from Greene's interests in South American politics, as detailed in *Getting to Know the General*. A comparison of the respective hero and heroine of *The Captain and the Enemy* and *The Man Within* also demonstrates just how powerfully his first published novel was occupying Greene's mind as he composed his last novel. It is as though this element of *The Captain and the Enemy* was intended as an implicit *hommage* to his earliest published novel. Hence, this last work offers a neatly circular concluding act of authorial closure to a long and successful literary career. At the end of his 60-year journey as a writer, Greene finds himself face to face with his youthful self.

In *The Man Within* the hero, Andrews, escapes from a hated school-life and meets a mercurial seafaring smuggler, Carlyon. Similarly, in *The Captain and the Enemy* a school-boy, Victor 'Jim' Baxter, whose absent father is persistently described as the 'Devil' (12, 25, 30, 53, 56, 70, etc.), also falls into the company of a mysterious (and nominally seafaring) stranger, the Captain, who takes him away from an uncongenial school-life. Carlyon and the Captain have much in common, even if the former operates as a smuggler along the Sussex shorelines during the early-1800s while the latter moves between the suburban anonymity of Camden Town, London, and the fraught modern worlds of Panama and Nicaragua. Like Carylon who seems untrammelled by conventional codes, the Captain offers an attractively fatalistic form of personal morality gleaning from hard-won experience. He recalls, for example, the kindness of monks at a monastery in the Pyrenees when during the war he was escaping to Spain from the Germans: 'When you are not a good man yourself you respect a good man . . . A good man teaches a lot of nonsense and a bad man teaches truth, but what the hell is the difference when you come to die?' (61).

Two mysteriously iconic young women dominate the emotional and spiritual sensibilities of Andrews and Baxter. In the earlier novel, Elizabeth lacks a solidly fleshed-out character and seems intended more to embody a sense of moral self-sufficiency. As a resolute young woman of apparently saint-like purity, Elizabeth recalls the potent virtue of St Thérèse of Lisieux, as she lives a nun-like existence in a small cottage set within the pastoral isolation of the Sussex Downs. In *The Captain and the Enemy* this inspirational role is taken by a devoted young woman called Liza (modernizing her earlier counterpart's name). She also lives a solitary existence, this time as befits the novel's urban context in a basement flat in Camden Town. Liza is more careworn by the world's vicissitudes than Elizabeth; and, as later revealed, she has even been exploited briefly as the casual mistress of Jim's devilish father who made her have an abortion (99–101). Nevertheless, she remains an unwaveringly loyal figure towards the Captain and the boy. Recalling Elizabeth's habitual biblical reading, Liz asks Jim to read sections from the Bible out loud to her every Sunday (69). Although the 1929 Elizabeth is heavily idealized and the 1988 Liza is worldlier, both young women are consistently placed, both metaphorically and spiritually, above the adventure-story narratives of their respective novels. In seeking to create an idealized female figure for his last published fiction, Greene seems instinctively to have turned back to the ideal of female virtue embodied in the heroine of his first published novel.

This self-referential circularity back to *The Man Within* embedded in *The Captain and the Enemy* is reinforced by the memories of the adult Jim (now a disillusioned hack journalist) of his own early writings. As Liza lies dying in hospital after a road accident, he returns to her flat and finds there one of his long-neglected manuscripts, variously described (like *The Man Within*) as a 'story', or 'fiction' or 'autobiography'. He recalls how in his youth he had harboured a 'vain ambition' of becoming a 'real writer' (84) and how years later he had started to revise this 'history which I had written of my childhood' (105–6). He even describes the Captain at one point, recalling Carlyon, as like a character who could exist only on the page of a 'youthful manuscript' (125). Carlyon is a pirate and smuggler and, when in Panama, Baxter and the Captain (now known as Señor Smith) recall fond memories (shared by Greene) of their boyhood admiration for the piracies of Morgan and Drake and the latter's raid on the 'Spanish treasure house in Portobello' (135) on the Panama coast. The third part of the novel, set in Panama, echoes numerous elements of Greene's more recent trips to that country, even to the adoption of his habitual flight-route there via Amsterdam and the naming of Baxter's guide (and CIA informant) as 'Quigly', a name specifically noted in *Getting to Know the General* as one that Greene might reuse 'one day, in God knows what story' (103).

Baxter's words at the close of the third part of the novel mark the end of his (and perhaps Greene's) career as a writer, as he symbolically throws the manuscript account of his life in the wastepaper basket: 'I write a line under all this scroll . . . The line means Finis' (180). Later examining this manuscript for secret, encoded meanings, the local security officer, Colonel Martinez, seems to comment upon the dangers of a literary figure (like Greene) encroaching into the dangerous world of Latin American politics: 'The boy seems to have had a certain talent and it's a pity he didn't stick to writing, for writing is a safe occupation' (183). Martinez reminds readers of *The Captain and the Enemy* that a writer's published works will always live on beyond the natural life of their creator. This is proved true even for Baxter since in the last words of the novel it becomes clear that he, like the Captain, has also been killed in an 'accident' (189).

Notes

Preface

1. Greene's (mis)quotations from Robert Browning's 'Bishop Blougram's Apology', in a letter to Evelyn Waugh, see Watts, 69; and Cardinal John Henry Newman's *The Idea of a University*, see Ker, 115.
2. The Pollinger papers are in the Harry Ransom Center, University of Texas at Austin; and the Elliott Collection, Brotherton Library, University of Leeds.
3. *A Sort of Life*, 114, 124.
4. *Ibid.*, 54–68.
5. *Dream Diary*, vii. See *A Sort of Life*, 73–6.
6. Quoted in Sherry, I.97; Watts, 11–12.
7. *A Sort of Life*, 84.
8. *Ibid.*, 73.
9. *The Other Man*, 30.

Chapter 1

1. Sherry, I.254.
2. See *The Other Man*, 41.
3. Sherry, I.3–4.
4. *Collected Essays*, 85–6.
5. Jarrett, 21, 53.
6. Sherry, I.127.
7. *The Cherwell* (22 November 1924), 11.
8. Sherry, I.168–71; Shelden, 92–4; Mockler, 52–3; *Babbling April*, copy in the Elliott Collection, Brotherton Library, University of Leeds, dedicated: 'To Helen Laws from Graham Greene. Feb. 26' (the month of Greene's conversion to Catholicism).
9. Shakespeare provides the title In *The Name of Action* (1930), 'and lose the name of action' (Hamlet); and lines from Eliot's 'The Hollow Men', 'Between the idea/And the reality/Between the motion/And the act/Falls the Shadow', form its epigraph.
10. *Ways of Escape*, 40.
11. See Sherry, I.141–2 for Greene's 'Sitwellianism'.
12. *Ibid.*, I.164–5.
13. *Ibid.*, I.76–9, 83–4, 165–6, 314. The typescripts of 'Prologue to Pilgrimage' and 'Anthony Sant' are at the Harry Ransom Humanities Research Centre, University of Texas-Austin, Graham Greene Collection (box 27/7); and the Lauinger Library, Georgetown University, Special Collections, Catherine Walston and Graham Greene Papers (box 62/1).
14. Sherry, I.314–16. The typescript of 'The Episode' is at the Lauinger Library, Georgetown University, Special Collections, Walston and Greene Papers (box 57/1–6).
15. *Ibid.*, I.361.
16. *Ibid.*, I.316, 700.
17. *A Sort of Life*, 40.
18. West, 46.

19. See the proof copy of *Loser Takes All* (1955), sent to Vivien in October 1954 and bearing her manuscript corrections and emendations. Elliott Collection, Brotherton Library, University of Leeds.
20. Sherry, I.179–80.
21. *Ibid.*, I.369–71.
22. O'Prey, 16; Shelden, 116; Watts, 19.
23. See p. xxx.
24. Sherry, I.385.
25. *Ibid.*, I.352–3.
26. West, 35.
27. Elliott Collection, Brotherton Library, University of Leeds.
28. Brennan (2006), 134–57.
29. In 1922 Basil Blackwell took over the publication of the Dominican magazine, *Blackfriars*, when Vivien was working for the firm.
30. Now this author's copy.
31. This illustration is printed in *Les Annales de Ste Thérèse de Lisieux* (Lisieux, 1 June 1925).
32. Sherry, I.269–74; Shelden, 114–15.
33. Hoskins, 4.

Chapter 2

1. *A Sort of Life*, 143.
2. Johnstone, 66; O'Prey, 20.
3. Watts, 14; West, 26.
4. Sherry, I.382.
5. Watts, 22.
6. *Ibid.*, 22.
7. Shelden, 156.
8. Sherry, I.384, 391–2.
9. Watts, 124; *Ways of Escape*, 19.
10. *Conversations*, 46.
11. Stratford, 104–5, 172.
12. See Watts, 24 for publication figures.
13. Shelden, 97; Bergonzi (2006), 23; Watts, 25, 27; Sherry, I.407.
14. Sherry, I.408–9.
15. Quoted in Sherry, I.426–7.
16. Smith, 25.
17. *John Gerard. The Autobiography of an Elizabethan*, x.
18. Watts, 26.
19. *Ways of Escape*, 68.
20. *A Sort of Life*, 25.
21. *Ibid.*, 37; Watts, 32, 128–34. 206; Shelden, 70.
22. Bergonzi (2006), 40.
23. *Ways of Escape*, 32; Sherry, I.457–8.
24. Sherry, I.457.
25. Watts, 28–9.
26. Sherry, I.161–5.
27. Watts, 125, 145.
28. Sherry, I.463; West, 56–8.
29. O'Prey, 37.
30. Sherry, I.484.
31. *Ways of Escape*, 37.
32. Sherry, I.471–2, 500–1.
33. *Ways of Escape*, 36; Watts, 23.
34. *Ways of Escape*, 37.

35. Sherry, I.472.
36. *Ways of Escape*, 37.

Chapter 3

1. Quoted in Sherry, I.510.
2. Sherry, I.421.
3. Sykes, 109–10, 128, 136, 165–6.
4. Sherry, I.510–11, 570; West, 66–7.
5. Sherry, I.563–5. Greene's annotated copy of this edition, excising the problematic passages, is now in the Elliott Collection, Brotherton Library, University of Leeds.
6. Chesterton provided a preface to Vivien's poetic collection, *Little Wings* (1921) and also wrote 'A Meditation on the Manichees' (included in his 1933 study of St Thomas Aquinas). Greene published in 1944 a defence of Chesterton's *Orthodoxy* (1908) and Vivien carefully annotated her 1922 edition of *Orthodoxy* (now this author's copy).
7. Sherry, I.571–2, 580. Watts, 38.
8. *Ways of Escape*, 72.
9. Bergonzi (2006), 64.
10. West, 69–72.
11. Sherry, I.96. Cf. the pig in Greene's short-story, 'A Shocking Incident'.
12. Sherry, I.241.
13. Watts, 40; *Night and Day*, vii–xiv.
14. Sherry, I.649–50, 655–6.
15. Watts, 172.
16. *The Pleasure-Dome*, 75.
17. Greene had included the idea of a joint suicide pact in his short story, 'A Drive in the Country' (1937).

Chapter 4

1. Sherry, I.698.
2. *Ibid.*, I.656.
3. Sherry, I.663–4, 704; Brennan (2002b), 7–23.
4. *Articles of Faith*, xiv–vi, 1–18.
5. Sherry, I, 479, 576; II.14; Sharrock, 77.
6. Sherry, II.83–4; *Ways of Escape*, 76.
7. *Ibid.*, 88.
8. DeVitis, 37.
9. Sherry, I.700–1; II.29–31.
10. DeVitis, 77–8.
11. *The Other Man*, 136; Bergonzi (2007), 11–18.
12. De Vitis, 84.
13. Sherry, II.91–4.
14. Smith, 41.
15. Ben Greene's papers (private collection). Shelden, 20.
16. West, 94–103.

Chapter 5

1. Sherry, II.159–64, 166–87, 209, 211–12, 239–42.
2. *Ibid.*, II.257

3. *Ibid.*, II. 215, 225–6, 275, 283.
4. Stannard, 215–16.
5. *The Other Man*, 158.
6. Waugh (1979), 702.
7. Quoted in Sherry, II.293.
8. *Ibid.*, II.293; *Ways of Escape*, 121.
9. Quoted from 1948 edition; omitted from 2004 Vintage edition.
10. *Conversations*, ed. Donaghy, 62.
11. *Ways of Escape*, 113, 118, 120–1.
12. DeVitis, 87.
13. *Ways of Escape*, 120–1.
14. Quoted in Hynes, 107.
15. Quoted in Stannard, 216n.
16. Waugh (1983), 360–6; Bergonzi (2006), 121–4.
17. Sherry, II.243–51.
18. *Ibid.*, II.247, 304–6.
19. 29 October 1951, quoted in DeVitis, 93.
20. Lodge, 9–10.
21. *Ways of Escape*, 135; DeVitis, 94–9; Bergonzi (2006), 125–34.
22. 4 August 1948, quoted in Sherry, II.253.
23. Bosco, 61.
24. 1951 edition, 94; later revised to: 'gross liver spots which covered his left cheek', Vintage (2004), 63.
25. 1951 edition, 228; later revised to 'one insignificant spot', Vintage (2004), 154.
26. *Ways of Escape*, 137.
27. *Ibid.*, 137.
28. Watts, 93; Bosco, 46.
29. Sherry, II.450–4; Watts, 52–5.

Chapter 6

1. *Ways of Escape*, 219.
2. Sherry, II.335; III.73.
3. *Ways of Escape*, 140.
4. Sherry, II.339–53, 376–7, 441–2.
5. *Ibid.*, II.413, 472.
6. Bergonzi (2006), 148.
7. Bosco, 72.
8. *Ways of Escape*, 216; O'Prey, 109–110.
9. *Ways of Escape*, 217; Sherry, II.381–2; Watts, 38, 52, 202.
10. DeVitis, 46; Shelden, 214.
11. Quoted in Falk, 126.
12. Sherry, III.73–86.
13. *Ibid.*, III.12.
14. Watts, 71–2; Sherry, III.13–19.
15. See p. xxx.
16. DeVitis, 158; Waugh and *Life* article quoted in Sherry, III.29–30.
17. Sherry, III.131; Sharrock, 220.
18. DeVitis, 48; Bosco, 75.
19. Sherry III, 96–8, 113, 118, 125, 137, 141. Greene drafted another play set in a brothel, 'A House of Reputation'. See *Ibid.*, III.103, 301–10.
20. *Ibid.*, III.217; 209–10, 237.
21. Sharrock, 195.
22. Lodge, 10.
23. Brennan (2002a), 279.
24. Watts, 67.

25. DeVitis, 118.
26. Shelden, 70.
27. Watts, 73.
28. DeVitis, 162.

Chapter 7

1. Quoted in Sherry, III.375.
2. *Reflections*, 221–8.
3. Sherry, III.318–19.
4. DeVitis, 127, 129.
5. *Ways of Escape*, 270.
6. Sherry, III.405, 421.
7. Quoted in Falk, 156.
8. *Ways of Escape*, 274.
9. Sherry, III.403, 408–12.
10. *Ibid.*, III. 491, 493.
11. Watts, 74; Sherry, III.498–500; *Ways of Escape*, 286.
12. Bosco, 73.
13. *Ibid.*, 99.
14. *Reflections*, 257–65; West, 210–13.
15. West, 214.
16. *Reflections*, 266–70.
17. West, 214.
18. Sharrock, 238.
19. Sherry, III.510–14, 544.
20. Quoted in Sherry, III.526–7.
21. Watts, 104.
22. Bosco, 114.
23. *Ibid.*, 117.

Chapter 8

1. *Ways of Escape*, 238; Watts, 81.
2. Sherry, III.601–8; Watts, 79.
3. Bosco, 125.
4. *Ibid.*, 119, 123.
5. Bergonzi (2006), 175.
6. Brennan (forthcoming).
7. Quoted in Sherry, III.614.
8. Sharrock, 270.
9. Durán, 134–5.
10. *Ways of Escape*, 258.
11. Quoted in Bosco, 141.
12. Sherry, I.185–6.
13. Durán, 83–4, 247–59.
14. See also 'The Country with Five Frontiers', *New York Review of Books* (17 February 1977).
15. Sherry, III.561–97; Watts, 74–81; Durán, 53–74.
16. Shelden, 10.

Bibliography

Bergonzi, B. *A Study in Greene: Graham Greene and the Art of the Novel*, Oxford: Oxford UP, 2006.

—. 'The Power and the Glory – The Dramatic Heritage'. *Plus sur Greene. The Power and the Glory: The Sorbonne Conference*. Paris: Atlande, 2007. 11–18.

Bosco, M. *Graham Greene's Catholic Imagination*. Oxford and New York: Oxford UP, 2005.

Brennan, M. G. 'Damnation and Divine Providence: The Consolations of Catholicism for Graham Greene and Evelyn Waugh'. *Perceptions of Religious Faith in the Work of Graham Greene*. Ed. Wm. Thomas Hill. Bern: Peter Lang Publishers, 2002a. 255–287.

—. 'Graham Greene, Evelyn Waugh and Mexico'. *Renascence*, 55 (2002b): 7–23.

—. 'Graham Greene's Catholic Conversion. The Early Writings (1923–29) and The Man Within', *Logos*, 9 (2006):134–57.

—. 'Graham Greene's Monsignor Quixote (1982): A Pilgrimage of Doubt and Reason towards Faith and Belief'. In *Essays in Contemporary Catholic Literature*. Ed. M. R. Reichardt (forthcoming).

DeVitis, A. A. *Graham Greene. Revised Edition*. New York and London: Twyne Publishers and Prentice Hall International, 1986.

Durán, Leopoldo. *Graham Greene. Friend and Brother*. Trans. Euan Cameron. London: Fount (Harper Collins), 1995.

Falk, Quentin. *Travels in Greeneland. The Cinema of Graham Greene*. London and New York: Quartet Books, 1984, rpt. 1990.

Greene, Barbara. *Land Benighted*. London: Geoffrey Bles, 1938.

Greene, Henry Graham (London: Vintage Classics, unless otherwise stated).

—. 'The Trial of Pan'. *The Oxford Outlook* 5 (February, 1923): 47–50.

—. 'The Improbable Tale of the Archbishop of Canterbridge'. *The Cherwell* 12 (15 November, 1924): 187–91.

—. *Babbling April*. Oxford: B. Blackwell, 1925.

—. *The Man Within*, 1929, rpt. 2001.

—. *The Name of Action*. London: William Heinemann, 1930.

—. *Rumour at Nightfall*. New York: Doubleday, Doran & Co., 1931, rpt. 1932.

—. *Stamboul Train*, 1932, rpt. 2004.

—. *It's a Battlefield*. Harmondsworth: Penguin Books, 1934, rpt. n.d.

—. *England Made Me*, 1935, rpt. 2006.

—. 'Review of Evelyn Waugh, *Life of Campion*, and Pierre Janelle's *Life of Robert Southwell*'. *Spectator* (1 November, 1935). Rpt. Evelyn Waugh, *Edmund Campion*. London: Cassell Publishers Ltd., 1987.

—. *Journey Without Maps*, 1936, rpt. 2006.

—. *A Gun for Sale*, 1936, rpt. 2001.

—. *Brighton Rock*, 1938, rpt. 2004.

—. *The Confidential Agent*, 1939, rpt. 2006.

—. *The Lawless Roads*, 1939, rpt. 2002.

—. *The Power and the Glory*, 1940, rpt. 2004.

—. *The Ministry of Fear*, 1943, rpt. 2001.

—. *The Heart of the Matter*, 1948, rpt. 2004.

—. *The Lost Childhood and Other Essays.* Harmondsworth: Penguin Books, 1951, rpt. 1962.

—. *Introduction to John Gerard. The Autobiography of an Elizabethan.* Translated from the Latin by Philip Caraman. London, New York, Toronto: Longmans, Green and Co., 1951.

—. *The End of the Affair.* Melbourne, London, Toronto: Heinemann Ltd., 1951

—. *The End of the Affair.* 1951, rpt. 2004.

—. *Essais Catholiques.* Paris: Editions du Seuil, 1953.

—. *The Quiet American.* 1955, rpt. 2004.

—. *Our Man in Havana*, 1958, rpt. 2004.

—. *A Burnt Out Case*, 1960, rpt. 2004.

—. *In Search of a Character: Two African Journals.* Harmondsworth: Penguin Books, 1961, rpt. 1986.

—. *The Comedians*, 1966, rpt. 2004.

—. *Travels With My Aunt*, 1969, rpt. 1999.

—. *Collected Essays.* Harmondsworth: Penguin Books, 1969, rpt. 1978.

—. *A Sort of Life*, 1971, rpt. 1999.

—. *The Honorary Consul*, 1973, rpt. 2004.

—. *The Third Man.* Graham Greene. Directed by Carol Reed, London and Boston: Faber and Faber, 1973; rpt. 1989.

—. *Lord Rochester's Monkey.* London: Futura Publications, 1974, rpt. 1976.

—. *The Human Factor*, 1978, rpt. 2005.

—. *The Pleasure-Dome . . . The Collected Film Criticism 1935–40.* Ed. J. R. Taylor. Oxford: Oxford UP, 1980.

—. *Doctor Fischer of Geneva or The Bomb Party*, 1980, rpt. 1999.

—. *Ways of Escape*,1980, rpt. 1999.

—. *Monsignor Quixote*, 1982, rpt. 2006.

—. *The Other Man. Conversations with Graham Greene by Marie-Françoise Allain.* London, Sydney, Toronto: The Bodley Head, 1983.

—. *Getting to Know the General.* Harmondsworth: Penguin Books, 1984, rpt. 1986.

—. *The Tenth Man*, 1985, rpt. 2000.

—. *The Collected Plays of Graham Greene.* Harmondsworth: Penguin Books, 1985.

—. *Collected Short Stories* [*Twenty-One Stories, A Sense of Reality, May We Borrow Your Husband*]. Harmondsworth: Penguin Books, 1986.

—. *The Captain and the Enemy.* Harmondsworth: Penguin Books, 1988, rpt. 1989.

—. *Reflections.* London and New York: Reinhardt Books and Viking, 1990.

—. *Conversations with Graham Greene.* Ed. H. J. Donaghy. Jackson: UP of Mississippi, 1992.

—. *A World of My Own. A Dream Diary.* London and Toronto: Reinhardt Books and Viking, 1992.

—. *Articles of Faith. The Collected Tablet Journalism of Graham Greene.* Ed. I. Thomson. Oxford: Signal Books, 2006.

Hoskins, R. *Graham Greene: An Approach to the Novels*. New York and London: Garland Publishing, 1999.

Hynes, S., ed. *Graham Greene: A Collection of Critical Essays*. Englewood Cliffs, NJ: Prentice-Hall, 1973.

Jarrett, B. *Life of St Dominic (1170–1221)*. London: Burns, Oates & Washbourne Ltd., 1924.

Johnstone, R. *The Will to Believe. Novelists of the Nineteen-Thirties*. Oxford: Oxford UP, 1982.

Ker, I. *The Catholic Revival in English Literature, 1845–1961*. Notre Dame, IN: U of Notre Dame P, 2003.

Lodge, D. 'Graham Greene: A Personal View. Encounters between Two Catholic Novelists', *Times Literary Supplement*, 12 April 1991: 9–10.

Mockler, A. *Graham Greene: Three Lives 1904–1945*. Arbroath: Hunter MacKay, 1994.

—. *Night and Day*. Edited and with an introduction by Christopher Hawtree. Preface by Graham Greene. London: Chatto & Windus, 1985.

Norman, E. R. *Roman Catholicism in England: From the Elizabethan Settlement to the Second Vatican Council*. Oxford: Oxford UP, 1985.

O'Prey, P. *A Reader's Guide to Graham Greene*. London: Thames and Hudson, 1988.

Oxford Dictionary of National Biography: From The Earliest Times to the Year 2000. Ed. H. C. G. Matthew and Brian Harrison Oxford: Oxford UP, 2004 (online edition).

Parsons, W. *Mexican Martyrdom*. New York: Macmillan, 1936.

Sharrock, R. *Saints, Sinners and Comedians: The Novels of Graham Greene*. Tunbridge Wells and Notre Dame, Indiana: Burns & Oates and U of Notre Dame P, 1984.

Shelden, M. *Graham Greene: The Man Within*. London: Heinemann, 1994.

Sherry, N. *The Life of Graham Greene Volume One: 1904–1939*. London and Toronto: Jonathan Cape and Lester & Orpen Dennys Limited, 1989.

Smith, G. *The Achievement of Graham Greene*. Sussex and New Jersey: The Harvester Press and Barnes & Noble Books, 1986.

Stannard, M. *Evelyn Waugh: No Abiding City 1939–1966*. London: J. M. Dent & Sons, 1992.

Sykes, C. *Evelyn Waugh*. A Biography. London: William Collins & Sons, 1975.

Waterfield's Vivien & Graham Greene Centenary Catalogue (2004), Oxford: Waterfield's Antiquarian Booksellers.

Watts, C. *A Preface to Greene*. Harlow: Pearson Education Limited, 1997.

Waugh, E. *Edmund Campion*. London: Cassell Publishers Limited, 1935, rpt. 1987.

—. *The Essays, Articles and Reviews*. Ed. D. Gallagher. London: Methuen, 1983.

—. *The Diaries of Evelyn Waugh*. Ed. M. Davie. Harmondsworth: Penguin Books, 1979.

West, W. J. *The Quest for Graham Greene*. London: Weidenfeld & Nicolson, 1997.

Wilson, R. G. *Greene King. A Business and Family History*. London: The Bodley Head Ltd. and Jonathan Cape, 1983.

Woodman, T. *Faithful Fictions: The Catholic Novel in British Literature*. Milton Keynes: Open UP, 1991.

Index